2024

PLANNER

NEW YEAR, NEW YOU

This is a new
year and this will
be a new you!

2 0 2 4

PLANNER

MY YEAR

Name

Phone

Email

Address

2024

JANUARY

SU	MO	TU	WE	TH	FR	SA
	01	02	03	04	05	06
07	08	09	10	11	12	13
14	15	16	17	18	19	20
21	22	23	24	25	26	27
28	29	30	31			

FEBRUARY

SU	MO	TU	WE	TH	FR	SA
				01	02	03
04	05	06	07	08	09	10
11	12	13	14	15	16	17
18	19	20	21	22	23	24
25	26	27	28			

MARCH

SU	MO	TU	WE	TH	FR	SA
					01	02
03	04	05	06	07	08	09
10	11	12	13	14	15	16
17	18	19	20	21	22	23
24	25	26	27	28	29	30
31						

APRIL

SU	MO	TU	WE	TH	FR	SA
	01	02	03	04	05	06
07	08	09	10	11	12	13
14	15	16	17	18	19	20
21	22	23	24	25	26	27
28	29	30				

MAY

SU	MO	TU	WE	TH	FR	SA
			01	02	03	04
05	06	07	08	09	10	11
12	13	14	15	16	17	18
19	20	21	22	23	24	25
26	27	28	29	30	31	

JUNE

SU	MO	TU	WE	TH	FR	SA
						01
02	03	04	05	06	07	08
09	10	11	12	13	14	15
16	17	18	19	20	21	22
23	24	25	26	27	28	29
30						

JULY

SU	MO	TU	WE	TH	FR	SA
	01	02	03	04	05	06
07	08	09	10	11	12	13
14	15	16	17	18	19	20
21	22	23	24	25	26	27
28	29	30	31			

AUGUST

SU	MO	TU	WE	TH	FR	SA
				01	02	03
04	05	06	07	08	09	10
11	12	13	14	15	16	17
18	19	20	21	22	23	24
25	26	27	28	29	30	31

SEPTEMBER

SU	MO	TU	WE	TH	FR	SA
01	02	03	04	05	06	07
08	09	10	11	12	13	14
15	16	17	18	19	20	21
22	23	24	25	26	27	28
29	30					

OCTOBER

SU	MO	TU	WE	TH	FR	SA
		01	02	03	04	05
06	07	08	09	10	11	12
13	14	15	16	17	18	19
20	21	22	23	24	25	26
27	28	29	30	31		

NOVEMBER

SU	MO	TU	WE	TH	FR	SA
					01	02
03	04	05	06	07	08	09
10	11	12	13	14	15	16
17	18	19	20	21	22	23
24	25	26	27	28	29	30

DECEMBER

SU	MO	TU	WE	TH	FR	SA
01	02	03	04	05	06	07
08	09	10	11	12	13	14
15	16	17	18	19	20	21
22	23	24	25	26	27	28
29	30	31				

JANUARY 2024

Sunday	Monday	Tuesday	Wednesday
	01	02	03
07	08	09	10
14	15	16	17
21	22	23	24
28	29	30	31

JANUARY 2024

Thursday	Friday	Saturday	Notes
04	05	06	
11	12	13	
18	19	20	
25	26	27	

JANUARY

Goal

Action Plan

Date

....
....
....
....
....

....
....
....
....
....

Grateful For

....
....
....
....
....

To Improve

....
....
....
....

Notes

....
....
....

DAILY PLANNER

JANUARY 1, 2024

Monday

TODAY'S AFFIRMATION

WEATHER

MOOD

TOP 3 PRIORITIES

1 _____

2 _____

3 _____

TO-DO LIST

- ☐
- ☐
- ☐
- ☐
- ☐
- ☐
- ☐
- ☐

DON'T FORGET

TIME	PLANS & SCHEDULE
6:00 am	
6:30 am	
7:00 am	
7:30 am	
8:00 am	
8:30 am	
9:00 am	
9:30 am	
10:00 am	
10:30 am	
11:00 am	
11:30 am	
12:00 pm	
12:30 pm	
1:00 pm	
1:30 pm	
2:00 pm	
2:30 pm	
3:00 pm	
3:30 pm	
4:00 pm	
4:30 pm	
5:00 pm	
5:30 pm	
6:00 pm	
6:30 pm	
7:00 pm	
7:30 pm	
8:00 pm	
8:30 pm	
9:00 pm	
9:30 pm	
10:00 pm	

DAILY PLANNER

JANUARY 2, 2024

Tuesday

TODAY'S AFFIRMATION

WEATHER

MOOD

TOP 3 PRIORITIES

1 _____

2 _____

3 _____

TO-DO LIST

- _____
- _____
- _____
- _____
- _____
- _____
- _____
- _____

DON'T FORGET

_____

_____

_____

TIME	PLANS & SCHEDULE
6:00 am	
6:30 am	
7:00 am	
7:30 am	
8:00 am	
8:30 am	
9:00 am	
9:30 am	
10:00 am	
10:30 am	
11:00 am	
11:30 am	
12:00 pm	
12:30 pm	
1:00 pm	
1:30 pm	
2:00 pm	
2:30 pm	
3:00 pm	
3:30 pm	
4:00 pm	
4:30 pm	
5:00 pm	
5:30 pm	
6:00 pm	
6:30 pm	
7:00 pm	
7:30 pm	
8:00 pm	
8:30 pm	
9:00 pm	
9:30 pm	
10:00 pm	

DAILY PLANNER

JANUARY 3, 2024

Wednesday

TODAY'S AFFIRMATION

TOP 3 PRIORITIES

1
2
3

TO-DO LIST

- ☐
- ☐
- ☐
- ☐
- ☐
- ☐
- ☐
- ☐

DON'T FORGET

WEATHER

MOOD

TIME	PLANS & SCHEDULE
6:00 am	
6:30 am	
7:00 am	
7:30 am	
8:00 am	
8:30 am	
9:00 am	
9:30 am	
10:00 am	
10:30 am	
11:00 am	
11:30 am	
12:00 pm	
12:30 pm	
1:00 pm	
1:30 pm	
2:00 pm	
2:30 pm	
3:00 pm	
3:30 pm	
4:00 pm	
4:30 pm	
5:00 pm	
5:30 pm	
6:00 pm	
6:30 pm	
7:00 pm	
7:30 pm	
8:00 pm	
8:30 pm	
9:00 pm	
9:30 pm	
10:00 pm	

DAILY PLANNER

JANUARY 4, 2024

Thursday

TODAY'S AFFIRMATION

WEATHER

MOOD

TOP 3 PRIORITIES

1 _____
_____

2 _____
_____

3 _____
_____

TO-DO LIST

- ☐ _____
- ☐ _____
- ☐ _____
- ☐ _____
- ☐ _____
- ☐ _____
- ☐ _____
- ☐ _____

DON'T FORGET

_____
_____
_____

TIME	PLANS & SCHEDULE
6:00 am	
6:30 am	
7:00 am	
7:30 am	
8:00 am	
8:30 am	
9:00 am	
9:30 am	
10:00 am	
10:30 am	
11:00 am	
11:30 am	
12:00 pm	
12:30 pm	
1:00 pm	
1:30 pm	
2:00 pm	
2:30 pm	
3:00 pm	
3:30 pm	
4:00 pm	
4:30 pm	
5:00 pm	
5:30 pm	
6:00 pm	
6:30 pm	
7:00 pm	
7:30 pm	
8:00 pm	
8:30 pm	
9:00 pm	
9:30 pm	
10:00 pm	

DAILY PLANNER

JANUARY 5, 2024

Friday

TODAY'S AFFIRMATION

WEATHER

MOOD

TOP 3 PRIORITIES

1 _____

2 _____

3 _____

TO-DO LIST

- ☐ _____
- ☐ _____
- ☐ _____
- ☐ _____
- ☐ _____
- ☐ _____
- ☐ _____
- ☐ _____

DON'T FORGET

_____

_____

_____

TIME	PLANS & SCHEDULE
6:00 am	
6:30 am	
7:00 am	
7:30 am	
8:00 am	
8:30 am	
9:00 am	
9:30 am	
10:00 am	
10:30 am	
11:00 am	
11:30 am	
12:00 pm	
12:30 pm	
1:00 pm	
1:30 pm	
2:00 pm	
2:30 pm	
3:00 pm	
3:30 pm	
4:00 pm	
4:30 pm	
5:00 pm	
5:30 pm	
6:00 pm	
6:30 pm	
7:00 pm	
7:30 pm	
8:00 pm	
8:30 pm	
9:00 pm	
9:30 pm	
10:00 pm	

DAILY PLANNER

JANUARY 6, 2024

Saturday

TODAY'S AFFIRMATION

WEATHER	

MOOD	

TOP 3 PRIORITIES

1 _____

_____

2 _____

_____

3 _____

_____

TO-DO LIST

■ _____

■ _____

■ _____

■ _____

■ _____

■ _____

■ _____

■ _____

DON'T FORGET

_____

_____

_____

TIME	PLANS & SCHEDULE
6:00 am	
6:30 am	
7:00 am	
7:30 am	
8:00 am	
8:30 am	
9:00 am	
9:30 am	
10:00 am	
10:30 am	
11:00 am	
11:30 am	
12:00 pm	
12:30 pm	
1:00 pm	
1:30 pm	
2:00 pm	
2:30 pm	
3:00 pm	
3:30 pm	
4:00 pm	
4:30 pm	
5:00 pm	
5:30 pm	
6:00 pm	
6:30 pm	
7:00 pm	
7:30 pm	
8:00 pm	
8:30 pm	
9:00 pm	
9:30 pm	
10:00 pm	

DAILY PLANNER

JANUARY 7, 2024

Sunday

TODAY'S AFFIRMATION

WEATHER

MOOD

TOP 3 PRIORITIES

1

2

3

TO-DO LIST

-
-
-
-
-
-
-
-

DON'T FORGET

TIME	PLANS & SCHEDULE
6:00 am	
6:30 am	
7:00 am	
7:30 am	
8:00 am	
8:30 am	
9:00 am	
9:30 am	
10:00 am	
10:30 am	
11:00 am	
11:30 am	
12:00 pm	
12:30 pm	
1:00 pm	
1:30 pm	
2:00 pm	
2:30 pm	
3:00 pm	
3:30 pm	
4:00 pm	
4:30 pm	
5:00 pm	
5:30 pm	
6:00 pm	
6:30 pm	
7:00 pm	
7:30 pm	
8:00 pm	
8:30 pm	
9:00 pm	
9:30 pm	
10:00 pm	

DAILY PLANNER

JANUARY 8, 2024

Monday

TODAY'S AFFIRMATION

WEATHER

MOOD

TOP 3 PRIORITIES

1 _____
_____

2 _____
_____

3 _____
_____

TO-DO LIST

- ☐ _____
- ☐ _____
- ☐ _____
- ☐ _____
- ☐ _____
- ☐ _____
- ☐ _____
- ☐ _____

DON'T FORGET

_____
_____
_____

TIME	PLANS & SCHEDULE
6:00 am	
6:30 am	
7:00 am	
7:30 am	
8:00 am	
8:30 am	
9:00 am	
9:30 am	
10:00 am	
10:30 am	
11:00 am	
11:30 am	
12:00 pm	
12:30 pm	
1:00 pm	
1:30 pm	
2:00 pm	
2:30 pm	
3:00 pm	
3:30 pm	
4:00 pm	
4:30 pm	
5:00 pm	
5:30 pm	
6:00 pm	
6:30 pm	
7:00 pm	
7:30 pm	
8:00 pm	
8:30 pm	
9:00 pm	
9:30 pm	
10:00 pm	

DAILY PLANNER

JANUARY 9, 2024

Tuesday

TODAY'S AFFIRMATION

WEATHER

MOOD

TOP 3 PRIORITIES

1 _____
_____

2 _____
_____

3 _____
_____

TO-DO LIST

- ▪ _____
- ▪ _____
- ▪ _____
- ▪ _____
- ▪ _____
- ▪ _____
- ▪ _____
- ▪ _____

DON'T FORGET

_____
_____
_____

TIME	PLANS & SCHEDULE
6:00 am	
6:30 am	
7:00 am	
7:30 am	
8:00 am	
8:30 am	
9:00 am	
9:30 am	
10:00 am	
10:30 am	
11:00 am	
11:30 am	
12:00 pm	
12:30 pm	
1:00 pm	
1:30 pm	
2:00 pm	
2:30 pm	
3:00 pm	
3:30 pm	
4:00 pm	
4:30 pm	
5:00 pm	
5:30 pm	
6:00 pm	
6:30 pm	
7:00 pm	
7:30 pm	
8:00 pm	
8:30 pm	
9:00 pm	
9:30 pm	
10:00 pm	

JANUARY 10, 2024

Wednesday

TODAY'S AFFIRMATION

WEATHER

MOOD

TOP 3 PRIORITIES

1 _____
_____

2 _____
_____

3 _____
_____

TO-DO LIST

- ▪ _____
- ▪ _____
- ▪ _____
- ▪ _____
- ▪ _____
- ▪ _____
- ▪ _____
- ▪ _____

DON'T FORGET

_____
_____
_____

TIME	PLANS & SCHEDULE
6:00 am	
6:30 am	
7:00 am	
7:30 am	
8:00 am	
8:30 am	
9:00 am	
9:30 am	
10:00 am	
10:30 am	
11:00 am	
11:30 am	
12:00 pm	
12:30 pm	
1:00 pm	
1:30 pm	
2:00 pm	
2:30 pm	
3:00 pm	
3:30 pm	
4:00 pm	
4:30 pm	
5:00 pm	
5:30 pm	
6:00 pm	
6:30 pm	
7:00 pm	
7:30 pm	
8:00 pm	
8:30 pm	
9:00 pm	
9:30 pm	
10:00 pm	

DAILY PLANNER

JANUARY 11, 2024

Thursday

TODAY'S AFFIRMATION

WEATHER

MOOD

TOP 3 PRIORITIES

1 _____
_____

2 _____
_____

3 _____
_____

TO-DO LIST

- ▪ _____
- ▪ _____
- ▪ _____
- ▪ _____
- ▪ _____
- ▪ _____
- ▪ _____
- ▪ _____

DON'T FORGET

_____
_____
_____

TIME	PLANS & SCHEDULE
6:00 am	
6:30 am	
7:00 am	
7:30 am	
8:00 am	
8:30 am	
9:00 am	
9:30 am	
10:00 am	
10:30 am	
11:00 am	
11:30 am	
12:00 pm	
12:30 pm	
1:00 pm	
1:30 pm	
2:00 pm	
2:30 pm	
3:00 pm	
3:30 pm	
4:00 pm	
4:30 pm	
5:00 pm	
5:30 pm	
6:00 pm	
6:30 pm	
7:00 pm	
7:30 pm	
8:00 pm	
8:30 pm	
9:00 pm	
9:30 pm	
10:00 pm	

DAILY PLANNER

JANUARY 12, 2024

Friday

TODAY'S AFFIRMATION

WEATHER

MOOD

TOP 3 PRIORITIES

1. _____
   _____
2. _____
   _____
3. _____
   _____

TO-DO LIST

- ▪ _____
- ▪ _____
- ▪ _____
- ▪ _____
- ▪ _____
- ▪ _____
- ▪ _____
- ▪ _____

DON'T FORGET

_____
_____
_____

TIME	PLANS & SCHEDULE
6:00 am	
6:30 am	
7:00 am	
7:30 am	
8:00 am	
8:30 am	
9:00 am	
9:30 am	
10:00 am	
10:30 am	
11:00 am	
11:30 am	
12:00 pm	
12:30 pm	
1:00 pm	
1:30 pm	
2:00 pm	
2:30 pm	
3:00 pm	
3:30 pm	
4:00 pm	
4:30 pm	
5:00 pm	
5:30 pm	
6:00 pm	
6:30 pm	
7:00 pm	
7:30 pm	
8:00 pm	
8:30 pm	
9:00 pm	
9:30 pm	
10:00 pm	

DAILY PLANNER

JANUARY 13, 2024

Saturday

TODAY'S AFFIRMATION

WEATHER

MOOD

TOP 3 PRIORITIES

1
2
3

TO-DO LIST

-
-
-
-
-
-
-
-

DON'T FORGET

TIME	PLANS & SCHEDULE
6:00 am	
6:30 am	
7:00 am	
7:30 am	
8:00 am	
8:30 am	
9:00 am	
9:30 am	
10:00 am	
10:30 am	
11:00 am	
11:30 am	
12:00 pm	
12:30 pm	
1:00 pm	
1:30 pm	
2:00 pm	
2:30 pm	
3:00 pm	
3:30 pm	
4:00 pm	
4:30 pm	
5:00 pm	
5:30 pm	
6:00 pm	
6:30 pm	
7:00 pm	
7:30 pm	
8:00 pm	
8:30 pm	
9:00 pm	
9:30 pm	
10:00 pm	

DAILY PLANNER

JANUARY 14, 2024

Sunday

TODAY'S AFFIRMATION

WEATHER

MOOD

TOP 3 PRIORITIES

1 _____
_____

2 _____
_____

3 _____
_____

TO-DO LIST

▪ _____

▪ _____

▪ _____

▪ _____

▪ _____

▪ _____

▪ _____

▪ _____

DON'T FORGET

_____
_____
_____

TIME	PLANS & SCHEDULE
6:00 am	
6:30 am	
7:00 am	
7:30 am	
8:00 am	
8:30 am	
9:00 am	
9:30 am	
10:00 am	
10:30 am	
11:00 am	
11:30 am	
12:00 pm	
12:30 pm	
1:00 pm	
1:30 pm	
2:00 pm	
2:30 pm	
3:00 pm	
3:30 pm	
4:00 pm	
4:30 pm	
5:00 pm	
5:30 pm	
6:00 pm	
6:30 pm	
7:00 pm	
7:30 pm	
8:00 pm	
8:30 pm	
9:00 pm	
9:30 pm	
10:00 pm	

DAILY PLANNER

JANUARY 15, 2024

Monday

TODAY'S AFFIRMATION

WEATHER

MOOD

TOP 3 PRIORITIES

1 _____

2 _____

3 _____

TO-DO LIST

- _____
- _____
- _____
- _____
- _____
- _____
- _____
- _____

DON'T FORGET

_____

_____

_____

TIME	PLANS & SCHEDULE
6:00 am	
6:30 am	
7:00 am	
7:30 am	
8:00 am	
8:30 am	
9:00 am	
9:30 am	
10:00 am	
10:30 am	
11:00 am	
11:30 am	
12:00 pm	
12:30 pm	
1:00 pm	
1:30 pm	
2:00 pm	
2:30 pm	
3:00 pm	
3:30 pm	
4:00 pm	
4:30 pm	
5:00 pm	
5:30 pm	
6:00 pm	
6:30 pm	
7:00 pm	
7:30 pm	
8:00 pm	
8:30 pm	
9:00 pm	
9:30 pm	
10:00 pm	

DAILY PLANNER

JANUARY 16, 2024

Tuesday

TODAY'S AFFIRMATION

WEATHER

MOOD

TOP 3 PRIORITIES

1 _____

_____

2 _____

_____

3 _____

_____

TO-DO LIST

- ■ _____
- ■ _____
- ■ _____
- ■ _____
- ■ _____
- ■ _____
- ■ _____
- ■ _____

DON'T FORGET

_____

_____

_____

TIME	PLANS & SCHEDULE
6:00 am	
6:30 am	
7:00 am	
7:30 am	
8:00 am	
8:30 am	
9:00 am	
9:30 am	
10:00 am	
10:30 am	
11:00 am	
11:30 am	
12:00 pm	
12:30 pm	
1:00 pm	
1:30 pm	
2:00 pm	
2:30 pm	
3:00 pm	
3:30 pm	
4:00 pm	
4:30 pm	
5:00 pm	
5:30 pm	
6:00 pm	
6:30 pm	
7:00 pm	
7:30 pm	
8:00 pm	
8:30 pm	
9:00 pm	
9:30 pm	
10:00 pm	

DAILY PLANNER

JANUARY 17, 2024

Wednesday

TODAY'S AFFIRMATION

WEATHER

MOOD

TOP 3 PRIORITIES

1 _____

2 _____

3 _____

TO-DO LIST

- _____
- _____
- _____
- _____
- _____
- _____
- _____
- _____

DON'T FORGET

TIME	PLANS & SCHEDULE
6:00 am	
6:30 am	
7:00 am	
7:30 am	
8:00 am	
8:30 am	
9:00 am	
9:30 am	
10:00 am	
10:30 am	
11:00 am	
11:30 am	
12:00 pm	
12:30 pm	
1:00 pm	
1:30 pm	
2:00 pm	
2:30 pm	
3:00 pm	
3:30 pm	
4:00 pm	
4:30 pm	
5:00 pm	
5:30 pm	
6:00 pm	
6:30 pm	
7:00 pm	
7:30 pm	
8:00 pm	
8:30 pm	
9:00 pm	
9:30 pm	
10:00 pm	

DAILY PLANNER

JANUARY 18, 2024

Thursday

TODAY'S AFFIRMATION

TOP 3 PRIORITIES

1 _____
   _____

2 _____
   _____

3 _____
   _____

TO-DO LIST

- _____
- _____
- _____
- _____
- _____
- _____
- _____
- _____

DON'T FORGET

_____
_____
_____

WEATHER

MOOD

TIME	PLANS & SCHEDULE
6:00 am	
6:30 am	
7:00 am	
7:30 am	
8:00 am	
8:30 am	
9:00 am	
9:30 am	
10:00 am	
10:30 am	
11:00 am	
11:30 am	
12:00 pm	
12:30 pm	
1:00 pm	
1:30 pm	
2:00 pm	
2:30 pm	
3:00 pm	
3:30 pm	
4:00 pm	
4:30 pm	
5:00 pm	
5:30 pm	
6:00 pm	
6:30 pm	
7:00 pm	
7:30 pm	
8:00 pm	
8:30 pm	
9:00 pm	
9:30 pm	
10:00 pm	

DAILY PLANNER

JANUARY 19, 2024

Friday

TODAY'S AFFIRMATION

WEATHER

MOOD

TOP 3 PRIORITIES

1 _____
_____

2 _____
_____

3 _____
_____

TO-DO LIST

▪ _____
▪ _____
▪ _____
▪ _____
▪ _____
▪ _____
▪ _____
▪ _____

DON'T FORGET

_____
_____
_____

TIME	PLANS & SCHEDULE
6:00 am	
6:30 am	
7:00 am	
7:30 am	
8:00 am	
8:30 am	
9:00 am	
9:30 am	
10:00 am	
10:30 am	
11:00 am	
11:30 am	
12:00 pm	
12:30 pm	
1:00 pm	
1:30 pm	
2:00 pm	
2:30 pm	
3:00 pm	
3:30 pm	
4:00 pm	
4:30 pm	
5:00 pm	
5:30 pm	
6:00 pm	
6:30 pm	
7:00 pm	
7:30 pm	
8:00 pm	
8:30 pm	
9:00 pm	
9:30 pm	
10:00 pm	

DAILY PLANNER

JANUARY 20, 2024

Saturday

TODAY'S AFFIRMATION

WEATHER

MOOD

TOP 3 PRIORITIES

1 _____
_____

2 _____
_____

3 _____
_____

TO-DO LIST

- ■ _____
- ■ _____
- ■ _____
- ■ _____
- ■ _____
- ■ _____
- ■ _____
- ■ _____

DON'T FORGET

_____
_____
_____

TIME	PLANS & SCHEDULE
6:00 am	
6:30 am	
7:00 am	
7:30 am	
8:00 am	
8:30 am	
9:00 am	
9:30 am	
10:00 am	
10:30 am	
11:00 am	
11:30 am	
12:00 pm	
12:30 pm	
1:00 pm	
1:30 pm	
2:00 pm	
2:30 pm	
3:00 pm	
3:30 pm	
4:00 pm	
4:30 pm	
5:00 pm	
5:30 pm	
6:00 pm	
6:30 pm	
7:00 pm	
7:30 pm	
8:00 pm	
8:30 pm	
9:00 pm	
9:30 pm	
10:00 pm	

DAILY PLANNER

JANUARY 21, 2024

Sunday

TODAY'S AFFIRMATION

WEATHER

MOOD

TOP 3 PRIORITIES

1 _____
_____

2 _____
_____

3 _____
_____

TO-DO LIST

- _____
- _____
- _____
- _____
- _____
- _____
- _____
- _____

DON'T FORGET

_____
_____
_____

TIME	PLANS & SCHEDULE
6:00 am	
6:30 am	
7:00 am	
7:30 am	
8:00 am	
8:30 am	
9:00 am	
9:30 am	
10:00 am	
10:30 am	
11:00 am	
11:30 am	
12:00 pm	
12:30 pm	
1:00 pm	
1:30 pm	
2:00 pm	
2:30 pm	
3:00 pm	
3:30 pm	
4:00 pm	
4:30 pm	
5:00 pm	
5:30 pm	
6:00 pm	
6:30 pm	
7:00 pm	
7:30 pm	
8:00 pm	
8:30 pm	
9:00 pm	
9:30 pm	
10:00 pm	

JANUARY 22, 2024

Monday

TODAY'S AFFIRMATION

WEATHER

MOOD

TOP 3 PRIORITIES

1 _____
_____

2 _____
_____

3 _____
_____

TO-DO LIST

- _____
- _____
- _____
- _____
- _____
- _____
- _____
- _____

DON'T FORGET

_____
_____
_____

TIME	PLANS & SCHEDULE
6:00 am	
6:30 am	
7:00 am	
7:30 am	
8:00 am	
8:30 am	
9:00 am	
9:30 am	
10:00 am	
10:30 am	
11:00 am	
11:30 am	
12:00 pm	
12:30 pm	
1:00 pm	
1:30 pm	
2:00 pm	
2:30 pm	
3:00 pm	
3:30 pm	
4:00 pm	
4:30 pm	
5:00 pm	
5:30 pm	
6:00 pm	
6:30 pm	
7:00 pm	
7:30 pm	
8:00 pm	
8:30 pm	
9:00 pm	
9:30 pm	
10:00 pm	

DAILY PLANNER

JANUARY 23, 2024

Tuesday

TODAY'S AFFIRMATION

WEATHER

MOOD

TOP 3 PRIORITIES

1 _____
_____

2 _____
_____

3 _____
_____

TO-DO LIST

- ◾ _____
- ◾ _____
- ◾ _____
- ◾ _____
- ◾ _____
- ◾ _____
- ◾ _____
- ◾ _____

DON'T FORGET

_____
_____
_____

TIME	PLANS & SCHEDULE
6:00 am	
6:30 am	
7:00 am	
7:30 am	
8:00 am	
8:30 am	
9:00 am	
9:30 am	
10:00 am	
10:30 am	
11:00 am	
11:30 am	
12:00 pm	
12:30 pm	
1:00 pm	
1:30 pm	
2:00 pm	
2:30 pm	
3:00 pm	
3:30 pm	
4:00 pm	
4:30 pm	
5:00 pm	
5:30 pm	
6:00 pm	
6:30 pm	
7:00 pm	
7:30 pm	
8:00 pm	
8:30 pm	
9:00 pm	
9:30 pm	
10:00 pm	

DAILY PLANNER

JANUARY 24, 2024

Wednesday

TODAY'S AFFIRMATION

WEATHER

MOOD

TIME	PLANS & SCHEDULE
6:00 am	
6:30 am	
7:00 am	
7:30 am	
8:00 am	
8:30 am	
9:00 am	
9:30 am	
10:00 am	
10:30 am	
11:00 am	
11:30 am	
12:00 pm	
12:30 pm	
1:00 pm	
1:30 pm	
2:00 pm	
2:30 pm	
3:00 pm	
3:30 pm	
4:00 pm	
4:30 pm	
5:00 pm	
5:30 pm	
6:00 pm	
6:30 pm	
7:00 pm	
7:30 pm	
8:00 pm	
8:30 pm	
9:00 pm	
9:30 pm	
10:00 pm	

TOP 3 PRIORITIES

1 _____
_____

2 _____
_____

3 _____
_____

TO-DO LIST

- _____
- _____
- _____
- _____
- _____
- _____
- _____
- _____

DON'T FORGET

_____
_____
_____

DAILY PLANNER

JANUARY 25, 2024

Thursday

TODAY'S AFFIRMATION

WEATHER

MOOD

TOP 3 PRIORITIES

1 _____

2 _____

3 _____

TO-DO LIST

- ☐
- ☐
- ☐
- ☐
- ☐
- ☐
- ☐
- ☐

DON'T FORGET

TIME	PLANS & SCHEDULE
6:00 am	
6:30 am	
7:00 am	
7:30 am	
8:00 am	
8:30 am	
9:00 am	
9:30 am	
10:00 am	
10:30 am	
11:00 am	
11:30 am	
12:00 pm	
12:30 pm	
1:00 pm	
1:30 pm	
2:00 pm	
2:30 pm	
3:00 pm	
3:30 pm	
4:00 pm	
4:30 pm	
5:00 pm	
5:30 pm	
6:00 pm	
6:30 pm	
7:00 pm	
7:30 pm	
8:00 pm	
8:30 pm	
9:00 pm	
9:30 pm	
10:00 pm	

JANUARY 26, 2024

Friday

TODAY'S AFFIRMATION

TOP 3 PRIORITIES

1 _____

_____

2 _____

_____

3 _____

_____

TO-DO LIST

☐ _____

☐ _____

☐ _____

☐ _____

☐ _____

☐ _____

☐ _____

☐ _____

DON'T FORGET

_____

_____

_____

WEATHER

MOOD

TIME	PLANS & SCHEDULE
6:00 am	
6:30 am	
7:00 am	
7:30 am	
8:00 am	
8:30 am	
9:00 am	
9:30 am	
10:00 am	
10:30 am	
11:00 am	
11:30 am	
12:00 pm	
12:30 pm	
1:00 pm	
1:30 pm	
2:00 pm	
2:30 pm	
3:00 pm	
3:30 pm	
4:00 pm	
4:30 pm	
5:00 pm	
5:30 pm	
6:00 pm	
6:30 pm	
7:00 pm	
7:30 pm	
8:00 pm	
8:30 pm	
9:00 pm	
9:30 pm	
10:00 pm	

DAILY PLANNER

JANUARY 27, 2024

Saturday

TODAY'S AFFIRMATION

WEATHER

MOOD

TOP 3 PRIORITIES

1 _____

2 _____

3 _____

TO-DO LIST

- ▪ _____
- ▪ _____
- ▪ _____
- ▪ _____
- ▪ _____
- ▪ _____
- ▪ _____
- ▪ _____

DON'T FORGET

_____
_____
_____

TIME	PLANS & SCHEDULE
6:00 am	
6:30 am	
7:00 am	
7:30 am	
8:00 am	
8:30 am	
9:00 am	
9:30 am	
10:00 am	
10:30 am	
11:00 am	
11:30 am	
12:00 pm	
12:30 pm	
1:00 pm	
1:30 pm	
2:00 pm	
2:30 pm	
3:00 pm	
3:30 pm	
4:00 pm	
4:30 pm	
5:00 pm	
5:30 pm	
6:00 pm	
6:30 pm	
7:00 pm	
7:30 pm	
8:00 pm	
8:30 pm	
9:00 pm	
9:30 pm	
10:00 pm	

DAILY PLANNER

JANUARY 28, 2024

Sunday

TODAY'S AFFIRMATION

WEATHER

MOOD

TOP 3 PRIORITIES

1 _____
_____

2 _____
_____

3 _____
_____

TO-DO LIST

- _____
- _____
- _____
- _____
- _____
- _____
- _____
- _____

DON'T FORGET

_____
_____
_____

TIME	PLANS & SCHEDULE
6:00 am	
6:30 am	
7:00 am	
7:30 am	
8:00 am	
8:30 am	
9:00 am	
9:30 am	
10:00 am	
10:30 am	
11:00 am	
11:30 am	
12:00 pm	
12:30 pm	
1:00 pm	
1:30 pm	
2:00 pm	
2:30 pm	
3:00 pm	
3:30 pm	
4:00 pm	
4:30 pm	
5:00 pm	
5:30 pm	
6:00 pm	
6:30 pm	
7:00 pm	
7:30 pm	
8:00 pm	
8:30 pm	
9:00 pm	
9:30 pm	
10:00 pm	

DAILY PLANNER

JANUARY 29, 2024

Monday

TODAY'S AFFIRMATION

WEATHER

MOOD

TOP 3 PRIORITIES

1 _____

2 _____

3 _____

TO-DO LIST

- ▪ _____
- ▪ _____
- ▪ _____
- ▪ _____
- ▪ _____
- ▪ _____
- ▪ _____
- ▪ _____

DON'T FORGET

_____

_____

_____

TIME	PLANS & SCHEDULE
6:00 am	
6:30 am	
7:00 am	
7:30 am	
8:00 am	
8:30 am	
9:00 am	
9:30 am	
10:00 am	
10:30 am	
11:00 am	
11:30 am	
12:00 pm	
12:30 pm	
1:00 pm	
1:30 pm	
2:00 pm	
2:30 pm	
3:00 pm	
3:30 pm	
4:00 pm	
4:30 pm	
5:00 pm	
5:30 pm	
6:00 pm	
6:30 pm	
7:00 pm	
7:30 pm	
8:00 pm	
8:30 pm	
9:00 pm	
9:30 pm	
10:00 pm	

DAILY PLANNER

JANUARY 30, 2024

Tuesday

TODAY'S AFFIRMATION

WEATHER

MOOD

TOP 3 PRIORITIES

1 _____
_____

2 _____
_____

3 _____
_____

TO-DO LIST

- ☐ _____
- ☐ _____
- ☐ _____
- ☐ _____
- ☐ _____
- ☐ _____
- ☐ _____
- ☐ _____

DON'T FORGET

_____
_____
_____

TIME	PLANS & SCHEDULE
6:00 am	
6:30 am	
7:00 am	
7:30 am	
8:00 am	
8:30 am	
9:00 am	
9:30 am	
10:00 am	
10:30 am	
11:00 am	
11:30 am	
12:00 pm	
12:30 pm	
1:00 pm	
1:30 pm	
2:00 pm	
2:30 pm	
3:00 pm	
3:30 pm	
4:00 pm	
4:30 pm	
5:00 pm	
5:30 pm	
6:00 pm	
6:30 pm	
7:00 pm	
7:30 pm	
8:00 pm	
8:30 pm	
9:00 pm	
9:30 pm	
10:00 pm	

JANUARY 31, 2024

Wednesday

TODAY'S AFFIRMATION

WEATHER

MOOD

TOP 3 PRIORITIES

1 _____
_____

2 _____
_____

3 _____
_____

TO-DO LIST

- ☐ _____
- ☐ _____
- ☐ _____
- ☐ _____
- ☐ _____
- ☐ _____
- ☐ _____
- ☐ _____
- ☐ _____

DON'T FORGET

_____
_____
_____

TIME	PLANS & SCHEDULE
6:00 am	
6:30 am	
7:00 am	
7:30 am	
8:00 am	
8:30 am	
9:00 am	
9:30 am	
10:00 am	
10:30 am	
11:00 am	
11:30 am	
12:00 pm	
12:30 pm	
1:00 pm	
1:30 pm	
2:00 pm	
2:30 pm	
3:00 pm	
3:30 pm	
4:00 pm	
4:30 pm	
5:00 pm	
5:30 pm	
6:00 pm	
6:30 pm	
7:00 pm	
7:30 pm	
8:00 pm	
8:30 pm	
9:00 pm	
9:30 pm	
10:00 pm	

MONTHLY BUDGET PLANNER

Budget Goal: _____

Month: _____

Income

Date	Description	Amount
Total		

Fixed Expenses

Date	Description	Amount
Total		

Other Expenses

Date	Description	Amount
Total		

Bills

Date	Description	Amount
Total		

Recap

	Goal	Actual	Difference
Earnt			
Spent			
Debt			
Saved			

Notes

Date:

GRATITUDE JOURNAL

DATE: _____   S M T W T F S

TODAY I'M GRATEFUL FOR

- _____
- _____
- _____

WATER INTAKE

1L   2L   3L

WEATHER

TODAY'S AFFIRMATION

- _____
- _____
- _____
- _____

NOTES / REMINDERS

SOMETHING I'M PROUD OF

- _____
- _____
- _____
- _____

TOMORROW I LOOK FORWARD TO

- _____
- _____
- _____
- _____

30 DAY
Self-Care Challenge

DAY 1	DAY 2	DAY 3	DAY 4	DAY 5
Start a gratitude journal	Learn to meditate	Spend the day social media free	Call someone you love	Take a 15 minute walk outdoors
DAY 6	**DAY 7**	**DAY 8**	**DAY 9**	**DAY 10**
Listen to a podcast	Learn to cook a new recipe	Stretch for 10-15 minutes	Listen to your favorite song	Practice deep breathing
DAY 11	**DAY 12**	**DAY 13**	**DAY 14**	**DAY 15**
Try a free online workout	Read a book for 15 minutes	Write a list of short-term goals	De-clutter a room or desk	Go to bed 30 minutes earlier
DAY 16	**DAY 17**	**DAY 18**	**DAY 19**	**DAY 20**
Have a game night	Wake up 15 minutes earlier	Make your favorite meal	Buy yourself something nice	Create a bucket list
DAY 21	**DAY 22**	**DAY 23**	**DAY 24**	**DAY 25**
Watch a movie or series	Write down your thoughts	Take a long shower or bath	Have a home spa day	Read inspirational quotes
DAY 26	**DAY 27**	**DAY 28**	**DAY 29**	**DAY 30**
Create a vision board	Spend some time outside	Do a hair mask	Write it all down in a journal	Take a power nap

FEBRUARY 2024

Sunday	Monday	Tuesday	Wednesday

04 	05 	06 	07 
11 	12 	13 	14 
18 	19 	20 	21 
25 	26 	27 	28 

FEBRUARY 2024

Thursday	Friday	Saturday	Notes
01	02	03	
08	09	10	
15	16	17	
22	23	24	
29			

FEBRUARY

Goal

Action Plan   Date

....

....

....

....

....

Grateful For

....

....

....

....

....

To Improve

....

....

....

....

Notes

....

....

....

DAILY PLANNER

FEBRUARY 1, 2024

Thursday

TODAY'S AFFIRMATION

WEATHER

MOOD

TOP 3 PRIORITIES

1 _____
_____

2 _____
_____

3 _____
_____

TO-DO LIST

- ■ _____
- ■ _____
- ■ _____
- ■ _____
- ■ _____
- ■ _____
- ■ _____
- ■ _____

DON'T FORGET

_____
_____
_____

TIME	PLANS & SCHEDULE
6:00 am	
6:30 am	
7:00 am	
7:30 am	
8:00 am	
8:30 am	
9:00 am	
9:30 am	
10:00 am	
10:30 am	
11:00 am	
11:30 am	
12:00 pm	
12:30 pm	
1:00 pm	
1:30 pm	
2:00 pm	
2:30 pm	
3:00 pm	
3:30 pm	
4:00 pm	
4:30 pm	
5:00 pm	
5:30 pm	
6:00 pm	
6:30 pm	
7:00 pm	
7:30 pm	
8:00 pm	
8:30 pm	
9:00 pm	
9:30 pm	
10:00 pm	

DAILY PLANNER

FEBRUARY 2, 2024

Friday

TODAY'S AFFIRMATION

WEATHER

MOOD

TOP 3 PRIORITIES

1. _____
   _____
2. _____
   _____
3. _____
   _____

TO-DO LIST

- ☐ _____
- ☐ _____
- ☐ _____
- ☐ _____
- ☐ _____
- ☐ _____
- ☐ _____
- ☐ _____

DON'T FORGET

_____
_____
_____

TIME	PLANS & SCHEDULE
6:00 am	
6:30 am	
7:00 am	
7:30 am	
8:00 am	
8:30 am	
9:00 am	
9:30 am	
10:00 am	
10:30 am	
11:00 am	
11:30 am	
12:00 pm	
12:30 pm	
1:00 pm	
1:30 pm	
2:00 pm	
2:30 pm	
3:00 pm	
3:30 pm	
4:00 pm	
4:30 pm	
5:00 pm	
5:30 pm	
6:00 pm	
6:30 pm	
7:00 pm	
7:30 pm	
8:00 pm	
8:30 pm	
9:00 pm	
9:30 pm	
10:00 pm	

FEBRUARY 3, 2024

Saturday

TODAY'S AFFIRMATION

WEATHER

MOOD

TOP 3 PRIORITIES

1 _____

2 _____

3 _____

TO-DO LIST

- _____
- _____
- _____
- _____
- _____
- _____
- _____
- _____

DON'T FORGET

_____

_____

_____

TIME	PLANS & SCHEDULE
6:00 am	
6:30 am	
7:00 am	
7:30 am	
8:00 am	
8:30 am	
9:00 am	
9:30 am	
10:00 am	
10:30 am	
11:00 am	
11:30 am	
12:00 pm	
12:30 pm	
1:00 pm	
1:30 pm	
2:00 pm	
2:30 pm	
3:00 pm	
3:30 pm	
4:00 pm	
4:30 pm	
5:00 pm	
5:30 pm	
6:00 pm	
6:30 pm	
7:00 pm	
7:30 pm	
8:00 pm	
8:30 pm	
9:00 pm	
9:30 pm	
10:00 pm	

DAILY PLANNER

FEBRUARY 4, 2024

Sunday

TODAY'S AFFIRMATION

WEATHER	

MOOD	

TOP 3 PRIORITIES

1 _____

_____

2 _____

_____

3 _____

_____

TO-DO LIST

- ▪ _____
- ▪ _____
- ▪ _____
- ▪ _____
- ▪ _____
- ▪ _____
- ▪ _____
- ▪ _____

DON'T FORGET

_____

_____

_____

TIME	PLANS & SCHEDULE
6:00 am	
6:30 am	
7:00 am	
7:30 am	
8:00 am	
8:30 am	
9:00 am	
9:30 am	
10:00 am	
10:30 am	
11:00 am	
11:30 am	
12:00 pm	
12:30 pm	
1:00 pm	
1:30 pm	
2:00 pm	
2:30 pm	
3:00 pm	
3:30 pm	
4:00 pm	
4:30 pm	
5:00 pm	
5:30 pm	
6:00 pm	
6:30 pm	
7:00 pm	
7:30 pm	
8:00 pm	
8:30 pm	
9:00 pm	
9:30 pm	
10:00 pm	

DAILY PLANNER

FEBRUARY 5, 2024

Monday

TODAY'S AFFIRMATION

WEATHER

MOOD

TOP 3 PRIORITIES

1 _____
_____

2 _____
_____

3 _____
_____

TO-DO LIST

- ▪ _____
- ▪ _____
- ▪ _____
- ▪ _____
- ▪ _____
- ▪ _____
- ▪ _____
- ▪ _____

DON'T FORGET

_____
_____
_____

TIME	PLANS & SCHEDULE
6:00 am	
6:30 am	
7:00 am	
7:30 am	
8:00 am	
8:30 am	
9:00 am	
9:30 am	
10:00 am	
10:30 am	
11:00 am	
11:30 am	
12:00 pm	
12:30 pm	
1:00 pm	
1:30 pm	
2:00 pm	
2:30 pm	
3:00 pm	
3:30 pm	
4:00 pm	
4:30 pm	
5:00 pm	
5:30 pm	
6:00 pm	
6:30 pm	
7:00 pm	
7:30 pm	
8:00 pm	
8:30 pm	
9:00 pm	
9:30 pm	
10:00 pm	

FEBRUARY 6, 2024

Tuesday

TODAY'S AFFIRMATION

WEATHER	
MOOD	

TOP 3 PRIORITIES

1 _____

_____

2 _____

_____

3 _____

_____

TO-DO LIST

- _____
- _____
- _____
- _____
- _____
- _____
- _____
- _____

DON'T FORGET

_____

_____

_____

TIME	PLANS & SCHEDULE
6:00 am	
6:30 am	
7:00 am	
7:30 am	
8:00 am	
8:30 am	
9:00 am	
9:30 am	
10:00 am	
10:30 am	
11:00 am	
11:30 am	
12:00 pm	
12:30 pm	
1:00 pm	
1:30 pm	
2:00 pm	
2:30 pm	
3:00 pm	
3:30 pm	
4:00 pm	
4:30 pm	
5:00 pm	
5:30 pm	
6:00 pm	
6:30 pm	
7:00 pm	
7:30 pm	
8:00 pm	
8:30 pm	
9:00 pm	
9:30 pm	
10:00 pm	

DAILY PLANNER

FEBRUARY 7, 2024

Wednesday

TODAY'S AFFIRMATION

WEATHER

MOOD

TOP 3 PRIORITIES

1 _____
_____

2 _____
_____

3 _____
_____

TO-DO LIST

■ _____

■ _____

■ _____

■ _____

■ _____

■ _____

■ _____

■ _____

DON'T FORGET

_____
_____
_____

TIME	PLANS & SCHEDULE
6:00 am	
6:30 am	
7:00 am	
7:30 am	
8:00 am	
8:30 am	
9:00 am	
9:30 am	
10:00 am	
10:30 am	
11:00 am	
11:30 am	
12:00 pm	
12:30 pm	
1:00 pm	
1:30 pm	
2:00 pm	
2:30 pm	
3:00 pm	
3:30 pm	
4:00 pm	
4:30 pm	
5:00 pm	
5:30 pm	
6:00 pm	
6:30 pm	
7:00 pm	
7:30 pm	
8:00 pm	
8:30 pm	
9:00 pm	
9:30 pm	
10:00 pm	

DAILY PLANNER

FEBRUARY 8, 2024

Thursday

TODAY'S AFFIRMATION

WEATHER

MOOD

TOP 3 PRIORITIES

1 _____
_____

2 _____
_____

3 _____
_____

TO-DO LIST

- ■ _____
- ■ _____
- ■ _____
- ■ _____
- ■ _____
- ■ _____
- ■ _____
- ■ _____

DON'T FORGET

_____
_____
_____

TIME	PLANS & SCHEDULE
6:00 am	
6:30 am	
7:00 am	
7:30 am	
8:00 am	
8:30 am	
9:00 am	
9:30 am	
10:00 am	
10:30 am	
11:00 am	
11:30 am	
12:00 pm	
12:30 pm	
1:00 pm	
1:30 pm	
2:00 pm	
2:30 pm	
3:00 pm	
3:30 pm	
4:00 pm	
4:30 pm	
5:00 pm	
5:30 pm	
6:00 pm	
6:30 pm	
7:00 pm	
7:30 pm	
8:00 pm	
8:30 pm	
9:00 pm	
9:30 pm	
10:00 pm	

DAILY PLANNER

FEBRUARY 9, 2024

Friday

TODAY'S AFFIRMATION

WEATHER

MOOD

TOP 3 PRIORITIES

1 _____

2 _____

3 _____

TO-DO LIST

- ☐ _____
- ☐ _____
- ☐ _____
- ☐ _____
- ☐ _____
- ☐ _____
- ☐ _____
- ☐ _____

DON'T FORGET

_____
_____
_____

TIME	PLANS & SCHEDULE
6:00 am	
6:30 am	
7:00 am	
7:30 am	
8:00 am	
8:30 am	
9:00 am	
9:30 am	
10:00 am	
10:30 am	
11:00 am	
11:30 am	
12:00 pm	
12:30 pm	
1:00 pm	
1:30 pm	
2:00 pm	
2:30 pm	
3:00 pm	
3:30 pm	
4:00 pm	
4:30 pm	
5:00 pm	
5:30 pm	
6:00 pm	
6:30 pm	
7:00 pm	
7:30 pm	
8:00 pm	
8:30 pm	
9:00 pm	
9:30 pm	
10:00 pm	

DAILY PLANNER

FEBRUARY 10, 2024

Saturday

TODAY'S AFFIRMATION

WEATHER	
MOOD	

TOP 3 PRIORITIES

1 _____

_____

2 _____

_____

3 _____

_____

TO-DO LIST

- ◼ _____
- ◼ _____
- ◼ _____
- ◼ _____
- ◼ _____
- ◼ _____
- ◼ _____
- ◼ _____

DON'T FORGET

_____

_____

_____

TIME	PLANS & SCHEDULE
6:00 am	
6:30 am	
7:00 am	
7:30 am	
8:00 am	
8:30 am	
9:00 am	
9:30 am	
10:00 am	
10:30 am	
11:00 am	
11:30 am	
12:00 pm	
12:30 pm	
1:00 pm	
1:30 pm	
2:00 pm	
2:30 pm	
3:00 pm	
3:30 pm	
4:00 pm	
4:30 pm	
5:00 pm	
5:30 pm	
6:00 pm	
6:30 pm	
7:00 pm	
7:30 pm	
8:00 pm	
8:30 pm	
9:00 pm	
9:30 pm	
10:00 pm	

DAILY PLANNER

FEBRUARY 11, 2024

Sunday

TODAY'S AFFIRMATION

WEATHER

MOOD

TOP 3 PRIORITIES

1 _____
_____

2 _____
_____

3 _____
_____

TO-DO LIST

- _____
- _____
- _____
- _____
- _____
- _____
- _____
- _____

DON'T FORGET

_____
_____
_____

TIME	PLANS & SCHEDULE
6:00 am	
6:30 am	
7:00 am	
7:30 am	
8:00 am	
8:30 am	
9:00 am	
9:30 am	
10:00 am	
10:30 am	
11:00 am	
11:30 am	
12:00 pm	
12:30 pm	
1:00 pm	
1:30 pm	
2:00 pm	
2:30 pm	
3:00 pm	
3:30 pm	
4:00 pm	
4:30 pm	
5:00 pm	
5:30 pm	
6:00 pm	
6:30 pm	
7:00 pm	
7:30 pm	
8:00 pm	
8:30 pm	
9:00 pm	
9:30 pm	
10:00 pm	

DAILY PLANNER

FEBRUARY 12, 2024

Monday

TODAY'S AFFIRMATION

WEATHER

MOOD

TOP 3 PRIORITIES

1

2

3

TO-DO LIST

-
-
-
-
-
-
-
-

DON'T FORGET

TIME	PLANS & SCHEDULE
6:00 am	
6:30 am	
7:00 am	
7:30 am	
8:00 am	
8:30 am	
9:00 am	
9:30 am	
10:00 am	
10:30 am	
11:00 am	
11:30 am	
12:00 pm	
12:30 pm	
1:00 pm	
1:30 pm	
2:00 pm	
2:30 pm	
3:00 pm	
3:30 pm	
4:00 pm	
4:30 pm	
5:00 pm	
5:30 pm	
6:00 pm	
6:30 pm	
7:00 pm	
7:30 pm	
8:00 pm	
8:30 pm	
9:00 pm	
9:30 pm	
10:00 pm	

DAILY PLANNER

FEBRUARY 13, 2024

Tuesday

TODAY'S AFFIRMATION

WEATHER

MOOD

TOP 3 PRIORITIES

1 _____

2 _____

3 _____

TO-DO LIST

- _____
- _____
- _____
- _____
- _____
- _____
- _____
- _____

DON'T FORGET

TIME	PLANS & SCHEDULE
6:00 am	
6:30 am	
7:00 am	
7:30 am	
8:00 am	
8:30 am	
9:00 am	
9:30 am	
10:00 am	
10:30 am	
11:00 am	
11:30 am	
12:00 pm	
12:30 pm	
1:00 pm	
1:30 pm	
2:00 pm	
2:30 pm	
3:00 pm	
3:30 pm	
4:00 pm	
4:30 pm	
5:00 pm	
5:30 pm	
6:00 pm	
6:30 pm	
7:00 pm	
7:30 pm	
8:00 pm	
8:30 pm	
9:00 pm	
9:30 pm	
10:00 pm	

DAILY PLANNER

FEBRUARY 14, 2024

Wednesday

TODAY'S AFFIRMATION

WEATHER	

MOOD	

TOP 3 PRIORITIES

1 _____
_____

2 _____
_____

3 _____
_____

TO-DO LIST

- _____
- _____
- _____
- _____
- _____
- _____
- _____
- _____

DON'T FORGET

_____
_____
_____

TIME	PLANS & SCHEDULE
6:00 am	
6:30 am	
7:00 am	
7:30 am	
8:00 am	
8:30 am	
9:00 am	
9:30 am	
10:00 am	
10:30 am	
11:00 am	
11:30 am	
12:00 pm	
12:30 pm	
1:00 pm	
1:30 pm	
2:00 pm	
2:30 pm	
3:00 pm	
3:30 pm	
4:00 pm	
4:30 pm	
5:00 pm	
5:30 pm	
6:00 pm	
6:30 pm	
7:00 pm	
7:30 pm	
8:00 pm	
8:30 pm	
9:00 pm	
9:30 pm	
10:00 pm	

DAILY PLANNER

FEBRUARY 15, 2024

Thursday

TODAY'S AFFIRMATION

WEATHER

MOOD

TOP 3 PRIORITIES

1 _____
   _____

2 _____
   _____

3 _____
   _____

TO-DO LIST

- _____
- _____
- _____
- _____
- _____
- _____
- _____
- _____

DON'T FORGET

_____
_____
_____

TIME	PLANS & SCHEDULE
6:00 am	
6:30 am	
7:00 am	
7:30 am	
8:00 am	
8:30 am	
9:00 am	
9:30 am	
10:00 am	
10:30 am	
11:00 am	
11:30 am	
12:00 pm	
12:30 pm	
1:00 pm	
1:30 pm	
2:00 pm	
2:30 pm	
3:00 pm	
3:30 pm	
4:00 pm	
4:30 pm	
5:00 pm	
5:30 pm	
6:00 pm	
6:30 pm	
7:00 pm	
7:30 pm	
8:00 pm	
8:30 pm	
9:00 pm	
9:30 pm	
10:00 pm	

DAILY PLANNER

FEBRUARY 16, 2024

Friday

TODAY'S AFFIRMATION

WEATHER	

MOOD	

TOP 3 PRIORITIES

1 _____

_____

2 _____

_____

3 _____

_____

TO-DO LIST

- ▪ _____
- ▪ _____
- ▪ _____
- ▪ _____
- ▪ _____
- ▪ _____
- ▪ _____
- ▪ _____

DON'T FORGET

_____

_____

_____

TIME	PLANS & SCHEDULE
6:00 am	
6:30 am	
7:00 am	
7:30 am	
8:00 am	
8:30 am	
9:00 am	
9:30 am	
10:00 am	
10:30 am	
11:00 am	
11:30 am	
12:00 pm	
12:30 pm	
1:00 pm	
1:30 pm	
2:00 pm	
2:30 pm	
3:00 pm	
3:30 pm	
4:00 pm	
4:30 pm	
5:00 pm	
5:30 pm	
6:00 pm	
6:30 pm	
7:00 pm	
7:30 pm	
8:00 pm	
8:30 pm	
9:00 pm	
9:30 pm	
10:00 pm	

DAILY PLANNER

FEBRUARY 17, 2024

Saturday

TODAY'S AFFIRMATION

WEATHER

MOOD

TOP 3 PRIORITIES

1

2

3

TO-DO LIST

-
-
-
-
-
-
-
-

DON'T FORGET

TIME	PLANS & SCHEDULE
6:00 am	
6:30 am	
7:00 am	
7:30 am	
8:00 am	
8:30 am	
9:00 am	
9:30 am	
10:00 am	
10:30 am	
11:00 am	
11:30 am	
12:00 pm	
12:30 pm	
1:00 pm	
1:30 pm	
2:00 pm	
2:30 pm	
3:00 pm	
3:30 pm	
4:00 pm	
4:30 pm	
5:00 pm	
5:30 pm	
6:00 pm	
6:30 pm	
7:00 pm	
7:30 pm	
8:00 pm	
8:30 pm	
9:00 pm	
9:30 pm	
10:00 pm	

DAILY PLANNER

FEBRUARY 18, 2024

Sunday

TODAY'S AFFIRMATION

TOP 3 PRIORITIES

1 _____

_____

2 _____

_____

3 _____

_____

TO-DO LIST

- ■ _____
- ■ _____
- ■ _____
- ■ _____
- ■ _____
- ■ _____
- ■ _____
- ■ _____

DON'T FORGET

_____

_____

_____

TIME	PLANS & SCHEDULE
6:00 am	
6:30 am	
7:00 am	
7:30 am	
8:00 am	
8:30 am	
9:00 am	
9:30 am	
10:00 am	
10:30 am	
11:00 am	
11:30 am	
12:00 pm	
12:30 pm	
1:00 pm	
1:30 pm	
2:00 pm	
2:30 pm	
3:00 pm	
3:30 pm	
4:00 pm	
4:30 pm	
5:00 pm	
5:30 pm	
6:00 pm	
6:30 pm	
7:00 pm	
7:30 pm	
8:00 pm	
8:30 pm	
9:00 pm	
9:30 pm	
10:00 pm	

DAILY PLANNER

FEBRUARY 19, 2024

Monday

TODAY'S AFFIRMATION

WEATHER

MOOD

TOP 3 PRIORITIES

1 _____

2 _____

3 _____

TO-DO LIST

- _____
- _____
- _____
- _____
- _____
- _____
- _____
- _____

DON'T FORGET

_____

_____

_____

TIME	PLANS & SCHEDULE
6:00 am	
6:30 am	
7:00 am	
7:30 am	
8:00 am	
8:30 am	
9:00 am	
9:30 am	
10:00 am	
10:30 am	
11:00 am	
11:30 am	
12:00 pm	
12:30 pm	
1:00 pm	
1:30 pm	
2:00 pm	
2:30 pm	
3:00 pm	
3:30 pm	
4:00 pm	
4:30 pm	
5:00 pm	
5:30 pm	
6:00 pm	
6:30 pm	
7:00 pm	
7:30 pm	
8:00 pm	
8:30 pm	
9:00 pm	
9:30 pm	
10:00 pm	

FEBRUARY 20, 2024

Tuesday

TODAY'S AFFIRMATION

| WEATHER |  |
| MOOD |  |

TOP 3 PRIORITIES

1 _____
_____

2 _____
_____

3 _____
_____

TO-DO LIST

■ _____
■ _____
■ _____
■ _____
■ _____
■ _____
■ _____
■ _____

DON'T FORGET

_____
_____
_____

TIME	PLANS & SCHEDULE
6:00 am	
6:30 am	
7:00 am	
7:30 am	
8:00 am	
8:30 am	
9:00 am	
9:30 am	
10:00 am	
10:30 am	
11:00 am	
11:30 am	
12:00 pm	
12:30 pm	
1:00 pm	
1:30 pm	
2:00 pm	
2:30 pm	
3:00 pm	
3:30 pm	
4:00 pm	
4:30 pm	
5:00 pm	
5:30 pm	
6:00 pm	
6:30 pm	
7:00 pm	
7:30 pm	
8:00 pm	
9:00 pm	
9:30 pm	
10:00 pm	
8:30 pm	

DAILY PLANNER

FEBRUARY 21, 2024

Wednesday

TODAY'S AFFIRMATION

WEATHER

MOOD

TOP 3 PRIORITIES

1 _____
_____

2 _____
_____

3 _____
_____

TO-DO LIST

- ▪ _____
- ▪ _____
- ▪ _____
- ▪ _____
- ▪ _____
- ▪ _____
- ▪ _____
- ▪ _____

DON'T FORGET

_____
_____
_____

TIME	PLANS & SCHEDULE
6:00 am	
6:30 am	
7:00 am	
7:30 am	
8:00 am	
8:30 am	
9:00 am	
9:30 am	
10:00 am	
10:30 am	
11:00 am	
11:30 am	
12:00 pm	
12:30 pm	
1:00 pm	
1:30 pm	
2:00 pm	
2:30 pm	
3:00 pm	
3:30 pm	
4:00 pm	
4:30 pm	
5:00 pm	
5:30 pm	
6:00 pm	
6:30 pm	
7:00 pm	
7:30 pm	
8:00 pm	
8:30 pm	
9:00 pm	
9:30 pm	
10:00 pm	

DAILY PLANNER

FEBRUARY 22, 2024

Thursday

TODAY'S AFFIRMATION

WEATHER	
MOOD	

TOP 3 PRIORITIES

1 _____

_____

2 _____

_____

3 _____

_____

TO-DO LIST

- ◼ _____
- ◼ _____
- ◼ _____
- ◼ _____
- ◼ _____
- ◼ _____
- ◼ _____
- ◼ _____

DON'T FORGET

_____

_____

_____

TIME	PLANS & SCHEDULE
6:00 am	
6:30 am	
7:00 am	
7:30 am	
8:00 am	
8:30 am	
9:00 am	
9:30 am	
10:00 am	
10:30 am	
11:00 am	
11:30 am	
12:00 pm	
12:30 pm	
1:00 pm	
1:30 pm	
2:00 pm	
2:30 pm	
3:00 pm	
3:30 pm	
4:00 pm	
4:30 pm	
5:00 pm	
5:30 pm	
6:00 pm	
6:30 pm	
7:00 pm	
7:30 pm	
8:00 pm	
8:30 pm	
9:00 pm	
9:30 pm	
10:00 pm	

DAILY PLANNER

FEBRUARY 23, 2024

Friday

TODAY'S AFFIRMATION

WEATHER

MOOD

TOP 3 PRIORITIES

1 _____

2 _____

3 _____

TO-DO LIST

- ☐ _____
- ☐ _____
- ☐ _____
- ☐ _____
- ☐ _____
- ☐ _____
- ☐ _____
- ☐ _____

DON'T FORGET

_____
_____
_____

TIME	PLANS & SCHEDULE
6:00 am	
6:30 am	
7:00 am	
7:30 am	
8:00 am	
8:30 am	
9:00 am	
9:30 am	
10:00 am	
10:30 am	
11:00 am	
11:30 am	
12:00 pm	
12:30 pm	
1:00 pm	
1:30 pm	
2:00 pm	
2:30 pm	
3:00 pm	
3:30 pm	
4:00 pm	
4:30 pm	
5:00 pm	
5:30 pm	
6:00 pm	
6:30 pm	
7:00 pm	
7:30 pm	
8:00 pm	
8:30 pm	
9:00 pm	
9:30 pm	
10:00 pm	

FEBRUARY 24, 2024

Saturday

TODAY'S AFFIRMATION

WEATHER	

MOOD	

TOP 3 PRIORITIES

1 _____
_____

2 _____
_____

3 _____
_____

TO-DO LIST

- _____
- _____
- _____
- _____
- _____
- _____
- _____
- _____

DON'T FORGET

_____
_____
_____

TIME	PLANS & SCHEDULE
6:00 am	
6:30 am	
7:00 am	
7:30 am	
8:00 am	
8:30 am	
9:00 am	
9:30 am	
10:00 am	
10:30 am	
11:00 am	
11:30 am	
12:00 pm	
12:30 pm	
1:00 pm	
1:30 pm	
2:00 pm	
2:30 pm	
3:00 pm	
3:30 pm	
4:00 pm	
4:30 pm	
5:00 pm	
5:30 pm	
6:00 pm	
6:30 pm	
7:00 pm	
7:30 pm	
8:00 pm	
8:30 pm	
9:00 pm	
9:30 pm	
10:00 pm	

DAILY PLANNER

FEBRUARY 25, 2024

Sunday

TODAY'S AFFIRMATION

WEATHER

MOOD

TOP 3 PRIORITIES

1 _____
_____

2 _____
_____

3 _____
_____

TO-DO LIST

- _____
- _____
- _____
- _____
- _____
- _____
- _____
- _____

DON'T FORGET

_____
_____
_____

TIME	PLANS & SCHEDULE
6:00 am	
6:30 am	
7:00 am	
7:30 am	
8:00 am	
8:30 am	
9:00 am	
9:30 am	
10:00 am	
10:30 am	
11:00 am	
11:30 am	
12:00 pm	
12:30 pm	
1:00 pm	
1:30 pm	
2:00 pm	
2:30 pm	
3:00 pm	
3:30 pm	
4:00 pm	
4:30 pm	
5:00 pm	
5:30 pm	
6:00 pm	
6:30 pm	
7:00 pm	
7:30 pm	
8:00 pm	
8:30 pm	
9:00 pm	
9:30 pm	
10:00 pm	

DAILY PLANNER

FEBRUARY 26, 2024

Monday

TODAY'S AFFIRMATION

WEATHER	

MOOD	

TOP 3 PRIORITIES

1 _____
_____

2 _____
_____

3 _____
_____

TO-DO LIST

- ▪ _____
- ▪ _____
- ▪ _____
- ▪ _____
- ▪ _____
- ▪ _____
- ▪ _____
- ▪ _____

DON'T FORGET

_____
_____
_____

TIME	PLANS & SCHEDULE
6:00 am	
6:30 am	
7:00 am	
7:30 am	
8:00 am	
8:30 am	
9:00 am	
9:30 am	
10:00 am	
10:30 am	
11:00 am	
11:30 am	
12:00 pm	
12:30 pm	
1:00 pm	
1:30 pm	
2:00 pm	
2:30 pm	
3:00 pm	
3:30 pm	
4:00 pm	
4:30 pm	
5:00 pm	
5:30 pm	
6:00 pm	
6:30 pm	
7:00 pm	
7:30 pm	
8:00 pm	
8:30 pm	
9:00 pm	
9:30 pm	
10:00 pm	

DAILY PLANNER

FEBRUARY 27, 2024

Tuesday

TODAY'S AFFIRMATION

WEATHER

MOOD

TOP 3 PRIORITIES

1 _____
  _____

2 _____
  _____

3 _____
  _____

TO-DO LIST

- _____
- _____
- _____
- _____
- _____
- _____
- _____
- _____

DON'T FORGET

_____
_____
_____

TIME	PLANS & SCHEDULE
6:00 am	
6:30 am	
7:00 am	
7:30 am	
8:00 am	
8:30 am	
9:00 am	
9:30 am	
10:00 am	
10:30 am	
11:00 am	
11:30 am	
12:00 pm	
12:30 pm	
1:00 pm	
1:30 pm	
2:00 pm	
2:30 pm	
3:00 pm	
3:30 pm	
4:00 pm	
4:30 pm	
5:00 pm	
5:30 pm	
6:00 pm	
6:30 pm	
7:00 pm	
7:30 pm	
8:00 pm	
8:30 pm	
9:00 pm	
9:30 pm	
10:00 pm	

FEBRUARY 28, 2024

Wednesday

TODAY'S AFFIRMATION

WEATHER	

MOOD	

TOP 3 PRIORITIES

1 _____
_____

2 _____
_____

3 _____
_____

TO-DO LIST

- ■ _____
- ■ _____
- ■ _____
- ■ _____
- ■ _____
- ■ _____
- ■ _____
- ■ _____

DON'T FORGET

_____
_____
_____

TIME	PLANS & SCHEDULE
6:00 am	
6:30 am	
7:00 am	
7:30 am	
8:00 am	
8:30 am	
9:00 am	
9:30 am	
10:00 am	
10:30 am	
11:00 am	
11:30 am	
12:00 pm	
12:30 pm	
1:00 pm	
1:30 pm	
2:00 pm	
2:30 pm	
3:00 pm	
3:30 pm	
4:00 pm	
4:30 pm	
5:00 pm	
5:30 pm	
6:00 pm	
6:30 pm	
7:00 pm	
7:30 pm	
8:00 pm	
8:30 pm	
9:00 pm	
9:30 pm	
10:00 pm	

DAILY PLANNER

FEBRUARY 29, 2024

Thursday

TODAY'S AFFIRMATION

WEATHER

MOOD

TOP 3 PRIORITIES

1 _____

2 _____

3 _____

TO-DO LIST

- ☐ _____
- ☐ _____
- ☐ _____
- ☐ _____
- ☐ _____
- ☐ _____
- ☐ _____
- ☐ _____

DON'T FORGET

_____

_____

_____

TIME	PLANS & SCHEDULE
6:00 am	
6:30 am	
7:00 am	
7:30 am	
8:00 am	
8:30 am	
9:00 am	
9:30 am	
10:00 am	
10:30 am	
11:00 am	
11:30 am	
12:00 pm	
12:30 pm	
1:00 pm	
1:30 pm	
2:00 pm	
2:30 pm	
3:00 pm	
3:30 pm	
4:00 pm	
4:30 pm	
5:00 pm	
5:30 pm	
6:00 pm	
6:30 pm	
7:00 pm	
7:30 pm	
8:00 pm	
8:30 pm	
9:00 pm	
9:30 pm	
10:00 pm	

MONTHLY BUDGET PLANNER

Budget Goal: _____   Month: _____

Income

Date	Description	Amount
Total		

Fixed Expenses

Date	Description	Amount
Total		

Other Expenses

Date	Description	Amount
Total		

Bills

Date	Description	Amount
Total		

Recap

	Goal	Actual	Difference
Earnt			
Spent			
Debt			
Saved			

Notes

Date:

GRATITUDE JOURNAL

DATE: _____   S M T W T F S

TODAY I'M GRATEFUL FOR

- _____
- _____
- _____

WATER INTAKE

1L   2L   3L

WEATHER

NOTES / REMINDERS

TODAY'S AFFIRMATION

- _____
- _____
- _____
- _____

SOMETHING I'M PROUD OF

- _____
- _____
- _____
- _____

TOMORROW I LOOK FORWARD TO

- _____
- _____
- _____
- _____

30 DAY
Self-Care Challenge

DAY 1 Start a gratitude journal	**DAY 2** Learn to meditate	**DAY 3** Spend the day social media free	**DAY 4** Call someone you love	**DAY 5** Take a 15 minute walk outdoors
DAY 6 Listen to a podcast	**DAY 7** Learn to cook a new recipe	**DAY 8** Stretch for 10-15 minutes	**DAY 9** Listen to your favorite song	**DAY 10** Practice deep breathing
DAY 11 Try a free online workout	**DAY 12** Read a book for 15 minutes	**DAY 13** Write a list of short-term goals	**DAY 14** De-clutter a room or desk	**DAY 15** Go to bed 30 minutes earlier
DAY 16 Have a game night	**DAY 17** Wake up 15 minutes earlier	**DAY 18** Make your favorite meal	**DAY 19** Buy yourself something nice	**DAY 20** Create a bucket list
DAY 21 Watch a movie or series	**DAY 22** Write down your thoughts	**DAY 23** Take a long shower or bath	**DAY 24** Have a home spa day	**DAY 25** Read inspirational quotes
DAY 26 Create a vision board	**DAY 27** Spend some time outside	**DAY 28** Do a hair mask	**DAY 29** Write it all down in a journal	**DAY 30** Take a power nap

MARCH 2024

Sunday	Monday	Tuesday	Wednesday
03	04	05	06
10	11	12	13
17	18	19	20
24	25	26	27
31			

MARCH 2024

Thursday	Friday	Saturday	Notes
	01	02	
07	08	09	
14	15	16	
21	22	23	
28	29	30	

MARCH

Goal

Action Plan

Date

....

....

....

....

....

....

....

....

....

....

Grateful For

To Improve

....

....

....

....

....

....

....

....

....

Notes

....

....

....

....

DAILY PLANNER

MARCH 1, 2024

Friday

TODAY'S AFFIRMATION

WEATHER

MOOD

TOP 3 PRIORITIES

1 _____
_____

2 _____
_____

3 _____
_____

TO-DO LIST

- ■ _____
- ■ _____
- ■ _____
- ■ _____
- ■ _____
- ■ _____
- ■ _____
- ■ _____

DON'T FORGET

_____
_____
_____

TIME	PLANS & SCHEDULE
6:00 am	
6:30 am	
7:00 am	
7:30 am	
8:00 am	
8:30 am	
9:00 am	
9:30 am	
10:00 am	
10:30 am	
11:00 am	
11:30 am	
12:00 pm	
12:30 pm	
1:00 pm	
1:30 pm	
2:00 pm	
2:30 pm	
3:00 pm	
3:30 pm	
4:00 pm	
4:30 pm	
5:00 pm	
5:30 pm	
6:00 pm	
6:30 pm	
7:00 pm	
7:30 pm	
8:00 pm	
8:30 pm	
9:00 pm	
9:30 pm	
10:00 pm	

DAILY PLANNER

MARCH 2, 2024

Saturday

TODAY'S AFFIRMATION

WEATHER

MOOD

TOP 3 PRIORITIES

1 _____
_____

2 _____
_____

3 _____
_____

TO-DO LIST

- ☐ _____
- ☐ _____
- ☐ _____
- ☐ _____
- ☐ _____
- ☐ _____
- ☐ _____
- ☐ _____

DON'T FORGET

_____
_____
_____

TIME	PLANS & SCHEDULE
6:00 am	
6:30 am	
7:00 am	
7:30 am	
8:00 am	
8:30 am	
9:00 am	
9:30 am	
10:00 am	
10:30 am	
11:00 am	
11:30 am	
12:00 pm	
12:30 pm	
1:00 pm	
1:30 pm	
2:00 pm	
2:30 pm	
3:00 pm	
3:30 pm	
4:00 pm	
4:30 pm	
5:00 pm	
5:30 pm	
6:00 pm	
6:30 pm	
7:00 pm	
7:30 pm	
8:00 pm	
8:30 pm	
9:00 pm	
9:30 pm	
10:00 pm	

DAILY PLANNER

MARCH 3, 2024

Sunday

TODAY'S AFFIRMATION

WEATHER

MOOD

TOP 3 PRIORITIES

1 _____
_____

2 _____
_____

3 _____
_____

TO-DO LIST

- ▪ _____
- ▪ _____
- ▪ _____
- ▪ _____
- ▪ _____
- ▪ _____
- ▪ _____
- ▪ _____

DON'T FORGET

_____
_____
_____

TIME	PLANS & SCHEDULE
6:00 am	
6:30 am	
7:00 am	
7:30 am	
8:00 am	
8:30 am	
9:00 am	
9:30 am	
10:00 am	
10:30 am	
11:00 am	
11:30 am	
12:00 pm	
12:30 pm	
1:00 pm	
1:30 pm	
2:00 pm	
2:30 pm	
3:00 pm	
3:30 pm	
4:00 pm	
4:30 pm	
5:00 pm	
5:30 pm	
6:00 pm	
6:30 pm	
7:00 pm	
7:30 pm	
8:00 pm	
8:30 pm	
9:00 pm	
9:30 pm	
10:00 pm	

DAILY PLANNER

MARCH 4, 2024

Monday

TODAY'S AFFIRMATION

TOP 3 PRIORITIES

1 _____
_____

2 _____
_____

3 _____
_____

TO-DO LIST

- ■ _____
- ■ _____
- ■ _____
- ■ _____
- ■ _____
- ■ _____
- ■ _____
- ■ _____

DON'T FORGET

_____
_____
_____

TIME	PLANS & SCHEDULE
6:00 am	
6:30 am	
7:00 am	
7:30 am	
8:00 am	
8:30 am	
9:00 am	
9:30 am	
10:00 am	
10:30 am	
11:00 am	
11:30 am	
12:00 pm	
12:30 pm	
1:00 pm	
1:30 pm	
2:00 pm	
2:30 pm	
3:00 pm	
3:30 pm	
4:00 pm	
4:30 pm	
5:00 pm	
5:30 pm	
6:00 pm	
6:30 pm	
7:00 pm	
7:30 pm	
8:00 pm	
8:30 pm	
9:00 pm	
9:30 pm	
10:00 pm	

DAILY PLANNER

MARCH 5, 2024

Tuesday

TODAY'S AFFIRMATION

WEATHER

MOOD

TOP 3 PRIORITIES

1 _____
_____

2 _____
_____

3 _____
_____

TO-DO LIST

- _____
- _____
- _____
- _____
- _____
- _____
- _____
- _____

DON'T FORGET

_____
_____
_____

TIME	PLANS & SCHEDULE
6:00 am	
6:30 am	
7:00 am	
7:30 am	
8:00 am	
8:30 am	
9:00 am	
9:30 am	
10:00 am	
10:30 am	
11:00 am	
11:30 am	
12:00 pm	
12:30 pm	
1:00 pm	
1:30 pm	
2:00 pm	
2:30 pm	
3:00 pm	
3:30 pm	
4:00 pm	
4:30 pm	
5:00 pm	
5:30 pm	
6:00 pm	
6:30 pm	
7:00 pm	
7:30 pm	
8:00 pm	
8:30 pm	
9:00 pm	
9:30 pm	
10:00 pm	

DAILY PLANNER

MARCH 6, 2024

Wednesday

TODAY'S AFFIRMATION

WEATHER	
MOOD	

TOP 3 PRIORITIES

1 _____
_____

2 _____
_____

3 _____
_____

TO-DO LIST

☐ _____

☐ _____

☐ _____

☐ _____

☐ _____

☐ _____

☐ _____

☐ _____

DON'T FORGET

_____
_____
_____

TIME	PLANS & SCHEDULE
6:00 am	
6:30 am	
7:00 am	
7:30 am	
8:00 am	
8:30 am	
9:00 am	
9:30 am	
10:00 am	
10:30 am	
11:00 am	
11:30 am	
12:00 pm	
12:30 pm	
1:00 pm	
1:30 pm	
2:00 pm	
2:30 pm	
3:00 pm	
3:30 pm	
4:00 pm	
4:30 pm	
5:00 pm	
5:30 pm	
6:00 pm	
6:30 pm	
7:00 pm	
7:30 pm	
8:00 pm	
8:30 pm	
9:00 pm	
9:30 pm	

10:00 pm

DAILY PLANNER

MARCH 7, 2024

Thursday

TODAY'S AFFIRMATION

WEATHER

MOOD

TOP 3 PRIORITIES

1 _____
_____

2 _____
_____

3 _____
_____

TO-DO LIST

- ▪ _____
- ▪ _____
- ▪ _____
- ▪ _____
- ▪ _____
- ▪ _____
- ▪ _____
- ▪ _____

DON'T FORGET

_____
_____
_____

TIME	PLANS & SCHEDULE
6:00 am	
6:30 am	
7:00 am	
7:30 am	
8:00 am	
8:30 am	
9:00 am	
9:30 am	
10:00 am	
10:30 am	
11:00 am	
11:30 am	
12:00 pm	
12:30 pm	
1:00 pm	
1:30 pm	
2:00 pm	
2:30 pm	
3:00 pm	
3:30 pm	
4:00 pm	
4:30 pm	
5:00 pm	
5:30 pm	
6:00 pm	
6:30 pm	
7:00 pm	
7:30 pm	
8:00 pm	
8:30 pm	
9:00 pm	
9:30 pm	
10:00 pm	

DAILY PLANNER

MARCH 8, 2024

Friday

TODAY'S AFFIRMATION

WEATHER	

MOOD	

TOP 3 PRIORITIES

1. _____
   _____
2. _____
   _____
3. _____
   _____

TO-DO LIST

- ☐ _____
- ☐ _____
- ☐ _____
- ☐ _____
- ☐ _____
- ☐ _____
- ☐ _____
- ☐ _____

DON'T FORGET

_____
_____
_____

TIME	PLANS & SCHEDULE
6:00 am	
6:30 am	
7:00 am	
7:30 am	
8:00 am	
8:30 am	
9:00 am	
9:30 am	
10:00 am	
10:30 am	
11:00 am	
11:30 am	
12:00 pm	
12:30 pm	
1:00 pm	
1:30 pm	
2:00 pm	
2:30 pm	
3:00 pm	
3:30 pm	
4:00 pm	
4:30 pm	
5:00 pm	
5:30 pm	
6:00 pm	
6:30 pm	
7:00 pm	
7:30 pm	
8:30 pm	
9:00 pm	
9:30 pm	
10:00 pm	

DAILY PLANNER

MARCH 9, 2024

Saturday

TODAY'S AFFIRMATION

WEATHER

MOOD

TOP 3 PRIORITIES

1 _____
_____

2 _____
_____

3 _____
_____

TO-DO LIST

- ☐ _____
- ☐ _____
- ☐ _____
- ☐ _____
- ☐ _____
- ☐ _____
- ☐ _____
- ☐ _____

DON'T FORGET

_____
_____
_____

TIME	PLANS & SCHEDULE
6:00 am	
6:30 am	
7:00 am	
7:30 am	
8:00 am	
8:30 am	
9:00 am	
9:30 am	
10:00 am	
10:30 am	
11:00 am	
11:30 am	
12:00 pm	
12:30 pm	
1:00 pm	
1:30 pm	
2:00 pm	
2:30 pm	
3:00 pm	
3:30 pm	
4:00 pm	
4:30 pm	
5:00 pm	
5:30 pm	
6:00 pm	
6:30 pm	
7:00 pm	
7:30 pm	
8:30 pm	
9:00 pm	
9:30 pm	
10:00 pm	
8:00 pm	

DAILY PLANNER

MARCH 10, 2024

Sunday

TODAY'S AFFIRMATION

WEATHER

MOOD

TOP 3 PRIORITIES

1 _____
_____

2 _____
_____

3 _____
_____

TO-DO LIST

- _____
- _____
- _____
- _____
- _____
- _____
- _____
- _____

DON'T FORGET

_____
_____
_____

TIME	PLANS & SCHEDULE
6:00 am	
6:30 am	
7:00 am	
7:30 am	
8:00 am	
8:30 am	
9:00 am	
9:30 am	
10:00 am	
10:30 am	
11:00 am	
11:30 am	
12:00 pm	
12:30 pm	
1:00 pm	
1:30 pm	
2:00 pm	
2:30 pm	
3:00 pm	
3:30 pm	
4:00 pm	
4:30 pm	
5:00 pm	
5:30 pm	
6:00 pm	
6:30 pm	
7:00 pm	
7:30 pm	
8:00 pm	
8:30 pm	
9:00 pm	
9:30 pm	
10:00 pm	

DAILY PLANNER

MARCH 11, 2024

Monday

TODAY'S AFFIRMATION

WEATHER

MOOD

TOP 3 PRIORITIES

1 _____
_____

2 _____
_____

3 _____
_____

TO-DO LIST

- _____
- _____
- _____
- _____
- _____
- _____
- _____
- _____

DON'T FORGET

_____
_____
_____

TIME	PLANS & SCHEDULE
6:00 am	
6:30 am	
7:00 am	
7:30 am	
8:00 am	
8:30 am	
9:00 am	
9:30 am	
10:00 am	
10:30 am	
11:00 am	
11:30 am	
12:00 pm	
12:30 pm	
1:00 pm	
1:30 pm	
2:00 pm	
2:30 pm	
3:00 pm	
3:30 pm	
4:00 pm	
4:30 pm	
5:00 pm	
5:30 pm	
6:00 pm	
6:30 pm	
7:00 pm	
7:30 pm	
8:00 pm	
8:30 pm	
9:00 pm	
9:30 pm	
10:00 pm	

DAILY PLANNER

MARCH 12, 2024

Tuesday

TODAY'S AFFIRMATION

WEATHER

MOOD

TOP 3 PRIORITIES

1 _____
_____

2 _____
_____

3 _____
_____

TO-DO LIST

- ◼ _____
- ◼ _____
- ◼ _____
- ◼ _____
- ◼ _____
- ◼ _____
- ◼ _____
- ◼ _____

DON'T FORGET

_____
_____
_____

TIME	PLANS & SCHEDULE
6:00 am	
6:30 am	
7:00 am	
7:30 am	
8:00 am	
8:30 am	
9:00 am	
9:30 am	
10:00 am	
10:30 am	
11:00 am	
11:30 am	
12:00 pm	
12:30 pm	
1:00 pm	
1:30 pm	
2:00 pm	
2:30 pm	
3:00 pm	
3:30 pm	
4:00 pm	
4:30 pm	
5:00 pm	
5:30 pm	
6:00 pm	
6:30 pm	
7:00 pm	
7:30 pm	
8:00 pm	
8:30 pm	
9:00 pm	
9:30 pm	
10:00 pm	

DAILY PLANNER

MARCH 13, 2024

Wednesday

TODAY'S AFFIRMATION

WEATHER

MOOD

TOP 3 PRIORITIES

1 _____
_____

2 _____
_____

3 _____
_____

TO-DO LIST

- ▪ _____
- ▪ _____
- ▪ _____
- ▪ _____
- ▪ _____
- ▪ _____
- ▪ _____
- ▪ _____

DON'T FORGET

_____
_____
_____

TIME	PLANS & SCHEDULE
6:00 am	
6:30 am	
7:00 am	
7:30 am	
8:00 am	
8:30 am	
9:00 am	
9:30 am	
10:00 am	
10:30 am	
11:00 am	
11:30 am	
12:00 pm	
12:30 pm	
1:00 pm	
1:30 pm	
2:00 pm	
2:30 pm	
3:00 pm	
3:30 pm	
4:00 pm	
4:30 pm	
5:00 pm	
5:30 pm	
6:00 pm	
6:30 pm	
7:00 pm	
7:30 pm	
8:00 pm	
8:30 pm	
9:00 pm	
9:30 pm	
10:00 pm	

DAILY PLANNER

MARCH 14, 2024

Thursday

TODAY'S AFFIRMATION

WEATHER	

MOOD	

TOP 3 PRIORITIES

1 _____

_____

2 _____

_____

3 _____

_____

TO-DO LIST

- _____
- _____
- _____
- _____
- _____
- _____
- _____
- _____

DON'T FORGET

_____

_____

_____

TIME	PLANS & SCHEDULE
6:00 am	
6:30 am	
7:00 am	
7:30 am	
8:00 am	
8:30 am	
9:00 am	
9:30 am	
10:00 am	
10:30 am	
11:00 am	
11:30 am	
12:00 pm	
12:30 pm	
1:00 pm	
1:30 pm	
2:00 pm	
2:30 pm	
3:00 pm	
3:30 pm	
4:00 pm	
4:30 pm	
5:00 pm	
5:30 pm	
6:00 pm	
6:30 pm	
7:00 pm	
7:30 pm	
8:00 pm	
8:30 pm	
9:00 pm	
9:30 pm	
10:00 pm	

DAILY PLANNER

MARCH 15, 2024

Friday

TODAY'S AFFIRMATION

WEATHER

MOOD

TIME	PLANS & SCHEDULE
6:00 am	
6:30 am	
7:00 am	
7:30 am	
8:00 am	
8:30 am	
9:00 am	
9:30 am	
10:00 am	
10:30 am	
11:00 am	
11:30 am	
12:00 pm	
12:30 pm	
1:00 pm	
1:30 pm	
2:00 pm	
2:30 pm	
3:00 pm	
3:30 pm	
4:00 pm	
4:30 pm	
5:00 pm	
5:30 pm	
6:00 pm	
6:30 pm	
7:00 pm	
7:30 pm	
8:00 pm	
8:30 pm	
9:00 pm	
9:30 pm	
10:00 pm	

TOP 3 PRIORITIES

1

2

3

TO-DO LIST

-
-
-
-
-
-
-
-

DON'T FORGET

DAILY PLANNER

MARCH 16, 2024

Saturday

TODAY'S AFFIRMATION

WEATHER	

MOOD	

TOP 3 PRIORITIES

1 _____
_____

2 _____
_____

3 _____
_____

TO-DO LIST

- ☐ _____
- ☐ _____
- ☐ _____
- ☐ _____
- ☐ _____
- ☐ _____
- ☐ _____
- ☐ _____

DON'T FORGET

_____
_____
_____

TIME	PLANS & SCHEDULE
6:00 am	
6:30 am	
7:00 am	
7:30 am	
8:00 am	
8:30 am	
9:00 am	
9:30 am	
10:00 am	
10:30 am	
11:00 am	
11:30 am	
12:00 pm	
12:30 pm	
1:00 pm	
1:30 pm	
2:00 pm	
2:30 pm	
3:00 pm	
3:30 pm	
4:00 pm	
4:30 pm	
5:00 pm	
5:30 pm	
6:00 pm	
6:30 pm	
7:00 pm	
7:30 pm	
8:00 pm	
8:30 pm	
9:00 pm	
9:30 pm	
10:00 pm	

DAILY PLANNER

MARCH 17, 2024

Sunday

TODAY'S AFFIRMATION

WEATHER

MOOD

TOP 3 PRIORITIES

1 _____
_____

2 _____
_____

3 _____
_____

TO-DO LIST

- ◼ _____
- ◼ _____
- ◼ _____
- ◼ _____
- ◼ _____
- ◼ _____
- ◼ _____
- ◼ _____

DON'T FORGET

_____
_____
_____

TIME	PLANS & SCHEDULE
6:00 am	
6:30 am	
7:00 am	
7:30 am	
8:00 am	
8:30 am	
9:00 am	
9:30 am	
10:00 am	
10:30 am	
11:00 am	
11:30 am	
12:00 pm	
12:30 pm	
1:00 pm	
1:30 pm	
2:00 pm	
2:30 pm	
3:00 pm	
3:30 pm	
4:00 pm	
4:30 pm	
5:00 pm	
5:30 pm	
6:00 pm	
6:30 pm	
7:00 pm	
7:30 pm	
8:00 pm	
8:30 pm	
9:00 pm	
9:30 pm	
10:00 pm	

DAILY PLANNER

MARCH 18, 2024

Monday

TODAY'S AFFIRMATION

WEATHER	

MOOD	

TOP 3 PRIORITIES

1 _____
_____

2 _____
_____

3 _____
_____

TO-DO LIST

- ☐
- ☐
- ☐
- ☐
- ☐
- ☐
- ☐
- ☐

DON'T FORGET

TIME	PLANS & SCHEDULE
6:00 am	
6:30 am	
7:00 am	
7:30 am	
8:00 am	
8:30 am	
9:00 am	
9:30 am	
10:00 am	
10:30 am	
11:00 am	
11:30 am	
12:00 pm	
12:30 pm	
1:00 pm	
1:30 pm	
2:00 pm	
2:30 pm	
3:00 pm	
3:30 pm	
4:00 pm	
4:30 pm	
5:00 pm	
5:30 pm	
6:00 pm	
6:30 pm	
7:00 pm	
7:30 pm	
8:00 pm	
8:30 pm	
9:00 pm	
9:30 pm	
10:00 pm	

DAILY PLANNER

MARCH 19, 2024

Tuesday

TODAY'S AFFIRMATION

WEATHER

MOOD

TOP 3 PRIORITIES

1 _____
_____

2 _____
_____

3 _____
_____

TO-DO LIST

- _____
- _____
- _____
- _____
- _____
- _____
- _____
- _____

DON'T FORGET

_____
_____
_____

TIME	PLANS & SCHEDULE
6:00 am	
6:30 am	
7:00 am	
7:30 am	
8:00 am	
8:30 am	
9:00 am	
9:30 am	
10:00 am	
10:30 am	
11:00 am	
11:30 am	
12:00 pm	
12:30 pm	
1:00 pm	
1:30 pm	
2:00 pm	
2:30 pm	
3:00 pm	
3:30 pm	
4:00 pm	
4:30 pm	
5:00 pm	
5:30 pm	
6:00 pm	
6:30 pm	
7:00 pm	
7:30 pm	
8:00 pm	
8:30 pm	
9:00 pm	
9:30 pm	
10:00 pm	

DAILY PLANNER

MARCH 20, 2024

Wednesday

TODAY'S AFFIRMATION

WEATHER

MOOD

TOP 3 PRIORITIES

1 _____
_____

2 _____
_____

3 _____
_____

TO-DO LIST

■ _____

■ _____

■ _____

■ _____

■ _____

■ _____

■ _____

■ _____

DON'T FORGET

_____
_____
_____

TIME	PLANS & SCHEDULE
6:00 am	
6:30 am	
7:00 am	
7:30 am	
8:00 am	
8:30 am	
9:00 am	
9:30 am	
10:00 am	
10:30 am	
11:00 am	
11:30 am	
12:00 pm	
12:30 pm	
1:00 pm	
1:30 pm	
2:00 pm	
2:30 pm	
3:00 pm	
3:30 pm	
4:00 pm	
4:30 pm	
5:00 pm	
5:30 pm	
6:00 pm	
6:30 pm	
7:00 pm	
7:30 pm	
8:00 pm	
8:30 pm	
9:00 pm	
9:30 pm	
10:00 pm	

DAILY PLANNER

MARCH 21, 2024

Thursday

TODAY'S AFFIRMATION

WEATHER

MOOD

TOP 3 PRIORITIES

1 _____
_____

2 _____
_____

3 _____
_____

TO-DO LIST

■ _____

■ _____

■ _____

■ _____

■ _____

■ _____

■ _____

■ _____

DON'T FORGET

_____

_____

_____

TIME	PLANS & SCHEDULE
6:00 am	
6:30 am	
7:00 am	
7:30 am	
8:00 am	
8:30 am	
9:00 am	
9:30 am	
10:00 am	
10:30 am	
11:00 am	
11:30 am	
12:00 pm	
12:30 pm	
1:00 pm	
1:30 pm	
2:00 pm	
2:30 pm	
3:00 pm	
3:30 pm	
4:00 pm	
4:30 pm	
5:00 pm	
5:30 pm	
6:00 pm	
6:30 pm	
7:00 pm	
7:30 pm	
8:00 pm	
8:30 pm	
9:00 pm	
9:30 pm	
10:00 pm	

DAILY PLANNER

MARCH 22, 2024

Friday

TODAY'S AFFIRMATION

WEATHER

MOOD

TOP 3 PRIORITIES

1 _____
_____

2 _____
_____

3 _____
_____

TO-DO LIST

- ■ _____
- ■ _____
- ■ _____
- ■ _____
- ■ _____
- ■ _____
- ■ _____
- ■ _____

DON'T FORGET

_____
_____
_____

TIME	PLANS & SCHEDULE
6:00 am	
6:30 am	
7:00 am	
7:30 am	
8:00 am	
8:30 am	
9:00 am	
9:30 am	
10:00 am	
10:30 am	
11:00 am	
11:30 am	
12:00 pm	
12:30 pm	
1:00 pm	
1:30 pm	
2:00 pm	
2:30 pm	
3:00 pm	
3:30 pm	
4:00 pm	
4:30 pm	
5:00 pm	
5:30 pm	
6:00 pm	
6:30 pm	
7:00 pm	
7:30 pm	
8:00 pm	
8:30 pm	
9:00 pm	
9:30 pm	
10:00 pm	

DAILY PLANNER

MARCH 23, 2024

Saturday

TODAY'S AFFIRMATION

WEATHER

MOOD

TOP 3 PRIORITIES

1 _____
_____

2 _____
_____

3 _____
_____

TO-DO LIST

- ◼ _____
- ◼ _____
- ◼ _____
- ◼ _____
- ◼ _____
- ◼ _____
- ◼ _____
- ◼ _____

DON'T FORGET

_____
_____
_____

TIME	PLANS & SCHEDULE
6:00 am	
6:30 am	
7:00 am	
7:30 am	
8:00 am	
8:30 am	
9:00 am	
9:30 am	
10:00 am	
10:30 am	
11:00 am	
11:30 am	
12:00 pm	
12:30 pm	
1:00 pm	
1:30 pm	
2:00 pm	
2:30 pm	
3:00 pm	
3:30 pm	
4:00 pm	
4:30 pm	
5:00 pm	
5:30 pm	
6:00 pm	
6:30 pm	
7:00 pm	
7:30 pm	
8:00 pm	
8:30 pm	
9:00 pm	
9:30 pm	
10:00 pm	

DAILY PLANNER

MARCH 24, 2024

Sunday

TODAY'S AFFIRMATION

WEATHER	
MOOD	

TOP 3 PRIORITIES

1 _____

_____

2 _____

_____

3 _____

_____

TO-DO LIST

■ _____

■ _____

■ _____

■ _____

■ _____

■ _____

■ _____

■ _____

DON'T FORGET

_____

_____

_____

TIME	PLANS & SCHEDULE
6:00 am	
6:30 am	
7:00 am	
7:30 am	
8:00 am	
8:30 am	
9:00 am	
9:30 am	
10:00 am	
10:30 am	
11:00 am	
11:30 am	
12:00 pm	
12:30 pm	
1:00 pm	
1:30 pm	
2:00 pm	
2:30 pm	
3:00 pm	
3:30 pm	
4:00 pm	
4:30 pm	
5:00 pm	
5:30 pm	
6:00 pm	
6:30 pm	
7:00 pm	
7:30 pm	
8:00 pm	
8:30 pm	
9:00 pm	
9:30 pm	
10:00 pm	

DAILY PLANNER

MARCH 25, 2024

Monday

TODAY'S AFFIRMATION

WEATHER

MOOD

TOP 3 PRIORITIES

1 _____
_____

2 _____
_____

3 _____
_____

TO-DO LIST

- _____
- _____
- _____
- _____
- _____
- _____
- _____
- _____

DON'T FORGET

_____
_____
_____
_____

TIME	PLANS & SCHEDULE
6:00 am	
6:30 am	
7:00 am	
7:30 am	
8:00 am	
8:30 am	
9:00 am	
9:30 am	
10:00 am	
10:30 am	
11:00 am	
11:30 am	
12:00 pm	
12:30 pm	
1:00 pm	
1:30 pm	
2:00 pm	
2:30 pm	
3:00 pm	
3:30 pm	
4:00 pm	
4:30 pm	
5:00 pm	
5:30 pm	
6:00 pm	
6:30 pm	
7:00 pm	
7:30 pm	
8:00 pm	
8:30 pm	
9:00 pm	
9:30 pm	
10:00 pm	

DAILY PLANNER

MARCH 26, 2024

Tuesday

TODAY'S AFFIRMATION

WEATHER	
MOOD	

TOP 3 PRIORITIES

1 _____
_____

2 _____
_____

3 _____
_____

TO-DO LIST

- ■ _____
- ■ _____
- ■ _____
- ■ _____
- ■ _____
- ■ _____
- ■ _____
- ■ _____

DON'T FORGET

_____
_____
_____

TIME	PLANS & SCHEDULE
6:00 am	
6:30 am	
7:00 am	
7:30 am	
8:00 am	
8:30 am	
9:00 am	
9:30 am	
10:00 am	
10:30 am	
11:00 am	
11:30 am	
12:00 pm	
12:30 pm	
1:00 pm	
1:30 pm	
2:00 pm	
2:30 pm	
3:00 pm	
3:30 pm	
4:00 pm	
4:30 pm	
5:00 pm	
5:30 pm	
6:00 pm	
6:30 pm	
7:00 pm	
7:30 pm	
8:00 pm	
8:30 pm	
9:00 pm	
9:30 pm	
10:00 pm	

DAILY PLANNER

MARCH 27, 2024

Wednesday

TODAY'S AFFIRMATION

WEATHER

MOOD

TOP 3 PRIORITIES

1 _____

2 _____

3 _____

TO-DO LIST

- ▪ _____
- ▪ _____
- ▪ _____
- ▪ _____
- ▪ _____
- ▪ _____
- ▪ _____
- ▪ _____

DON'T FORGET

TIME	PLANS & SCHEDULE
6:00 am	
6:30 am	
7:00 am	
7:30 am	
8:00 am	
8:30 am	
9:00 am	
9:30 am	
10:00 am	
10:30 am	
11:00 am	
11:30 am	
12:00 pm	
12:30 pm	
1:00 pm	
1:30 pm	
2:00 pm	
2:30 pm	
3:00 pm	
3:30 pm	
4:00 pm	
4:30 pm	
5:00 pm	
5:30 pm	
6:00 pm	
6:30 pm	
7:00 pm	
7:30 pm	
8:00 pm	
8:30 pm	
9:00 pm	
9:30 pm	
10:00 pm	

DAILY PLANNER

MARCH 28, 2024

Thursday

TODAY'S AFFIRMATION

WEATHER

MOOD

TOP 3 PRIORITIES

1 _____
_____

2 _____
_____

3 _____
_____

TO-DO LIST

■ _____

■ _____

■ _____

■ _____

■ _____

■ _____

■ _____

■ _____

DON'T FORGET

_____

_____

_____

TIME	PLANS & SCHEDULE
6:00 am	
6:30 am	
7:00 am	
7:30 am	
8:00 am	
8:30 am	
9:00 am	
9:30 am	
10:00 am	
10:30 am	
11:00 am	
11:30 am	
12:00 pm	
12:30 pm	
1:00 pm	
1:30 pm	
2:00 pm	
2:30 pm	
3:00 pm	
3:30 pm	
4:00 pm	
4:30 pm	
5:00 pm	
5:30 pm	
6:00 pm	
6:30 pm	
7:00 pm	
7:30 pm	
8:00 pm	
8:30 pm	
9:00 pm	
9:30 pm	
10:00 pm	

DAILY PLANNER

MARCH 29, 2024

Friday

TODAY'S AFFIRMATION

WEATHER

MOOD

TOP 3 PRIORITIES

1 _____

2 _____

3 _____

TO-DO LIST

- _____
- _____
- _____
- _____
- _____
- _____
- _____
- _____

DON'T FORGET

_____

_____

_____

TIME	PLANS & SCHEDULE
6:00 am	
6:30 am	
7:00 am	
7:30 am	
8:00 am	
8:30 am	
9:00 am	
9:30 am	
10:00 am	
10:30 am	
11:00 am	
11:30 am	
12:00 pm	
12:30 pm	
1:00 pm	
1:30 pm	
2:00 pm	
2:30 pm	
3:00 pm	
3:30 pm	
4:00 pm	
4:30 pm	
5:00 pm	
5:30 pm	
6:00 pm	
6:30 pm	
7:00 pm	
7:30 pm	
8:00 pm	
8:30 pm	
9:00 pm	
9:30 pm	
10:00 pm	

DAILY PLANNER

MARCH 30, 2024

Saturday

TODAY'S AFFIRMATION

WEATHER

MOOD

TOP 3 PRIORITIES

1 _____
_____

2 _____
_____

3 _____
_____

TO-DO LIST

- _____
- _____
- _____
- _____
- _____
- _____
- _____
- _____

DON'T FORGET

_____
_____
_____

TIME	PLANS & SCHEDULE
6:00 am	
6:30 am	
7:00 am	
7:30 am	
8:00 am	
8:30 am	
9:00 am	
9:30 am	
10:00 am	
10:30 am	
11:00 am	
11:30 am	
12:00 pm	
12:30 pm	
1:00 pm	
1:30 pm	
2:00 pm	
2:30 pm	
3:00 pm	
3:30 pm	
4:00 pm	
4:30 pm	
5:00 pm	
5:30 pm	
6:00 pm	
6:30 pm	
7:00 pm	
7:30 pm	
8:00 pm	
8:30 pm	
9:00 pm	
9:30 pm	
10:00 pm	

DAILY PLANNER

MARCH 31, 2024

Sunday

TODAY'S AFFIRMATION

WEATHER

MOOD

TOP 3 PRIORITIES

1 _____
_____

2 _____
_____

3 _____
_____

TO-DO LIST

- ◼ _____
- ◼ _____
- ◼ _____
- ◼ _____
- ◼ _____
- ◼ _____
- ◼ _____
- ◼ _____

DON'T FORGET

_____
_____
_____

TIME	PLANS & SCHEDULE
6:00 am	
6:30 am	
7:00 am	
7:30 am	
8:00 am	
8:30 am	
9:00 am	
9:30 am	
10:00 am	
10:30 am	
11:00 am	
11:30 am	
12:00 pm	
12:30 pm	
1:00 pm	
1:30 pm	
2:00 pm	
2:30 pm	
3:00 pm	
3:30 pm	
4:00 pm	
4:30 pm	
5:00 pm	
5:30 pm	
6:00 pm	
6:30 pm	
7:00 pm	
7:30 pm	
8:00 pm	
8:30 pm	
9:00 pm	
9:30 pm	
10:00 pm	

MONTHLY BUDGET PLANNER

Budget Goal: _____   Month: _____

Income

Date	Description	Amount
Total		

Fixed Expenses

Date	Description	Amount
Total		

Other Expenses

Date	Description	Amount
Total		

Bills

Date	Description	Amount
Total		

Recap

	Goal	Actual	Difference
Earnt			
Spent			
Debt			
Saved			

Notes

Date:

GRATITUDE JOURNAL

DATE: _____   S M T W T F S

TODAY I'M GRATEFUL FOR

- _____
- _____
- _____

WATER INTAKE

◇◇◇◇ ◇◇◇◇ ◇◇
     1L   2L   3L

WEATHER

TODAY'S AFFIRMATION

- _____
- _____
- _____
- _____

NOTES / REMINDERS

SOMETHING I'M PROUD OF

- _____
- _____
- _____
- _____

TOMORROW I LOOK FORWARD TO

- _____
- _____
- _____
- _____

30 DAY
Self-Care Challenge

DAY 1	DAY 2	DAY 3	DAY 4	DAY 5
Start a gratitude journal	Learn to meditate	Spend the day social media free	Call someone you love	Take a 15 minute walk outdoors
DAY 6	**DAY 7**	**DAY 8**	**DAY 9**	**DAY 10**
Listen to a podcast	Learn to cook a new recipe	Stretch for 10-15 minutes	Listen to your favorite song	Practice deep breathing
DAY 11	**DAY 12**	**DAY 13**	**DAY 14**	**DAY 15**
Try a free online workout	Read a book for 15 minutes	Write a list of short-term goals	De-clutter a room or desk	Go to bed 30 minutes earlier
DAY 16	**DAY 17**	**DAY 18**	**DAY 19**	**DAY 20**
Have a game night	Wake up 15 minutes earlier	Make your favorite meal	Buy yourself something nice	Create a bucket list
DAY 21	**DAY 22**	**DAY 23**	**DAY 24**	**DAY 25**
Watch a movie or series	Write down your thoughts	Take a long shower or bath	Have a home spa day	Read inspirational quotes
DAY 26	**DAY 27**	**DAY 28**	**DAY 29**	**DAY 30**
Create a vision board	Spend some time outside	Do a hair mask	Write it all down in a journal	Take a power nap

APRIL 2024

Sunday	Monday	Tuesday	Wednesday
	01	02	03
07	08	09	10
14	15	16	17
21	22	23	24
28	29	30	

APRIL 2024

Thursday	Friday	Saturday	Notes
04	05	06	....
11	12	13	....
18	19	20	....
25	26	27	....

APRIL

Goal

Action Plan

Date

Grateful For

To Improve

Notes

DAILY PLANNER

APRIL 1, 2024

Monday

TODAY'S AFFIRMATION

WEATHER

MOOD

TOP 3 PRIORITIES
1 _____
_____
2 _____
_____
3 _____
_____

TO-DO LIST

- ▪ _____
- ▪ _____
- ▪ _____
- ▪ _____
- ▪ _____
- ▪ _____
- ▪ _____
- ▪ _____

DON'T FORGET

_____

_____

_____

TIME	PLANS & SCHEDULE
6:00 am	
6:30 am	
7:00 am	
7:30 am	
8:00 am	
8:30 am	
9:00 am	
9:30 am	
10:00 am	
10:30 am	
11:00 am	
11:30 am	
12:00 pm	
12:30 pm	
1:00 pm	
1:30 pm	
2:00 pm	
2:30 pm	
3:00 pm	
3:30 pm	
4:00 pm	
4:30 pm	
5:00 pm	
5:30 pm	
6:00 pm	
6:30 pm	
7:00 pm	
7:30 pm	
8:00 pm	
8:30 pm	
9:00 pm	
9:30 pm	
10:00 pm	

DAILY PLANNER

APRIL 2, 2024

Tuesday

TODAY'S AFFIRMATION

WEATHER

MOOD

TOP 3 PRIORITIES

1 _____
_____

2 _____
_____

3 _____
_____

TO-DO LIST

- ■ _____
- ■ _____
- ■ _____
- ■ _____
- ■ _____
- ■ _____
- ■ _____
- ■ _____

DON'T FORGET

_____
_____
_____

TIME	PLANS & SCHEDULE
6:00 am	
6:30 am	
7:00 am	
7:30 am	
8:00 am	
8:30 am	
9:00 am	
9:30 am	
10:00 am	
10:30 am	
11:00 am	
11:30 am	
12:00 pm	
12:30 pm	
1:00 pm	
1:30 pm	
2:00 pm	
2:30 pm	
3:00 pm	
3:30 pm	
4:00 pm	
4:30 pm	
5:00 pm	
5:30 pm	
6:00 pm	
6:30 pm	
7:00 pm	
7:30 pm	
8:00 pm	
8:30 pm	
9:00 pm	
9:30 pm	
10:00 pm	

DAILY PLANNER

APRIL 3, 2024

Wednesday

TODAY'S AFFIRMATION

WEATHER

MOOD

TOP 3 PRIORITIES

1 _____
_____

2 _____
_____

3 _____
_____

TO-DO LIST

- ◼ _____
- ◼ _____
- ◼ _____
- ◼ _____
- ◼ _____
- ◼ _____
- ◼ _____
- ◼ _____

DON'T FORGET

_____
_____
_____

TIME	PLANS & SCHEDULE
6:00 am	
6:30 am	
7:00 am	
7:30 am	
8:00 am	
8:30 am	
9:00 am	
9:30 am	
10:00 am	
10:30 am	
11:00 am	
11:30 am	
12:00 pm	
12:30 pm	
1:00 pm	
1:30 pm	
2:00 pm	
2:30 pm	
3:00 pm	
3:30 pm	
4:00 pm	
4:30 pm	
5:00 pm	
5:30 pm	
6:00 pm	
6:30 pm	
7:00 pm	
7:30 pm	
8:00 pm	
8:30 pm	
9:00 pm	
9:30 pm	
10:00 pm	

DAILY PLANNER

APRIL 4, 2024

Thursday

TODAY'S AFFIRMATION

WEATHER	
MOOD	

TOP 3 PRIORITIES

1 _____
_____

2 _____
_____

3 _____
_____

TO-DO LIST

- ▪ _____
- ▪ _____
- ▪ _____
- ▪ _____
- ▪ _____
- ▪ _____
- ▪ _____
- ▪ _____

DON'T FORGET

_____
_____
_____

TIME	PLANS & SCHEDULE
6:00 am	
6:30 am	
7:00 am	
7:30 am	
8:00 am	
8:30 am	
9:00 am	
9:30 am	
10:00 am	
10:30 am	
11:00 am	
11:30 am	
12:00 pm	
12:30 pm	
1:00 pm	
1:30 pm	
2:00 pm	
2:30 pm	
3:00 pm	
3:30 pm	
4:00 pm	
4:30 pm	
5:00 pm	
5:30 pm	
6:00 pm	
6:30 pm	
7:00 pm	
7:30 pm	
8:00 pm	
8:30 pm	
9:00 pm	
9:30 pm	
10:00 pm	

DAILY PLANNER

APRIL 5, 2024

Friday

TODAY'S AFFIRMATION

WEATHER

MOOD

TOP 3 PRIORITIES

1
2
3

TO-DO LIST

-
-
-
-
-
-
-
-

DON'T FORGET

TIME	PLANS & SCHEDULE
6:00 am	
6:30 am	
7:00 am	
7:30 am	
8:00 am	
8:30 am	
9:00 am	
9:30 am	
10:00 am	
10:30 am	
11:00 am	
11:30 am	
12:00 pm	
12:30 pm	
1:00 pm	
1:30 pm	
2:00 pm	
2:30 pm	
3:00 pm	
3:30 pm	
4:00 pm	
4:30 pm	
5:00 pm	
5:30 pm	
6:00 pm	
6:30 pm	
7:00 pm	
7:30 pm	
8:00 pm	
8:30 pm	
9:00 pm	
9:30 pm	
10:00 pm	

DAILY PLANNER

APRIL 6, 2024

Saturday

TODAY'S AFFIRMATION

WEATHER	

MOOD	

TOP 3 PRIORITIES

1 _____
  _____

2 _____
  _____

3 _____
  _____

TO-DO LIST

- ▪ _____
- ▪ _____
- ▪ _____
- ▪ _____
- ▪ _____
- ▪ _____
- ▪ _____
- ▪ _____

DON'T FORGET

_____
_____
_____

TIME	PLANS & SCHEDULE
6:00 am	
6:30 am	
7:00 am	
7:30 am	
8:00 am	
8:30 am	
9:00 am	
9:30 am	
10:00 am	
10:30 am	
11:00 am	
11:30 am	
12:00 pm	
12:30 pm	
1:00 pm	
1:30 pm	
2:00 pm	
2:30 pm	
3:00 pm	
3:30 pm	
4:00 pm	
4:30 pm	
5:00 pm	
5:30 pm	
6:00 pm	
6:30 pm	
7:00 pm	
7:30 pm	
8:00 pm	
8:30 pm	
9:00 pm	
9:30 pm	
10:00 pm	

DAILY PLANNER

APRIL 7, 2024

Sunday

TODAY'S AFFIRMATION

WEATHER

MOOD

TOP 3 PRIORITIES

1 _____
_____

2 _____
_____

3 _____
_____

TO-DO LIST

- _____
- _____
- _____
- _____
- _____
- _____
- _____
- _____

DON'T FORGET

_____
_____
_____

TIME	PLANS & SCHEDULE
6:00 am	
6:30 am	
7:00 am	
7:30 am	
8:00 am	
8:30 am	
9:00 am	
9:30 am	
10:00 am	
10:30 am	
11:00 am	
11:30 am	
12:00 pm	
12:30 pm	
1:00 pm	
1:30 pm	
2:00 pm	
2:30 pm	
3:00 pm	
3:30 pm	
4:00 pm	
4:30 pm	
5:00 pm	
5:30 pm	
6:00 pm	
6:30 pm	
7:00 pm	
7:30 pm	
8:00 pm	
8:30 pm	
9:00 pm	
9:30 pm	
10:00 pm	

DAILY PLANNER

APRIL 8, 2024

Monday

TODAY'S AFFIRMATION

WEATHER	

MOOD	

TOP 3 PRIORITIES

1. _____
   _____

2. _____
   _____

3. _____
   _____

TO-DO LIST

- ☐ _____
- ☐ _____
- ☐ _____
- ☐ _____
- ☐ _____
- ☐ _____
- ☐ _____
- ☐ _____

DON'T FORGET

_____
_____
_____

TIME	PLANS & SCHEDULE
6:00 am	
6:30 am	
7:00 am	
7:30 am	
8:00 am	
8:30 am	
9:00 am	
9:30 am	
10:00 am	
10:30 am	
11:00 am	
11:30 am	
12:00 pm	
12:30 pm	
1:00 pm	
1:30 pm	
2:00 pm	
2:30 pm	
3:00 pm	
3:30 pm	
4:00 pm	
4:30 pm	
5:00 pm	
5:30 pm	
6:00 pm	
6:30 pm	
7:00 pm	
7:30 pm	
8:00 pm	
8:30 pm	
9:00 pm	
9:30 pm	
10:00 pm	

DAILY PLANNER

APRIL 9, 2024

Tuesday

TODAY'S AFFIRMATION

WEATHER

MOOD

TOP 3 PRIORITIES

1 _____
_____

2 _____
_____

3 _____
_____

TO-DO LIST

- ☐ _____
- ☐ _____
- ☐ _____
- ☐ _____
- ☐ _____
- ☐ _____
- ☐ _____
- ☐ _____

DON'T FORGET

_____
_____
_____

TIME	PLANS & SCHEDULE
6:00 am	
6:30 am	
7:00 am	
7:30 am	
8:00 am	
8:30 am	
9:00 am	
9:30 am	
10:00 am	
10:30 am	
11:00 am	
11:30 am	
12:00 pm	
12:30 pm	
1:00 pm	
1:30 pm	
2:00 pm	
2:30 pm	
3:00 pm	
3:30 pm	
4:00 pm	
4:30 pm	
5:00 pm	
5:30 pm	
6:00 pm	
6:30 pm	
7:00 pm	
7:30 pm	
8:00 pm	
8:30 pm	
9:00 pm	
9:30 pm	
10:00 pm	

DAILY PLANNER

APRIL 10, 2024

Wednesday

TODAY'S AFFIRMATION

WEATHER

MOOD

TOP 3 PRIORITIES

1 _____

_____

2 _____

_____

3 _____

_____

TO-DO LIST

- ■ _____
- ■ _____
- ■ _____
- ■ _____
- ■ _____
- ■ _____
- ■ _____
- ■ _____

DON'T FORGET

_____

_____

_____

TIME	PLANS & SCHEDULE
6:00 am	
6:30 am	
7:00 am	
7:30 am	
8:00 am	
8:30 am	
9:00 am	
9:30 am	
10:00 am	
10:30 am	
11:00 am	
11:30 am	
12:00 pm	
12:30 pm	
1:00 pm	
1:30 pm	
2:00 pm	
2:30 pm	
3:00 pm	
3:30 pm	
4:00 pm	
4:30 pm	
5:00 pm	
5:30 pm	
6:00 pm	
6:30 pm	
7:00 pm	
7:30 pm	
8:00 pm	
8:30 pm	
9:00 pm	
9:30 pm	
10:00 pm	

DAILY PLANNER

APRIL 11, 2024

Thursday

TODAY'S AFFIRMATION

WEATHER

MOOD

TOP 3 PRIORITIES

1 _____
_____

2 _____
_____

3 _____
_____

TO-DO LIST

- _____
- _____
- _____
- _____
- _____
- _____
- _____
- _____

DON'T FORGET

_____
_____
_____

TIME	PLANS & SCHEDULE
6:00 am	
6:30 am	
7:00 am	
7:30 am	
8:00 am	
8:30 am	
9:00 am	
9:30 am	
10:00 am	
10:30 am	
11:00 am	
11:30 am	
12:00 pm	
12:30 pm	
1:00 pm	
1:30 pm	
2:00 pm	
2:30 pm	
3:00 pm	
3:30 pm	
4:00 pm	
4:30 pm	
5:00 pm	
5:30 pm	
6:00 pm	
6:30 pm	
7:00 pm	
7:30 pm	
8:00 pm	
8:30 pm	
9:00 pm	
9:30 pm	
10:00 pm	

DAILY PLANNER

APRIL 12, 2024

Friday

TODAY'S AFFIRMATION

WEATHER	

MOOD	

TOP 3 PRIORITIES

1 _____

_____

2 _____

_____

3 _____

_____

TO-DO LIST

- ■ _____
- ■ _____
- ■ _____
- ■ _____
- ■ _____
- ■ _____
- ■ _____
- ■ _____

DON'T FORGET

_____

_____

_____

TIME	PLANS & SCHEDULE
6:00 am	
6:30 am	
7:00 am	
7:30 am	
8:00 am	
8:30 am	
9:00 am	
9:30 am	
10:00 am	
10:30 am	
11:00 am	
11:30 am	
12:00 pm	
12:30 pm	
1:00 pm	
1:30 pm	
2:00 pm	
2:30 pm	
3:00 pm	
3:30 pm	
4:00 pm	
4:30 pm	
5:00 pm	
5:30 pm	
6:00 pm	
6:30 pm	
7:00 pm	
7:30 pm	
8:00 pm	
8:30 pm	
9:00 pm	
9:30 pm	
10:00 pm	

DAILY PLANNER

APRIL 13, 2024

Saturday

TODAY'S AFFIRMATION

TOP 3 PRIORITIES

1. _____
_____

2. _____
_____

3. _____
_____

TO-DO LIST

- ▪ _____
- ▪ _____
- ▪ _____
- ▪ _____
- ▪ _____
- ▪ _____
- ▪ _____
- ▪ _____

DON'T FORGET

_____
_____
_____

TIME	PLANS & SCHEDULE
6:00 am	
6:30 am	
7:00 am	
7:30 am	
8:00 am	
8:30 am	
9:00 am	
9:30 am	
10:00 am	
10:30 am	
11:00 am	
11:30 am	
12:00 pm	
12:30 pm	
1:00 pm	
1:30 pm	
2:00 pm	
2:30 pm	
3:00 pm	
3:30 pm	
4:00 pm	
4:30 pm	
5:00 pm	
5:30 pm	
6:00 pm	
6:30 pm	
7:00 pm	
7:30 pm	
8:00 pm	
8:30 pm	
9:00 pm	
9:30 pm	
10:00 pm	

DAILY PLANNER

APRIL 14, 2024

Sunday

TODAY'S AFFIRMATION

WEATHER

MOOD

TOP 3 PRIORITIES

1 _____
_____

2 _____
_____

3 _____
_____

TO-DO LIST

- ◼ _____
- ◼ _____
- ◼ _____
- ◼ _____
- ◼ _____
- ◼ _____
- ◼ _____
- ◼ _____

DON'T FORGET

_____
_____
_____

TIME	PLANS & SCHEDULE
6:00 am	
6:30 am	
7:00 am	
7:30 am	
8:00 am	
8:30 am	
9:00 am	
9:30 am	
10:00 am	
10:30 am	
11:00 am	
11:30 am	
12:00 pm	
12:30 pm	
1:00 pm	
1:30 pm	
2:00 pm	
2:30 pm	
3:00 pm	
3:30 pm	
4:00 pm	
4:30 pm	
5:00 pm	
5:30 pm	
6:00 pm	
6:30 pm	
7:00 pm	
7:30 pm	
8:00 pm	
8:30 pm	
9:00 pm	
9:30 pm	
10:00 pm	

DAILY PLANNER

APRIL 15, 2024

Monday

WEATHER

MOOD

TOP 3 PRIORITIES

1 _____

2 _____

3 _____

TO-DO LIST

- ▪ _____
- ▪ _____
- ▪ _____
- ▪ _____
- ▪ _____
- ▪ _____
- ▪ _____
- ▪ _____

DON'T FORGET

_____

_____

_____

TIME	PLANS & SCHEDULE
6:00 am	
6:30 am	
7:00 am	
7:30 am	
8:00 am	
8:30 am	
9:00 am	
9:30 am	
10:00 am	
10:30 am	
11:00 am	
11:30 am	
12:00 pm	
12:30 pm	
1:00 pm	
1:30 pm	
2:00 pm	
2:30 pm	
3:00 pm	
3:30 pm	
4:00 pm	
4:30 pm	
5:00 pm	
5:30 pm	
6:00 pm	
6:30 pm	
7:00 pm	
7:30 pm	
8:00 pm	
8:30 pm	
9:00 pm	
9:30 pm	
10:00 pm	

DAILY PLANNER

APRIL 16, 2024

Tuesday

TODAY'S AFFIRMATION

WEATHER	

MOOD	

TOP 3 PRIORITIES

1 _____
  _____

2 _____
  _____

3 _____
  _____

TO-DO LIST

- ■ _____
- ■ _____
- ■ _____
- ■ _____
- ■ _____
- ■ _____
- ■ _____
- ■ _____

DON'T FORGET

_____
_____
_____

TIME	PLANS & SCHEDULE
6:00 am	
6:30 am	
7:00 am	
7:30 am	
8:00 am	
8:30 am	
9:00 am	
9:30 am	
10:00 am	
10:30 am	
11:00 am	
11:30 am	
12:00 pm	
12:30 pm	
1:00 pm	
1:30 pm	
2:00 pm	
2:30 pm	
3:00 pm	
3:30 pm	
4:00 pm	
4:30 pm	
5:00 pm	
5:30 pm	
6:00 pm	
6:30 pm	
7:00 pm	
7:30 pm	
8:00 pm	
8:30 pm	
9:00 pm	
9:30 pm	
10:00 pm	

DAILY PLANNER

APRIL 17, 2024

Wednesday

TODAY'S AFFIRMATION

WEATHER

MOOD

TOP 3 PRIORITIES

1 _____
_____

2 _____
_____

3 _____
_____

TO-DO LIST

▪ _____

▪ _____

▪ _____

▪ _____

▪ _____

▪ _____

▪ _____

▪ _____

DON'T FORGET

_____

_____

_____

TIME	PLANS & SCHEDULE
6:00 am	
6:30 am	
7:00 am	
7:30 am	
8:00 am	
8:30 am	
9:00 am	
9:30 am	
10:00 am	
10:30 am	
11:00 am	
11:30 am	
12:00 pm	
12:30 pm	
1:00 pm	
1:30 pm	
2:00 pm	
2:30 pm	
3:00 pm	
3:30 pm	
4:00 pm	
4:30 pm	
5:00 pm	
5:30 pm	
6:00 pm	
6:30 pm	
7:00 pm	
7:30 pm	
8:00 pm	
8:30 pm	
9:00 pm	
9:30 pm	
10:00 pm	

DAILY PLANNER

APRIL 18, 2024

Thursday

TODAY'S AFFIRMATION

WEATHER

MOOD

TOP 3 PRIORITIES

1 _____

2 _____

3 _____

TO-DO LIST

- _____
- _____
- _____
- _____
- _____
- _____
- _____
- _____

DON'T FORGET

_____
_____
_____

TIME	PLANS & SCHEDULE
6:00 am	
6:30 am	
7:00 am	
7:30 am	
8:00 am	
8:30 am	
9:00 am	
9:30 am	
10:00 am	
10:30 am	
11:00 am	
11:30 am	
12:00 pm	
12:30 pm	
1:00 pm	
1:30 pm	
2:00 pm	
2:30 pm	
3:00 pm	
3:30 pm	
4:00 pm	
4:30 pm	
5:00 pm	
5:30 pm	
6:00 pm	
6:30 pm	
7:00 pm	
7:30 pm	
8:00 pm	
8:30 pm	
9:00 pm	
9:30 pm	
10:00 pm	

DAILY PLANNER

APRIL 19, 2024

Friday

TODAY'S AFFIRMATION

WEATHER

MOOD

TOP 3 PRIORITIES

1 _____
_____

2 _____
_____

3 _____
_____

TO-DO LIST

- _____
- _____
- _____
- _____
- _____
- _____
- _____
- _____

DON'T FORGET

_____
_____
_____

TIME	PLANS & SCHEDULE
6:00 am	
6:30 am	
7:00 am	
7:30 am	
8:00 am	
8:30 am	
9:00 am	
9:30 am	
10:00 am	
10:30 am	
11:00 am	
11:30 am	
12:00 pm	
12:30 pm	
1:00 pm	
1:30 pm	
2:00 pm	
2:30 pm	
3:00 pm	
3:30 pm	
4:00 pm	
4:30 pm	
5:00 pm	
5:30 pm	
6:00 pm	
6:30 pm	
7:00 pm	
7:30 pm	
8:00 pm	
8:30 pm	
9:00 pm	
9:30 pm	
10:00 pm	

DAILY PLANNER

APRIL 20, 2024

Saturday

TODAY'S AFFIRMATION

WEATHER	

MOOD	

TOP 3 PRIORITIES

1 _____
_____

2 _____
_____

3 _____
_____

TO-DO LIST

- ◼ _____
- ◼ _____
- ◼ _____
- ◼ _____
- ◼ _____
- ◼ _____
- ◼ _____
- ◼ _____

DON'T FORGET

_____
_____
_____

TIME	PLANS & SCHEDULE
6:00 am	
6:30 am	
7:00 am	
7:30 am	
8:00 am	
8:30 am	
9:00 am	
9:30 am	
10:00 am	
10:30 am	
11:00 am	
11:30 am	
12:00 pm	
12:30 pm	
1:00 pm	
1:30 pm	
2:00 pm	
2:30 pm	
3:00 pm	
3:30 pm	
4:00 pm	
4:30 pm	
5:00 pm	
5:30 pm	
6:00 pm	
6:30 pm	
7:00 pm	
7:30 pm	
8:00 pm	
8:30 pm	
9:00 pm	
9:30 pm	
10:00 pm	

DAILY PLANNER

APRIL 21, 2024

Sunday

TODAY'S AFFIRMATION

TOP 3 PRIORITIES

1 _____
_____

2 _____
_____

3 _____
_____

TO-DO LIST

- ▪ _____
- ▪ _____
- ▪ _____
- ▪ _____
- ▪ _____
- ▪ _____
- ▪ _____
- ▪ _____

DON'T FORGET

_____
_____
_____

TIME	PLANS & SCHEDULE
6:00 am	
6:30 am	
7:00 am	
7:30 am	
8:00 am	
8:30 am	
9:00 am	
9:30 am	
10:00 am	
10:30 am	
11:00 am	
11:30 am	
12:00 pm	
12:30 pm	
1:00 pm	
1:30 pm	
2:00 pm	
2:30 pm	
3:00 pm	
3:30 pm	
4:00 pm	
4:30 pm	
5:00 pm	
5:30 pm	
6:00 pm	
6:30 pm	
7:00 pm	
7:30 pm	
8:00 pm	
8:30 pm	
9:00 pm	
9:30 pm	
10:00 pm	

DAILY PLANNER

APRIL 22, 2024

Monday

TODAY'S AFFIRMATION

TOP 3 PRIORITIES

1 _____

_____

2 _____

_____

3 _____

_____

TO-DO LIST

- _____
- _____
- _____
- _____
- _____
- _____
- _____
- _____

DON'T FORGET

_____

_____

_____

TIME	PLANS & SCHEDULE
6:00 am	
6:30 am	
7:00 am	
7:30 am	
8:00 am	
8:30 am	
9:00 am	
9:30 am	
10:00 am	
10:30 am	
11:00 am	
11:30 am	
12:00 pm	
12:30 pm	
1:00 pm	
1:30 pm	
2:00 pm	
2:30 pm	
3:00 pm	
3:30 pm	
4:00 pm	
4:30 pm	
5:00 pm	
5:30 pm	
6:00 pm	
6:30 pm	
7:00 pm	
7:30 pm	
8:00 pm	
8:30 pm	
9:00 pm	
9:30 pm	
10:00 pm	

DAILY PLANNER

APRIL 23, 2024

Tuesday

TODAY'S AFFIRMATION

WEATHER

MOOD

TOP 3 PRIORITIES

1 _____
_____

2 _____
_____

3 _____
_____

TO-DO LIST

☐ _____

☐ _____

☐ _____

☐ _____

☐ _____

☐ _____

☐ _____

☐ _____

DON'T FORGET

_____

_____

_____

TIME	PLANS & SCHEDULE
6:00 am	
6:30 am	
7:00 am	
7:30 am	
8:00 am	
8:30 am	
9:00 am	
9:30 am	
10:00 am	
10:30 am	
11:00 am	
11:30 am	
12:00 pm	
12:30 pm	
1:00 pm	
1:30 pm	
2:00 pm	
2:30 pm	
3:00 pm	
3:30 pm	
4:00 pm	
4:30 pm	
5:00 pm	
5:30 pm	
6:00 pm	
6:30 pm	
7:00 pm	
7:30 pm	
8:00 pm	
8:30 pm	
9:00 pm	
9:30 pm	
10:00 pm	

DAILY PLANNER

APRIL 24, 2024

Wednesday

TODAY'S AFFIRMATION

WEATHER

MOOD

TOP 3 PRIORITIES

1 _____
_____

2 _____
_____

3 _____
_____

TO-DO LIST

- _____
- _____
- _____
- _____
- _____
- _____
- _____
- _____

DON'T FORGET

_____
_____
_____

TIME	PLANS & SCHEDULE
6:00 am	
6:30 am	
7:00 am	
7:30 am	
8:00 am	
8:30 am	
9:00 am	
9:30 am	
10:00 am	
10:30 am	
11:00 am	
11:30 am	
12:00 pm	
12:30 pm	
1:00 pm	
1:30 pm	
2:00 pm	
2:30 pm	
3:00 pm	
3:30 pm	
4:00 pm	
4:30 pm	
5:00 pm	
5:30 pm	
6:00 pm	
6:30 pm	
7:00 pm	
7:30 pm	
8:00 pm	
8:30 pm	
9:00 pm	
9:30 pm	
10:00 pm	

DAILY PLANNER

APRIL 25, 2024

Thursday

TODAY'S AFFIRMATION

WEATHER

MOOD

TOP 3 PRIORITIES

1 _____
_____

2 _____
_____

3 _____
_____

TO-DO LIST

▪ _____

▪ _____

▪ _____

▪ _____

▪ _____

▪ _____

▪ _____

▪ _____

DON'T FORGET

_____

_____

_____

TIME	PLANS & SCHEDULE
6:00 am	
6:30 am	
7:00 am	
7:30 am	
8:00 am	
8:30 am	
9:00 am	
9:30 am	
10:00 am	
10:30 am	
11:00 am	
11:30 am	
12:00 pm	
12:30 pm	
1:00 pm	
1:30 pm	
2:00 pm	
2:30 pm	
3:00 pm	
3:30 pm	
4:00 pm	
4:30 pm	
5:00 pm	
5:30 pm	
6:00 pm	
6:30 pm	
7:00 pm	
7:30 pm	
8:00 pm	
8:30 pm	
9:00 pm	
9:30 pm	
10:00 pm	

DAILY PLANNER

APRIL 26, 2024

Friday

TODAY'S AFFIRMATION

WEATHER

MOOD

TOP 3 PRIORITIES

1 _____
_____

2 _____
_____

3 _____
_____

TO-DO LIST

- _____
- _____
- _____
- _____
- _____
- _____
- _____
- _____

DON'T FORGET

_____
_____
_____

TIME	PLANS & SCHEDULE
6:00 am	
6:30 am	
7:00 am	
7:30 am	
8:00 am	
8:30 am	
9:00 am	
9:30 am	
10:00 am	
10:30 am	
11:00 am	
11:30 am	
12:00 pm	
12:30 pm	
1:00 pm	
1:30 pm	
2:00 pm	
2:30 pm	
3:00 pm	
3:30 pm	
4:00 pm	
4:30 pm	
5:00 pm	
5:30 pm	
6:00 pm	
6:30 pm	
7:00 pm	
7:30 pm	
8:00 pm	
8:30 pm	
9:00 pm	
9:30 pm	
10:00 pm	

DAILY PLANNER

APRIL 27, 2024

Saturday

TODAY'S AFFIRMATION

WEATHER

MOOD

TOP 3 PRIORITIES

1 _____
_____

2 _____
_____

3 _____
_____

TO-DO LIST

☐ _____
☐ _____
☐ _____
☐ _____
☐ _____
☐ _____
☐ _____
☐ _____

DON'T FORGET

_____
_____
_____

TIME	PLANS & SCHEDULE
6:00 am	
6:30 am	
7:00 am	
7:30 am	
8:00 am	
8:30 am	
9:00 am	
9:30 am	
10:00 am	
10:30 am	
11:00 am	
11:30 am	
12:00 pm	
12:30 pm	
1:00 pm	
1:30 pm	
2:00 pm	
2:30 pm	
3:00 pm	
3:30 pm	
4:00 pm	
4:30 pm	
5:00 pm	
5:30 pm	
6:00 pm	
6:30 pm	
7:00 pm	
7:30 pm	
8:00 pm	
8:30 pm	
9:00 pm	
9:30 pm	
10:00 pm	

DAILY PLANNER

APRIL 28, 2024

Sunday

TODAY'S AFFIRMATION

WEATHER

MOOD

TOP 3 PRIORITIES

1 _____
_____

2 _____
_____

3 _____
_____

TO-DO LIST

- _____
- _____
- _____
- _____
- _____
- _____
- _____
- _____

DON'T FORGET

_____
_____
_____

TIME	PLANS & SCHEDULE
6:00 am	
6:30 am	
7:00 am	
7:30 am	
8:00 am	
8:30 am	
9:00 am	
9:30 am	
10:00 am	
10:30 am	
11:00 am	
11:30 am	
12:00 pm	
12:30 pm	
1:00 pm	
1:30 pm	
2:00 pm	
2:30 pm	
3:00 pm	
3:30 pm	
4:00 pm	
4:30 pm	
5:00 pm	
5:30 pm	
6:00 pm	
6:30 pm	
7:00 pm	
7:30 pm	
8:00 pm	
8:30 pm	
9:00 pm	
9:30 pm	
10:00 pm	

DAILY PLANNER

APRIL 29, 2024

Monday

TODAY'S AFFIRMATION

WEATHER

MOOD

TOP 3 PRIORITIES

1 _____
_____

2 _____
_____

3 _____
_____

TO-DO LIST

- _____
- _____
- _____
- _____
- _____
- _____
- _____
- _____

DON'T FORGET

_____
_____
_____

TIME	PLANS & SCHEDULE
6:00 am	
6:30 am	
7:00 am	
7:30 am	
8:00 am	
8:30 am	
9:00 am	
9:30 am	
10:00 am	
10:30 am	
11:00 am	
11:30 am	
12:00 pm	
12:30 pm	
1:00 pm	
1:30 pm	
2:00 pm	
2:30 pm	
3:00 pm	
3:30 pm	
4:00 pm	
4:30 pm	
5:00 pm	
5:30 pm	
6:00 pm	
6:30 pm	
7:00 pm	
7:30 pm	
8:00 pm	
8:30 pm	
9:00 pm	
9:30 pm	
10:00 pm	

DAILY PLANNER

APRIL 30, 2024

Tuesday

TODAY'S AFFIRMATION

WEATHER

MOOD

TOP 3 PRIORITIES

1 _____
_____

2 _____
_____

3 _____
_____

TO-DO LIST

▪ _____

▪ _____

▪ _____

▪ _____

▪ _____

▪ _____

▪ _____

▪ _____

DON'T FORGET

_____
_____
_____

TIME	PLANS & SCHEDULE
6:00 am	
6:30 am	
7:00 am	
7:30 am	
8:00 am	
8:30 am	
9:00 am	
9:30 am	
10:00 am	
10:30 am	
11:00 am	
11:30 am	
12:00 pm	
12:30 pm	
1:00 pm	
1:30 pm	
2:00 pm	
2:30 pm	
3:00 pm	
3:30 pm	
4:00 pm	
4:30 pm	
5:00 pm	
5:30 pm	
6:00 pm	
6:30 pm	
7:00 pm	
7:30 pm	
8:00 pm	
8:30 pm	
9:00 pm	
9:30 pm	
10:00 pm	

Notes

Date:

☐
☐
☐
☐
☐

MONTHLY BUDGET PLANNER

Budget Goal: _____   Month: _____

Income

Date	Description	Amount
Total		

Fixed Expenses

Date	Description	Amount
Total		

Other Expenses

Date	Description	Amount
Total		

Bills

Date	Description	Amount
Total		

Recap

	Goal	Actual	Difference
Earnt			
Spent			
Debt			
Saved			

GRATITUDE JOURNAL

DATE: _____   S M T W T F S

TODAY I'M GRATEFUL FOR

- _____
- _____
- _____

WATER INTAKE

◊ ◊ ◊ ◊   ◊ ◊ ◊ ◊   ◊ ◊
     1L   2L   3L

WEATHER

TODAY'S AFFIRMATION

- _____
- _____
- _____
- _____

NOTES / REMINDERS

SOMETHING I'M PROUD OF

- _____
- _____
- _____
- _____

TOMORROW I LOOK FORWARD TO

- _____
- _____
- _____
- _____

30 DAY
Self-Care Challenge

DAY 1	DAY 2	DAY 3	DAY 4	DAY 5
Start a gratitude journal	Learn to meditate	Spend the day social media free	Call someone you love	Take a 15 minute walk outdoors
DAY 6	**DAY 7**	**DAY 8**	**DAY 9**	**DAY 10**
Listen to a podcast	Learn to cook a new recipe	Stretch for 10-15 minutes	Listen to your favorite song	Practice deep breathing
DAY 11	**DAY 12**	**DAY 13**	**DAY 14**	**DAY 15**
Try a free online workout	Read a book for 15 minutes	Write a list of short-term goals	De-clutter a room or desk	Go to bed 30 minutes earlier
DAY 16	**DAY 17**	**DAY 18**	**DAY 19**	**DAY 20**
Have a game night	Wake up 15 minutes earlier	Make your favorite meal	Buy yourself something nice	Create a bucket list
DAY 21	**DAY 22**	**DAY 23**	**DAY 24**	**DAY 25**
Watch a movie or series	Write down your thoughts	Take a long shower or bath	Have a home spa day	Read inspirational quotes
DAY 26	**DAY 27**	**DAY 28**	**DAY 29**	**DAY 30**
Create a vision board	Spend some time outside	Do a hair mask	Write it all down in a journal	Take a power nap

MAY 2024

Sunday	Monday	Tuesday	Wednesday
			01
05	06	07	08
12	13	14	15
19	20	21	22
26	27	28	29

MAY 2024

Thursday	Friday	Saturday	Notes
02	03	04	
09	10	11	
16	17	18	
23	24	25	
30	31		

MAY

Goal

Action Plan

Date

Grateful For

To Improve

Notes

DAILY PLANNER

MAY 1, 2024

Wednesday

TODAY'S AFFIRMATION

WEATHER

MOOD

TOP 3 PRIORITIES

1 _____

_____

2 _____

_____

3 _____

_____

TO-DO LIST

- ☐ _____
- ☐ _____
- ☐ _____
- ☐ _____
- ☐ _____
- ☐ _____
- ☐ _____
- ☐ _____

DON'T FORGET

_____

_____

_____

TIME	PLANS & SCHEDULE
6:00 am	
6:30 am	
7:00 am	
7:30 am	
8:00 am	
8:30 am	
9:00 am	
9:30 am	
10:00 am	
10:30 am	
11:00 am	
11:30 am	
12:00 pm	
12:30 pm	
1:00 pm	
1:30 pm	
2:00 pm	
2:30 pm	
3:00 pm	
3:30 pm	
4:00 pm	
4:30 pm	
5:00 pm	
5:30 pm	
6:00 pm	
6:30 pm	
7:00 pm	
7:30 pm	
8:00 pm	
8:30 pm	
9:00 pm	
9:30 pm	
10:00 pm	

DAILY PLANNER

MAY 2, 2024

Thursday

TODAY'S AFFIRMATION

WEATHER

MOOD

TOP 3 PRIORITIES

1 _____
_____

2 _____
_____

3 _____
_____

TO-DO LIST

- _____
- _____
- _____
- _____
- _____
- _____
- _____
- _____

DON'T FORGET

_____
_____
_____

TIME	PLANS & SCHEDULE
6:00 am	
6:30 am	
7:00 am	
7:30 am	
8:00 am	
8:30 am	
9:00 am	
9:30 am	
10:00 am	
10:30 am	
11:00 am	
11:30 am	
12:00 pm	
12:30 pm	
1:00 pm	
1:30 pm	
2:00 pm	
2:30 pm	
3:00 pm	
3:30 pm	
4:00 pm	
4:30 pm	
5:00 pm	
5:30 pm	
6:00 pm	
6:30 pm	
7:00 pm	
7:30 pm	
8:00 pm	
8:30 pm	
9:00 pm	
9:30 pm	
10:00 pm	

DAILY PLANNER

MAY 3, 2024

Friday

TODAY'S AFFIRMATION

WEATHER

MOOD

TOP 3 PRIORITIES

1 _____

_____

2 _____

_____

3 _____

_____

TO-DO LIST

- _____
- _____
- _____
- _____
- _____
- _____
- _____
- _____

DON'T FORGET

_____

_____

_____

TIME	PLANS & SCHEDULE
6:00 am	
6:30 am	
7:00 am	
7:30 am	
8:00 am	
8:30 am	
9:00 am	
9:30 am	
10:00 am	
10:30 am	
11:00 am	
11:30 am	
12:00 pm	
12:30 pm	
1:00 pm	
1:30 pm	
2:00 pm	
2:30 pm	
3:00 pm	
3:30 pm	
4:00 pm	
4:30 pm	
5:00 pm	
5:30 pm	
6:00 pm	
6:30 pm	
7:00 pm	
7:30 pm	
8:00 pm	
8:30 pm	
9:00 pm	
9:30 pm	
10:00 pm	

DAILY PLANNER

MAY 4, 2024

Saturday

TODAY'S AFFIRMATION

WEATHER

MOOD

TOP 3 PRIORITIES

1 _____
_____

2 _____
_____

3 _____
_____

TO-DO LIST

- _____
- _____
- _____
- _____
- _____
- _____
- _____
- _____

DON'T FORGET

_____
_____
_____

TIME	PLANS & SCHEDULE
6:00 am	
6:30 am	
7:00 am	
7:30 am	
8:00 am	
8:30 am	
9:00 am	
9:30 am	
10:00 am	
10:30 am	
11:00 am	
11:30 am	
12:00 pm	
12:30 pm	
1:00 pm	
1:30 pm	
2:00 pm	
2:30 pm	
3:00 pm	
3:30 pm	
4:00 pm	
4:30 pm	
5:00 pm	
5:30 pm	
6:00 pm	
6:30 pm	
7:00 pm	
7:30 pm	
8:00 pm	
8:30 pm	
9:00 pm	
9:30 pm	
10:00 pm	

DAILY PLANNER

MAY 5, 2024

Sunday

TODAY'S AFFIRMATION

WEATHER

MOOD

TOP 3 PRIORITIES

1 _____
_____

2 _____
_____

3 _____
_____

TO-DO LIST

☐ _____

☐ _____

☐ _____

☐ _____

☐ _____

☐ _____

☐ _____

☐ _____

DON'T FORGET

_____

_____

_____

TIME	PLANS & SCHEDULE
6:00 am	
6:30 am	
7:00 am	
7:30 am	
8:00 am	
8:30 am	
9:00 am	
9:30 am	
10:00 am	
10:30 am	
11:00 am	
11:30 am	
12:00 pm	
12:30 pm	
1:00 pm	
1:30 pm	
2:00 pm	
2:30 pm	
3:00 pm	
3:30 pm	
4:00 pm	
4:30 pm	
5:00 pm	
5:30 pm	
6:00 pm	
6:30 pm	
7:00 pm	
7:30 pm	
8:00 pm	
8:30 pm	
9:00 pm	
9:30 pm	
10:00 pm	

DAILY PLANNER

MAY 6, 2024

Monday

TODAY'S AFFIRMATION

WEATHER

MOOD

TOP 3 PRIORITIES

1 _____

_____

2 _____

_____

3 _____

_____

TO-DO LIST

☐ _____

☐ _____

☐ _____

☐ _____

☐ _____

☐ _____

☐ _____

☐ _____

DON'T FORGET

_____

_____

_____

TIME	PLANS & SCHEDULE
6:00 am	
6:30 am	
7:00 am	
7:30 am	
8:00 am	
8:30 am	
9:00 am	
9:30 am	
10:00 am	
10:30 am	
11:00 am	
11:30 am	
12:00 pm	
12:30 pm	
1:00 pm	
1:30 pm	
2:00 pm	
2:30 pm	
3:00 pm	
3:30 pm	
4:00 pm	
4:30 pm	
5:00 pm	
5:30 pm	
6:00 pm	
6:30 pm	
7:00 pm	
7:30 pm	
8:00 pm	
8:30 pm	
9:00 pm	
9:30 pm	
10:00 pm	

DAILY PLANNER

MAY 7, 2024

Tuesday

TODAY'S AFFIRMATION

WEATHER

MOOD

TOP 3 PRIORITIES

1 _____
_____

2 _____
_____

3 _____
_____

TO-DO LIST

- _____
- _____
- _____
- _____
- _____
- _____
- _____
- _____

DON'T FORGET

_____
_____
_____

TIME	PLANS & SCHEDULE
6:00 am	
6:30 am	
7:00 am	
7:30 am	
8:00 am	
8:30 am	
9:00 am	
9:30 am	
10:00 am	
10:30 am	
11:00 am	
11:30 am	
12:00 pm	
12:30 pm	
1:00 pm	
1:30 pm	
2:00 pm	
2:30 pm	
3:00 pm	
3:30 pm	
4:00 pm	
4:30 pm	
5:00 pm	
5:30 pm	
6:00 pm	
6:30 pm	
7:00 pm	
7:30 pm	
8:00 pm	
8:30 pm	
9:00 pm	
9:30 pm	
10:00 pm	

DAILY PLANNER

MAY 8, 2024

Wednesday

TODAY'S AFFIRMATION

WEATHER

MOOD

TOP 3 PRIORITIES

1 _____
_____

2 _____
_____

3 _____
_____

TO-DO LIST

☐ _____

☐ _____

☐ _____

☐ _____

☐ _____

☐ _____

☐ _____

☐ _____

DON'T FORGET

_____

_____

_____

TIME	PLANS & SCHEDULE
6:00 am	
6:30 am	
7:00 am	
7:30 am	
8:00 am	
8:30 am	
9:00 am	
9:30 am	
10:00 am	
10:30 am	
11:00 am	
11:30 am	
12:00 pm	
12:30 pm	
1:00 pm	
1:30 pm	
2:00 pm	
2:30 pm	
3:00 pm	
3:30 pm	
4:00 pm	
4:30 pm	
5:00 pm	
5:30 pm	
6:00 pm	
6:30 pm	
7:00 pm	
7:30 pm	
8:00 pm	
8:30 pm	
9:00 pm	
9:30 pm	
10:00 pm	

DAILY PLANNER

MAY 9, 2024

Thursday

TODAY'S AFFIRMATION

WEATHER

MOOD

TOP 3 PRIORITIES

1 _____

_____

2 _____

_____

3 _____

_____

TO-DO LIST

☐ _____

☐ _____

☐ _____

☐ _____

☐ _____

☐ _____

☐ _____

☐ _____

DON'T FORGET

_____

_____

_____

TIME	PLANS & SCHEDULE
6:00 am	
6:30 am	
7:00 am	
7:30 am	
8:00 am	
8:30 am	
9:00 am	
9:30 am	
10:00 am	
10:30 am	
11:00 am	
11:30 am	
12:00 pm	
12:30 pm	
1:00 pm	
1:30 pm	
2:00 pm	
2:30 pm	
3:00 pm	
3:30 pm	
4:00 pm	
4:30 pm	
5:00 pm	
5:30 pm	
6:00 pm	
6:30 pm	
7:00 pm	
7:30 pm	
8:00 pm	
8:30 pm	
9:00 pm	
9:30 pm	
10:00 pm	

DAILY PLANNER

MAY 10, 2024

Friday

TODAY'S AFFIRMATION

WEATHER

MOOD

TOP 3 PRIORITIES

1 _____
_____

2 _____
_____

3 _____
_____

TO-DO LIST

☐ _____

☐ _____

☐ _____

☐ _____

☐ _____

☐ _____

☐ _____

☐ _____

DON'T FORGET

_____

_____

_____

TIME	PLANS & SCHEDULE
6:00 am	
6:30 am	
7:00 am	
7:30 am	
8:00 am	
8:30 am	
9:00 am	
9:30 am	
10:00 am	
10:30 am	
11:00 am	
11:30 am	
12:00 pm	
12:30 pm	
1:00 pm	
1:30 pm	
2:00 pm	
2:30 pm	
3:00 pm	
3:30 pm	
4:00 pm	
4:30 pm	
5:00 pm	
5:30 pm	
6:00 pm	
6:30 pm	
7:00 pm	
7:30 pm	
8:00 pm	
8:30 pm	
9:00 pm	
9:30 pm	
10:00 pm	

DAILY PLANNER

MAY 11, 2024

Saturday

TODAY'S AFFIRMATION

WEATHER

MOOD

TOP 3 PRIORITIES

1 _____

_____

2 _____

_____

3 _____

_____

TO-DO LIST

▢ _____

▢ _____

▢ _____

▢ _____

▢ _____

▢ _____

▢ _____

▢ _____

DON'T FORGET

_____

_____

_____

TIME	PLANS & SCHEDULE
6:00 am	
6:30 am	
7:00 am	
7:30 am	
8:00 am	
8:30 am	
9:00 am	
9:30 am	
10:00 am	
10:30 am	
11:00 am	
11:30 am	
12:00 pm	
12:30 pm	
1:00 pm	
1:30 pm	
2:00 pm	
2:30 pm	
3:00 pm	
3:30 pm	
4:00 pm	
4:30 pm	
5:00 pm	
5:30 pm	
6:00 pm	
6:30 pm	
7:00 pm	
7:30 pm	
8:00 pm	
8:30 pm	
9:00 pm	
9:30 pm	
10:00 pm	

DAILY PLANNER

MAY 12, 2024

Sunday

TODAY'S AFFIRMATION

WEATHER	
MOOD	

TOP 3 PRIORITIES

1 _____

_____

2 _____

_____

3 _____

_____

TO-DO LIST

☐ _____

☐ _____

☐ _____

☐ _____

☐ _____

☐ _____

☐ _____

☐ _____

DON'T FORGET

_____

_____

_____

TIME	PLANS & SCHEDULE
6:00 am	
6:30 am	
7:00 am	
7:30 am	
8:00 am	
8:30 am	
9:00 am	
9:30 am	
10:00 am	
10:30 am	
11:00 am	
11:30 am	
12:00 pm	
12:30 pm	
1:00 pm	
1:30 pm	
2:00 pm	
2:30 pm	
3:00 pm	
3:30 pm	
4:00 pm	
4:30 pm	
5:00 pm	
5:30 pm	
6:00 pm	
6:30 pm	
7:00 pm	
7:30 pm	
8:00 pm	
8:30 pm	
9:00 pm	
9:30 pm	
10:00 pm	

DAILY PLANNER

MAY 13, 2024

Monday

TODAY'S AFFIRMATION

WEATHER

MOOD

TOP 3 PRIORITIES

1 _____
_____

2 _____
_____

3 _____
_____

TO-DO LIST

- _____
- _____
- _____
- _____
- _____
- _____
- _____
- _____

DON'T FORGET

_____
_____
_____

TIME	PLANS & SCHEDULE
6:00 am	
6:30 am	
7:00 am	
7:30 am	
8:00 am	
8:30 am	
9:00 am	
9:30 am	
10:00 am	
10:30 am	
11:00 am	
11:30 am	
12:00 pm	
12:30 pm	
1:00 pm	
1:30 pm	
2:00 pm	
2:30 pm	
3:00 pm	
3:30 pm	
4:00 pm	
4:30 pm	
5:00 pm	
5:30 pm	
6:00 pm	
6:30 pm	
7:00 pm	
7:30 pm	
8:00 pm	
8:30 pm	
9:00 pm	
9:30 pm	
10:00 pm	

DAILY PLANNER

MAY 14, 2024

Tuesday

TODAY'S AFFIRMATION

WEATHER

MOOD

TOP 3 PRIORITIES

1 _____
_____

2 _____
_____

3 _____
_____

TO-DO LIST

- _____
- _____
- _____
- _____
- _____
- _____
- _____
- _____

DON'T FORGET

_____
_____
_____

TIME	PLANS & SCHEDULE
6:00 am	
6:30 am	
7:00 am	
7:30 am	
8:00 am	
8:30 am	
9:00 am	
9:30 am	
10:00 am	
10:30 am	
11:00 am	
11:30 am	
12:00 pm	
12:30 pm	
1:00 pm	
1:30 pm	
2:00 pm	
2:30 pm	
3:00 pm	
3:30 pm	
4:00 pm	
4:30 pm	
5:00 pm	
5:30 pm	
6:00 pm	
6:30 pm	
7:00 pm	
7:30 pm	
8:00 pm	
8:30 pm	
9:00 pm	
9:30 pm	
10:00 pm	

DAILY PLANNER

MAY 15, 2024

Wednesday

TODAY'S AFFIRMATION

WEATHER

MOOD

TOP 3 PRIORITIES

1 _____
_____

2 _____
_____

3 _____
_____

TO-DO LIST

- _____
- _____
- _____
- _____
- _____
- _____
- _____
- _____

DON'T FORGET

_____
_____
_____

TIME	PLANS & SCHEDULE
6:00 am	
6:30 am	
7:00 am	
7:30 am	
8:00 am	
8:30 am	
9:00 am	
9:30 am	
10:00 am	
10:30 am	
11:00 am	
11:30 am	
12:00 pm	
12:30 pm	
1:00 pm	
1:30 pm	
2:00 pm	
2:30 pm	
3:00 pm	
3:30 pm	
4:00 pm	
4:30 pm	
5:00 pm	
5:30 pm	
6:00 pm	
6:30 pm	
7:00 pm	
7:30 pm	
8:00 pm	
8:30 pm	
9:00 pm	
9:30 pm	
10:00 pm	

MAY 16, 2024

Thursday

TODAY'S AFFIRMATION

WEATHER

MOOD

TOP 3 PRIORITIES

1 _____

_____

2 _____

_____

3 _____

_____

TO-DO LIST

☐ _____

☐ _____

☐ _____

☐ _____

☐ _____

☐ _____

☐ _____

☐ _____

DON'T FORGET

_____

_____

_____

TIME	PLANS & SCHEDULE
6:00 am	
6:30 am	
7:00 am	
7:30 am	
8:00 am	
8:30 am	
9:00 am	
9:30 am	
10:00 am	
10:30 am	
11:00 am	
11:30 am	
12:00 pm	
12:30 pm	
1:00 pm	
1:30 pm	
2:00 pm	
2:30 pm	
3:00 pm	
3:30 pm	
4:00 pm	
4:30 pm	
5:00 pm	
5:30 pm	
6:00 pm	
6:30 pm	
7:00 pm	
7:30 pm	
8:00 pm	
8:30 pm	
9:00 pm	
9:30 pm	
10:00 pm	

DAILY PLANNER

MAY 17, 2024

Friday

TODAY'S AFFIRMATION

WEATHER

MOOD

TOP 3 PRIORITIES

1 _____
_____

2 _____
_____

3 _____
_____

TO-DO LIST

☐ _____

☐ _____

☐ _____

☐ _____

☐ _____

☐ _____

☐ _____

☐ _____

DON'T FORGET

_____

_____

_____

TIME	PLANS & SCHEDULE
6:00 am	
6:30 am	
7:00 am	
7:30 am	
8:00 am	
8:30 am	
9:00 am	
9:30 am	
10:00 am	
10:30 am	
11:00 am	
11:30 am	
12:00 pm	
12:30 pm	
1:00 pm	
1:30 pm	
2:00 pm	
2:30 pm	
3:00 pm	
3:30 pm	
4:00 pm	
4:30 pm	
5:00 pm	
5:30 pm	
6:00 pm	
6:30 pm	
7:00 pm	
7:30 pm	
8:00 pm	
8:30 pm	
9:00 pm	
9:30 pm	
10:00 pm	

DAILY PLANNER

MAY 18, 2024

Saturday

TODAY'S AFFIRMATION

WEATHER

MOOD

TOP 3 PRIORITIES

1 _____

_____

2 _____

_____

3 _____

_____

TO-DO LIST

☐ _____

☐ _____

☐ _____

☐ _____

☐ _____

☐ _____

☐ _____

☐ _____

DON'T FORGET

_____

_____

_____

TIME	PLANS & SCHEDULE
6:00 am	
6:30 am	
7:00 am	
7:30 am	
8:00 am	
8:30 am	
9:00 am	
9:30 am	
10:00 am	
10:30 am	
11:00 am	
11:30 am	
12:00 pm	
12:30 pm	
1:00 pm	
1:30 pm	
2:00 pm	
2:30 pm	
3:00 pm	
3:30 pm	
4:00 pm	
4:30 pm	
5:00 pm	
5:30 pm	
6:00 pm	
6:30 pm	
7:00 pm	
7:30 pm	
8:00 pm	
8:30 pm	
9:00 pm	
9:30 pm	
10:00 pm	

DAILY PLANNER

MAY 19, 2024

Sunday

TODAY'S AFFIRMATION

WEATHER

MOOD

TOP 3 PRIORITIES

1 _____

_____

2 _____

_____

3 _____

_____

TO-DO LIST

☐ _____

☐ _____

☐ _____

☐ _____

☐ _____

☐ _____

☐ _____

☐ _____

DON'T FORGET

_____

_____

_____

TIME	PLANS & SCHEDULE
6:00 am	
6:30 am	
7:00 am	
7:30 am	
8:00 am	
8:30 am	
9:00 am	
9:30 am	
10:00 am	
10:30 am	
11:00 am	
11:30 am	
12:00 pm	
12:30 pm	
1:00 pm	
1:30 pm	
2:00 pm	
2:30 pm	
3:00 pm	
3:30 pm	
4:00 pm	
4:30 pm	
5:00 pm	
5:30 pm	
6:00 pm	
6:30 pm	
7:00 pm	
7:30 pm	
8:00 pm	
8:30 pm	
9:00 pm	
9:30 pm	
10:00 pm	

DAILY PLANNER

MAY 20, 2024

Monday

TODAY'S AFFIRMATION

WEATHER

MOOD

TOP 3 PRIORITIES

1 _____
_____

2 _____
_____

3 _____
_____

TO-DO LIST

- _____
- _____
- _____
- _____
- _____
- _____
- _____
- _____

DON'T FORGET

_____
_____
_____

TIME	PLANS & SCHEDULE
6:00 am	
6:30 am	
7:00 am	
7:30 am	
8:00 am	
8:30 am	
9:00 am	
9:30 am	
10:00 am	
10:30 am	
11:00 am	
11:30 am	
12:00 pm	
12:30 pm	
1:00 pm	
1:30 pm	
2:00 pm	
2:30 pm	
3:00 pm	
3:30 pm	
4:00 pm	
4:30 pm	
5:00 pm	
5:30 pm	
6:00 pm	
6:30 pm	
7:00 pm	
7:30 pm	
8:00 pm	
8:30 pm	
9:00 pm	
9:30 pm	
10:00 pm	

DAILY PLANNER

MAY 21, 2024

Tuesday

TODAY'S AFFIRMATION

WEATHER

MOOD

TOP 3 PRIORITIES

1 _____

_____

2 _____

_____

3 _____

_____

TO-DO LIST

☐ _____

☐ _____

☐ _____

☐ _____

☐ _____

☐ _____

☐ _____

☐ _____

DON'T FORGET

_____

_____

_____

TIME	PLANS & SCHEDULE
6:00 am	
6:30 am	
7:00 am	
7:30 am	
8:00 am	
8:30 am	
9:00 am	
9:30 am	
10:00 am	
10:30 am	
11:00 am	
11:30 am	
12:00 pm	
12:30 pm	
1:00 pm	
1:30 pm	
2:00 pm	
2:30 pm	
3:00 pm	
3:30 pm	
4:00 pm	
4:30 pm	
5:00 pm	
5:30 pm	
6:00 pm	
6:30 pm	
7:00 pm	
7:30 pm	
8:00 pm	
8:30 pm	
9:00 pm	
9:30 pm	
10:00 pm	

DAILY PLANNER

MAY 22, 2024

Wednesday

TODAY'S AFFIRMATION

WEATHER

MOOD

TOP 3 PRIORITIES

1 _____

_____

2 _____

_____

3 _____

_____

TO-DO LIST

- _____
- _____
- _____
- _____
- _____
- _____
- _____
- _____

DON'T FORGET

_____

_____

_____

TIME	PLANS & SCHEDULE
6:00 am	
6:30 am	
7:00 am	
7:30 am	
8:00 am	
8:30 am	
9:00 am	
9:30 am	
10:00 am	
10:30 am	
11:00 am	
11:30 am	
12:00 pm	
12:30 pm	
1:00 pm	
1:30 pm	
2:00 pm	
2:30 pm	
3:00 pm	
3:30 pm	
4:00 pm	
4:30 pm	
5:00 pm	
5:30 pm	
6:00 pm	
6:30 pm	
7:00 pm	
7:30 pm	
8:00 pm	
8:30 pm	
9:00 pm	
9:30 pm	
10:00 pm	

DAILY PLANNER

MAY 23, 2024

Thursday

TODAY'S AFFIRMATION

WEATHER

MOOD

TOP 3 PRIORITIES

1 _____
_____

2 _____
_____

3 _____
_____

TO-DO LIST

☐ _____

☐ _____

☐ _____

☐ _____

☐ _____

☐ _____

☐ _____

☐ _____

DON'T FORGET

_____

_____

_____

TIME	PLANS & SCHEDULE
6:00 am	
6:30 am	
7:00 am	
7:30 am	
8:00 am	
8:30 am	
9:00 am	
9:30 am	
10:00 am	
10:30 am	
11:00 am	
11:30 am	
12:00 pm	
12:30 pm	
1:00 pm	
1:30 pm	
2:00 pm	
2:30 pm	
3:00 pm	
3:30 pm	
4:00 pm	
4:30 pm	
5:00 pm	
5:30 pm	
6:00 pm	
6:30 pm	
7:00 pm	
7:30 pm	
8:00 pm	
8:30 pm	
9:00 pm	
9:30 pm	
10:00 pm	

DAILY PLANNER

MAY 24, 2024

Friday

TODAY'S AFFIRMATION

WEATHER

MOOD

TOP 3 PRIORITIES

1 _____

_____

2 _____

_____

3 _____

_____

TO-DO LIST

☐ _____

☐ _____

☐ _____

☐ _____

☐ _____

☐ _____

☐ _____

☐ _____

DON'T FORGET

_____

_____

_____

TIME	PLANS & SCHEDULE
6:00 am	
6:30 am	
7:00 am	
7:30 am	
8:00 am	
8:30 am	
9:00 am	
9:30 am	
10:00 am	
10:30 am	
11:00 am	
11:30 am	
12:00 pm	
12:30 pm	
1:00 pm	
1:30 pm	
2:00 pm	
2:30 pm	
3:00 pm	
3:30 pm	
4:00 pm	
4:30 pm	
5:00 pm	
5:30 pm	
6:00 pm	
6:30 pm	
7:00 pm	
7:30 pm	
8:00 pm	
8:30 pm	
9:00 pm	
9:30 pm	
10:00 pm	

DAILY PLANNER

MAY 25, 2024

Saturday

TODAY'S AFFIRMATION

WEATHER

MOOD

TOP 3 PRIORITIES

1 _____

_____

2 _____

_____

3 _____

_____

TO-DO LIST

- _____
- _____
- _____
- _____
- _____
- _____
- _____
- _____

DON'T FORGET

_____

_____

_____

TIME	PLANS & SCHEDULE
6:00 am	
6:30 am	
7:00 am	
7:30 am	
8:00 am	
8:30 am	
9:00 am	
9:30 am	
10:00 am	
10:30 am	
11:00 am	
11:30 am	
12:00 pm	
12:30 pm	
1:00 pm	
1:30 pm	
2:00 pm	
2:30 pm	
3:00 pm	
3:30 pm	
4:00 pm	
4:30 pm	
5:00 pm	
5:30 pm	
6:00 pm	
6:30 pm	
7:00 pm	
7:30 pm	
8:00 pm	
8:30 pm	
9:00 pm	
9:30 pm	
10:00 pm	

DAILY PLANNER

MAY 26, 2024

Sunday

TODAY'S AFFIRMATION

WEATHER

MOOD

TOP 3 PRIORITIES

1 _____
_____

2 _____
_____

3 _____
_____

TO-DO LIST

☐ _____

☐ _____

☐ _____

☐ _____

☐ _____

☐ _____

☐ _____

☐ _____

DON'T FORGET

_____

_____

_____

TIME	PLANS & SCHEDULE
6:00 am	
6:30 am	
7:00 am	
7:30 am	
8:00 am	
8:30 am	
9:00 am	
9:30 am	
10:00 am	
10:30 am	
11:00 am	
11:30 am	
12:00 pm	
12:30 pm	
1:00 pm	
1:30 pm	
2:00 pm	
2:30 pm	
3:00 pm	
3:30 pm	
4:00 pm	
4:30 pm	
5:00 pm	
5:30 pm	
6:00 pm	
6:30 pm	
7:00 pm	
7:30 pm	
8:00 pm	
8:30 pm	
9:00 pm	
9:30 pm	
10:00 pm	

DAILY PLANNER

MAY 27, 2024

Monday

TODAY'S AFFIRMATION

WEATHER

MOOD

TOP 3 PRIORITIES
1 _____
_____
2 _____
_____
3 _____
_____

TO-DO LIST

- ▣ _____
- ▣ _____
- ▣ _____
- ▣ _____
- ▣ _____
- ▣ _____
- ▣ _____
- ▣ _____

DON'T FORGET

_____

_____

_____

TIME	PLANS & SCHEDULE
6:00 am	
6:30 am	
7:00 am	
7:30 am	
8:00 am	
8:30 am	
9:00 am	
9:30 am	
10:00 am	
10:30 am	
11:00 am	
11:30 am	
12:00 pm	
12:30 pm	
1:00 pm	
1:30 pm	
2:00 pm	
2:30 pm	
3:00 pm	
3:30 pm	
4:00 pm	
4:30 pm	
5:00 pm	
5:30 pm	
6:00 pm	
6:30 pm	
7:00 pm	
7:30 pm	
8:00 pm	
8:30 pm	
9:00 pm	
9:30 pm	
10:00 pm	

DAILY PLANNER

MAY 28, 2024

Tuesday

TODAY'S AFFIRMATION

WEATHER

MOOD

TOP 3 PRIORITIES

1 _____

_____

2 _____

_____

3 _____

_____

TO-DO LIST

☐ _____

☐ _____

☐ _____

☐ _____

☐ _____

☐ _____

☐ _____

☐ _____

DON'T FORGET

_____

_____

_____

TIME	PLANS & SCHEDULE
6:00 am	
6:30 am	
7:00 am	
7:30 am	
8:00 am	
8:30 am	
9:00 am	
9:30 am	
10:00 am	
10:30 am	
11:00 am	
11:30 am	
12:00 pm	
12:30 pm	
1:00 pm	
1:30 pm	
2:00 pm	
2:30 pm	
3:00 pm	
3:30 pm	
4:00 pm	
4:30 pm	
5:00 pm	
5:30 pm	
6:00 pm	
6:30 pm	
7:00 pm	
7:30 pm	
8:00 pm	
8:30 pm	
9:00 pm	
9:30 pm	
10:00 pm	

DAILY PLANNER

MAY 29, 2024

Wednesday

TODAY'S AFFIRMATION

WEATHER

MOOD

TOP 3 PRIORITIES

1 _____
_____

2 _____
_____

3 _____
_____

TO-DO LIST

☐ _____

☐ _____

☐ _____

☐ _____

☐ _____

☐ _____

☐ _____

☐ _____

DON'T FORGET

_____

_____

_____

TIME	PLANS & SCHEDULE
6:00 am	
6:30 am	
7:00 am	
7:30 am	
8:00 am	
8:30 am	
9:00 am	
9:30 am	
10:00 am	
10:30 am	
11:00 am	
11:30 am	
12:00 pm	
12:30 pm	
1:00 pm	
1:30 pm	
2:00 pm	
2:30 pm	
3:00 pm	
3:30 pm	
4:00 pm	
4:30 pm	
5:00 pm	
5:30 pm	
6:00 pm	
6:30 pm	
7:00 pm	
7:30 pm	
8:00 pm	
8:30 pm	
9:00 pm	
9:30 pm	
10:00 pm	

DAILY PLANNER

MAY 30, 2024

Thursday

TODAY'S AFFIRMATION

WEATHER

MOOD

TIME	PLANS & SCHEDULE
6:00 am	
6:30 am	
7:00 am	
7:30 am	
8:00 am	
8:30 am	
9:00 am	
9:30 am	
10:00 am	
10:30 am	
11:00 am	
11:30 am	
12:00 pm	
12:30 pm	
1:00 pm	
1:30 pm	
2:00 pm	
2:30 pm	
3:00 pm	
3:30 pm	
4:00 pm	
4:30 pm	
5:00 pm	
5:30 pm	
6:00 pm	
6:30 pm	
7:00 pm	
7:30 pm	
8:00 pm	
8:30 pm	
9:00 pm	
9:30 pm	
10:00 pm	

TOP 3 PRIORITIES

1 _____
_____

2 _____
_____

3 _____
_____

TO-DO LIST

- _____
- _____
- _____
- _____
- _____
- _____
- _____
- _____

DON'T FORGET

_____
_____
_____

DAILY PLANNER

MAY 31, 2024

Friday

TODAY'S AFFIRMATION

WEATHER

MOOD

TOP 3 PRIORITIES

1 _____
_____

2 _____
_____

3 _____
_____

TO-DO LIST

☒ _____

☒ _____

☒ _____

☒ _____

☒ _____

☒ _____

☒ _____

☒ _____

DON'T FORGET

_____

_____

_____

TIME	PLANS & SCHEDULE
6:00 am	
6:30 am	
7:00 am	
7:30 am	
8:00 am	
8:30 am	
9:00 am	
9:30 am	
10:00 am	
10:30 am	
11:00 am	
11:30 am	
12:00 pm	
12:30 pm	
1:00 pm	
1:30 pm	
2:00 pm	
2:30 pm	
3:00 pm	
3:30 pm	
4:00 pm	
4:30 pm	
5:00 pm	
5:30 pm	
6:00 pm	
6:30 pm	
7:00 pm	
7:30 pm	
8:00 pm	
8:30 pm	
9:00 pm	
9:30 pm	
10:00 pm	

MONTHLY BUDGET PLANNER

Budget Goal: _____   Month: _____

Income

Date	Description	Amount
Total		

Fixed Expenses

Date	Description	Amount
Total		

Other Expenses

Date	Description	Amount
Total		

Bills

Date	Description	Amount
Total		

Recap

	Goal	Actual	Difference
Earnt			
Spent			
Debt			
Saved			

Notes

Date:

GRATITUDE JOURNAL

DATE: _____   S M T W T F S

TODAY I'M GRATEFUL FOR

- ● _____
- ● _____
- ● _____

WATER INTAKE

1L   2L   3L

WEATHER

NOTES / REMINDERS

TODAY'S AFFIRMATION

- ● _____
- ● _____
- ● _____
- ● _____

SOMETHING I'M PROUD OF

- ● _____
- ● _____
- ● _____
- ● _____

TOMORROW I LOOK FORWARD TO

- ● _____
- ● _____
- ● _____
- ● _____

30 DAY
Self-Care Challenge

DAY 1	DAY 2	DAY 3	DAY 4	DAY 5
Start a gratitude journal	Learn to meditate	Spend the day social media free	Call someone you love	Take a 15 minute walk outdoors
DAY 6	**DAY 7**	**DAY 8**	**DAY 9**	**DAY 10**
Listen to a podcast	Learn to cook a new recipe	Stretch for 10-15 minutes	Listen to your favorite song	Practice deep breathing
DAY 11	**DAY 12**	**DAY 13**	**DAY 14**	**DAY 15**
Try a free online workout	Read a book for 15 minutes	Write a list of short-term goals	De-clutter a room or desk	Go to bed 30 minutes earlier
DAY 16	**DAY 17**	**DAY 18**	**DAY 19**	**DAY 20**
Have a game night	Wake up 15 minutes earlier	Make your favorite meal	Buy yourself something nice	Create a bucket list
DAY 21	**DAY 22**	**DAY 23**	**DAY 24**	**DAY 25**
Watch a movie or series	Write down your thoughts	Take a long shower or bath	Have a home spa day	Read inspirational quotes
DAY 26	**DAY 27**	**DAY 28**	**DAY 29**	**DAY 30**
Create a vision board	Spend some time outside	Do a hair mask	Write it all down in a journal	Take a power nap

JUNE 2024

Sunday	Monday	Tuesday	Wednesday
02	03	04	05
09	10	11	12
16	17	18	19
23 / 30	24	25	26

JUNE 2024

Thursday	Friday	Saturday	Notes
		01	....
			....
			....
06	07	08	....
			....
			....
13	14	15	....
			....
			....
20	21	22	....
			....
			....
27	28	29	....
			....
			....

JUNE

Goal

Action Plan

Date

....

....

....

....

....

....

....

....

....

....

Grateful For

....

....

....

....

....

To Improve

....

....

....

....

....

Notes

....

....

....

....

DAILY PLANNER

JUNE 1, 2024

Saturday

TODAY'S AFFIRMATION

WEATHER

MOOD

TOP 3 PRIORITIES

1 _____
_____

2 _____
_____

3 _____
_____

TO-DO LIST

- ☐ _____
- ☐ _____
- ☐ _____
- ☐ _____
- ☐ _____
- ☐ _____
- ☐ _____
- ☐ _____

DON'T FORGET

_____
_____
_____

TIME	PLANS & SCHEDULE
6:00 am	
6:30 am	
7:00 am	
7:30 am	
8:00 am	
8:30 am	
9:00 am	
9:30 am	
10:00 am	
10:30 am	
11:00 am	
11:30 am	
12:00 pm	
12:30 pm	
1:00 pm	
1:30 pm	
2:00 pm	
2:30 pm	
3:00 pm	
3:30 pm	
4:00 pm	
4:30 pm	
5:00 pm	
5:30 pm	
6:00 pm	
6:30 pm	
7:00 pm	
7:30 pm	
8:00 pm	
8:30 pm	
9:00 pm	
9:30 pm	
10:00 pm	

DAILY PLANNER

JUNE 2, 2024

Sunday

TODAY'S AFFIRMATION

WEATHER

MOOD

TOP 3 PRIORITIES

1 _____

_____

2 _____

_____

3 _____

_____

TO-DO LIST

- _____
- _____
- _____
- _____
- _____
- _____
- _____
- _____

DON'T FORGET

_____

_____

_____

TIME	PLANS & SCHEDULE
6:00 am	
6:30 am	
7:00 am	
7:30 am	
8:00 am	
8:30 am	
9:00 am	
9:30 am	
10:00 am	
10:30 am	
11:00 am	
11:30 am	
12:00 pm	
12:30 pm	
1:00 pm	
1:30 pm	
2:00 pm	
2:30 pm	
3:00 pm	
3:30 pm	
4:00 pm	
4:30 pm	
5:00 pm	
5:30 pm	
6:00 pm	
6:30 pm	
7:00 pm	
7:30 pm	
8:00 pm	
8:30 pm	
9:00 pm	
9:30 pm	
10:00 pm	

DAILY PLANNER

JUNE 3, 2024

Monday

TODAY'S AFFIRMATION

WEATHER

MOOD

TOP 3 PRIORITIES

1 _____

_____

2 _____

_____

3 _____

_____

TO-DO LIST

☐ _____

☐ _____

☐ _____

☐ _____

☐ _____

☐ _____

☐ _____

☐ _____

DON'T FORGET

_____

_____

_____

TIME	PLANS & SCHEDULE
6:00 am	
6:30 am	
7:00 am	
7:30 am	
8:00 am	
8:30 am	
9:00 am	
9:30 am	
10:00 am	
10:30 am	
11:00 am	
11:30 am	
12:00 pm	
12:30 pm	
1:00 pm	
1:30 pm	
2:00 pm	
2:30 pm	
3:00 pm	
3:30 pm	
4:00 pm	
4:30 pm	
5:00 pm	
5:30 pm	
6:00 pm	
6:30 pm	
7:00 pm	
7:30 pm	
8:00 pm	
8:30 pm	
9:00 pm	
9:30 pm	
10:00 pm	

DAILY PLANNER

JUNE 4, 2024

Tuesday

TODAY'S AFFIRMATION

WEATHER

MOOD

TOP 3 PRIORITIES

1 _____

_____

2 _____

_____

3 _____

_____

TO-DO LIST

- ▪ _____
- ▪ _____
- ▪ _____
- ▪ _____
- ▪ _____
- ▪ _____
- ▪ _____
- ▪ _____

DON'T FORGET

_____

_____

_____

TIME	PLANS & SCHEDULE
6:00 am	
6:30 am	
7:00 am	
7:30 am	
8:00 am	
8:30 am	
9:00 am	
9:30 am	
10:00 am	
10:30 am	
11:00 am	
11:30 am	
12:00 pm	
12:30 pm	
1:00 pm	
1:30 pm	
2:00 pm	
2:30 pm	
3:00 pm	
3:30 pm	
4:00 pm	
4:30 pm	
5:00 pm	
5:30 pm	
6:00 pm	
6:30 pm	
7:00 pm	
7:30 pm	
8:00 pm	
8:30 pm	
9:00 pm	
9:30 pm	
10:00 pm	

DAILY PLANNER

JUNE 5, 2024

Wednesday

TODAY'S AFFIRMATION

WEATHER

MOOD

TOP 3 PRIORITIES

1 _____
   _____

2 _____
   _____

3 _____
   _____

TO-DO LIST

☐ _____

☐ _____

☐ _____

☐ _____

☐ _____

☐ _____

☐ _____

☐ _____

DON'T FORGET

_____

_____

_____

TIME	PLANS & SCHEDULE
6:00 am	
6:30 am	
7:00 am	
7:30 am	
8:00 am	
8:30 am	
9:00 am	
9:30 am	
10:00 am	
10:30 am	
11:00 am	
11:30 am	
12:00 pm	
12:30 pm	
1:00 pm	
1:30 pm	
2:00 pm	
2:30 pm	
3:00 pm	
3:30 pm	
4:00 pm	
4:30 pm	
5:00 pm	
5:30 pm	
6:00 pm	
6:30 pm	
7:00 pm	
7:30 pm	
8:00 pm	
8:30 pm	
9:00 pm	
9:30 pm	
10:00 pm	

DAILY PLANNER

JUNE 6, 2024

Thursday

TODAY'S AFFIRMATION

TOP 3 PRIORITIES

1 _____

_____

2 _____

_____

3 _____

_____

TO-DO LIST

☐ _____

☐ _____

☐ _____

☐ _____

☐ _____

☐ _____

☐ _____

☐ _____

DON'T FORGET

_____

_____

_____

WEATHER

MOOD

TIME	PLANS & SCHEDULE
6:00 am	
6:30 am	
7:00 am	
7:30 am	
8:00 am	
8:30 am	
9:00 am	
9:30 am	
10:00 am	
10:30 am	
11:00 am	
11:30 am	
12:00 pm	
12:30 pm	
1:00 pm	
1:30 pm	
2:00 pm	
2:30 pm	
3:00 pm	
3:30 pm	
4:00 pm	
4:30 pm	
5:00 pm	
5:30 pm	
6:00 pm	
6:30 pm	
7:00 pm	
7:30 pm	
8:00 pm	
8:30 pm	
9:00 pm	
9:30 pm	
10:00 pm	

DAILY PLANNER

JUNE 7, 2024

Friday

TODAY'S AFFIRMATION

WEATHER

MOOD

TOP 3 PRIORITIES

1 _____
_____

2 _____
_____

3 _____
_____

TO-DO LIST

☐ _____

☐ _____

☐ _____

☐ _____

☐ _____

☐ _____

☐ _____

☐ _____

DON'T FORGET

_____
_____
_____

TIME	PLANS & SCHEDULE
6:00 am	
6:30 am	
7:00 am	
7:30 am	
8:00 am	
8:30 am	
9:00 am	
9:30 am	
10:00 am	
10:30 am	
11:00 am	
11:30 am	
12:00 pm	
12:30 pm	
1:00 pm	
1:30 pm	
2:00 pm	
2:30 pm	
3:00 pm	
3:30 pm	
4:00 pm	
4:30 pm	
5:00 pm	
5:30 pm	
6:00 pm	
6:30 pm	
7:00 pm	
7:30 pm	
8:00 pm	
8:30 pm	
9:00 pm	
9:30 pm	
10:00 pm	

DAILY PLANNER

JUNE 8, 2024

Saturday

TODAY'S AFFIRMATION

WEATHER

MOOD

TOP 3 PRIORITIES

1. _____
   _____

2. _____
   _____

3. _____
   _____

TO-DO LIST

- _____
- _____
- _____
- _____
- _____
- _____
- _____
- _____

DON'T FORGET

_____
_____
_____

TIME	PLANS & SCHEDULE
6:00 am	
6:30 am	
7:00 am	
7:30 am	
8:00 am	
8:30 am	
9:00 am	
9:30 am	
10:00 am	
10:30 am	
11:00 am	
11:30 am	
12:00 pm	
12:30 pm	
1:00 pm	
1:30 pm	
2:00 pm	
2:30 pm	
3:00 pm	
3:30 pm	
4:00 pm	
4:30 pm	
5:00 pm	
5:30 pm	
6:00 pm	
6:30 pm	
7:00 pm	
7:30 pm	
8:00 pm	
8:30 pm	
9:00 pm	
9:30 pm	
10:00 pm	

DAILY PLANNER

JUNE 9, 2024

Sunday

TODAY'S AFFIRMATION

WEATHER

MOOD

TOP 3 PRIORITIES

1 _____
_____

2 _____
_____

3 _____
_____

TO-DO LIST

☐ _____

☐ _____

☐ _____

☐ _____

☐ _____

☐ _____

☐ _____

☐ _____

DON'T FORGET

_____

_____

_____

TIME	PLANS & SCHEDULE
6:00 am	
6:30 am	
7:00 am	
7:30 am	
8:00 am	
8:30 am	
9:00 am	
9:30 am	
10:00 am	
10:30 am	
11:00 am	
11:30 am	
12:00 pm	
12:30 pm	
1:00 pm	
1:30 pm	
2:00 pm	
2:30 pm	
3:00 pm	
3:30 pm	
4:00 pm	
4:30 pm	
5:00 pm	
5:30 pm	
6:00 pm	
6:30 pm	
7:00 pm	
7:30 pm	
8:00 pm	
8:30 pm	
9:00 pm	
9:30 pm	
10:00 pm	

DAILY PLANNER

JUNE 10, 2024

Monday

WEATHER

MOOD

TOP 3 PRIORITIES

1 _____

_____

2 _____

_____

3 _____

_____

TO-DO LIST

☐ _____

☐ _____

☐ _____

☐ _____

☐ _____

☐ _____

☐ _____

☐ _____

DON'T FORGET

_____

_____

_____

TIME	PLANS & SCHEDULE
6:00 am	
6:30 am	
7:00 am	
7:30 am	
8:00 am	
8:30 am	
9:00 am	
9:30 am	
10:00 am	
10:30 am	
11:00 am	
11:30 am	
12:00 pm	
12:30 pm	
1:00 pm	
1:30 pm	
2:00 pm	
2:30 pm	
3:00 pm	
3:30 pm	
4:00 pm	
4:30 pm	
5:00 pm	
5:30 pm	
6:00 pm	
6:30 pm	
7:00 pm	
7:30 pm	
8:00 pm	
8:30 pm	
9:00 pm	
9:30 pm	
10:00 pm	

DAILY PLANNER

JUNE 11, 2024

Tuesday

TODAY'S AFFIRMATION

WEATHER

MOOD

TOP 3 PRIORITIES

1 _____
_____

2 _____
_____

3 _____
_____

TO-DO LIST

☐ _____

☐ _____

☐ _____

☐ _____

☐ _____

☐ _____

☐ _____

☐ _____

DON'T FORGET

_____

_____

_____

TIME	PLANS & SCHEDULE
6:00 am	
6:30 am	
7:00 am	
7:30 am	
8:00 am	
8:30 am	
9:00 am	
9:30 am	
10:00 am	
10:30 am	
11:00 am	
11:30 am	
12:00 pm	
12:30 pm	
1:00 pm	
1:30 pm	
2:00 pm	
2:30 pm	
3:00 pm	
3:30 pm	
4:00 pm	
4:30 pm	
5:00 pm	
5:30 pm	
6:00 pm	
6:30 pm	
7:00 pm	
7:30 pm	
8:00 pm	
8:30 pm	
9:00 pm	
9:30 pm	
10:00 pm	

DAILY PLANNER

JUNE 12, 2024

Wednesday

WEATHER

MOOD

TOP 3 PRIORITIES

1 _____
_____

2 _____
_____

3 _____
_____

TO-DO LIST

- ▦ _____
- ▦ _____
- ▦ _____
- ▦ _____
- ▦ _____
- ▦ _____
- ▦ _____
- ▦ _____

DON'T FORGET

_____
_____
_____

TIME	PLANS & SCHEDULE
6:00 am	
6:30 am	
7:00 am	
7:30 am	
8:00 am	
8:30 am	
9:00 am	
9:30 am	
10:00 am	
10:30 am	
11:00 am	
11:30 am	
12:00 pm	
12:30 pm	
1:00 pm	
1:30 pm	
2:00 pm	
2:30 pm	
3:00 pm	
3:30 pm	
4:00 pm	
4:30 pm	
5:00 pm	
5:30 pm	
6:00 pm	
6:30 pm	
7:00 pm	
7:30 pm	
8:00 pm	
8:30 pm	
9:00 pm	
9:30 pm	
10:00 pm	

DAILY PLANNER

JUNE 13, 2024

Thursday

TODAY'S AFFIRMATION

WEATHER

MOOD

TOP 3 PRIORITIES

1 _____
_____

2 _____
_____

3 _____
_____

TO-DO LIST

☐ _____

☐ _____

☐ _____

☐ _____

☐ _____

☐ _____

☐ _____

☐ _____

DON'T FORGET

_____

_____

_____

TIME	PLANS & SCHEDULE
6:00 am	
6:30 am	
7:00 am	
7:30 am	
8:00 am	
8:30 am	
9:00 am	
9:30 am	
10:00 am	
10:30 am	
11:00 am	
11:30 am	
12:00 pm	
12:30 pm	
1:00 pm	
1:30 pm	
2:00 pm	
2:30 pm	
3:00 pm	
3:30 pm	
4:00 pm	
4:30 pm	
5:00 pm	
5:30 pm	
6:00 pm	
6:30 pm	
7:00 pm	
7:30 pm	
8:00 pm	
8:30 pm	
9:00 pm	
9:30 pm	
10:00 pm	

DAILY PLANNER

JUNE 14, 2024

Friday

TODAY'S AFFIRMATION

WEATHER

MOOD

TOP 3 PRIORITIES

1 _____

_____

2 _____

_____

3 _____

_____

TO-DO LIST

☐ _____

☐ _____

☐ _____

☐ _____

☐ _____

☐ _____

☐ _____

☐ _____

DON'T FORGET

_____

_____

_____

TIME	PLANS & SCHEDULE
6:00 am	
6:30 am	
7:00 am	
7:30 am	
8:00 am	
8:30 am	
9:00 am	
9:30 am	
10:00 am	
10:30 am	
11:00 am	
11:30 am	
12:00 pm	
12:30 pm	
1:00 pm	
1:30 pm	
2:00 pm	
2:30 pm	
3:00 pm	
3:30 pm	
4:00 pm	
4:30 pm	
5:00 pm	
5:30 pm	
6:00 pm	
6:30 pm	
7:00 pm	
7:30 pm	
8:00 pm	
8:30 pm	
9:00 pm	
9:30 pm	
10:00 pm	

DAILY PLANNER

JUNE 15, 2024

Saturday

TODAY'S AFFIRMATION

WEATHER

MOOD

TOP 3 PRIORITIES

1 _____

_____

2 _____

_____

3 _____

_____

TO-DO LIST

☐ _____

☐ _____

☐ _____

☐ _____

☐ _____

☐ _____

☐ _____

☐ _____

DON'T FORGET

_____

_____

_____

TIME	PLANS & SCHEDULE
6:00 am	
6:30 am	
7:00 am	
7:30 am	
8:00 am	
8:30 am	
9:00 am	
9:30 am	
10:00 am	
10:30 am	
11:00 am	
11:30 am	
12:00 pm	
12:30 pm	
1:00 pm	
1:30 pm	
2:00 pm	
2:30 pm	
3:00 pm	
3:30 pm	
4:00 pm	
4:30 pm	
5:00 pm	
5:30 pm	
6:00 pm	
6:30 pm	
7:00 pm	
7:30 pm	
8:00 pm	
8:30 pm	
9:00 pm	
9:30 pm	
10:00 pm	

DAILY PLANNER

JUNE 16, 2024

Sunday

TODAY'S AFFIRMATION

WEATHER

MOOD

TOP 3 PRIORITIES

1 _____

2 _____

3 _____

TO-DO LIST

- _____
- _____
- _____
- _____
- _____
- _____
- _____
- _____

DON'T FORGET

_____

_____

_____

TIME	PLANS & SCHEDULE
6:00 am	
6:30 am	
7:00 am	
7:30 am	
8:00 am	
8:30 am	
9:00 am	
9:30 am	
10:00 am	
10:30 am	
11:00 am	
11:30 am	
12:00 pm	
12:30 pm	
1:00 pm	
1:30 pm	
2:00 pm	
2:30 pm	
3:00 pm	
3:30 pm	
4:00 pm	
4:30 pm	
5:00 pm	
5:30 pm	
6:00 pm	
6:30 pm	
7:00 pm	
7:30 pm	
8:00 pm	
8:30 pm	
9:00 pm	
9:30 pm	
10:00 pm	

DAILY PLANNER

JUNE 17, 2024

Monday

TODAY'S AFFIRMATION

WEATHER

MOOD

TOP 3 PRIORITIES

1 _____
_____

2 _____
_____

3 _____
_____

TO-DO LIST

☐ _____

☐ _____

☐ _____

☐ _____

☐ _____

☐ _____

☐ _____

☐ _____

DON'T FORGET

_____

_____

_____

TIME	PLANS & SCHEDULE
6:00 am	
6:30 am	
7:00 am	
7:30 am	
8:00 am	
8:30 am	
9:00 am	
9:30 am	
10:00 am	
10:30 am	
11:00 am	
11:30 am	
12:00 pm	
12:30 pm	
1:00 pm	
1:30 pm	
2:00 pm	
2:30 pm	
3:00 pm	
3:30 pm	
4:00 pm	
4:30 pm	
5:00 pm	
5:30 pm	
6:00 pm	
6:30 pm	
7:00 pm	
7:30 pm	
8:00 pm	
8:30 pm	
9:00 pm	
9:30 pm	
10:00 pm	

DAILY PLANNER

JUNE 18, 2024

Tuesday

TODAY'S AFFIRMATION

WEATHER

MOOD

TOP 3 PRIORITIES

1 _____
_____

2 _____
_____

3 _____
_____

TO-DO LIST

☐ _____
☐ _____
☐ _____
☐ _____
☐ _____
☐ _____
☐ _____
☐ _____

DON'T FORGET

_____
_____
_____

TIME	PLANS & SCHEDULE
6:00 am	
6:30 am	
7:00 am	
7:30 am	
8:00 am	
8:30 am	
9:00 am	
9:30 am	
10:00 am	
10:30 am	
11:00 am	
11:30 am	
12:00 pm	
12:30 pm	
1:00 pm	
1:30 pm	
2:00 pm	
2:30 pm	
3:00 pm	
3:30 pm	
4:00 pm	
4:30 pm	
5:00 pm	
5:30 pm	
6:00 pm	
6:30 pm	
7:00 pm	
7:30 pm	
8:00 pm	
8:30 pm	
9:00 pm	
9:30 pm	
10:00 pm	

DAILY PLANNER

JUNE 19, 2024

Wednesday

TODAY'S AFFIRMATION

WEATHER

MOOD

TOP 3 PRIORITIES

1 _____
_____

2 _____
_____

3 _____
_____

TO-DO LIST

☐ _____

☐ _____

☐ _____

☐ _____

☐ _____

☐ _____

☐ _____

☐ _____

DON'T FORGET

_____

_____

_____

TIME	PLANS & SCHEDULE
6:00 am	
6:30 am	
7:00 am	
7:30 am	
8:00 am	
8:30 am	
9:00 am	
9:30 am	
10:00 am	
10:30 am	
11:00 am	
11:30 am	
12:00 pm	
12:30 pm	
1:00 pm	
1:30 pm	
2:00 pm	
2:30 pm	
3:00 pm	
3:30 pm	
4:00 pm	
4:30 pm	
5:00 pm	
5:30 pm	
6:00 pm	
6:30 pm	
7:00 pm	
7:30 pm	
8:00 pm	
8:30 pm	
9:00 pm	
9:30 pm	
10:00 pm	

DAILY PLANNER

JUNE 20, 2024

Thursday

TODAY'S AFFIRMATION

WEATHER

MOOD

TOP 3 PRIORITIES

1 _____

_____

2 _____

_____

3 _____

_____

TO-DO LIST

▪ _____

▪ _____

▪ _____

▪ _____

▪ _____

▪ _____

▪ _____

▪ _____

DON'T FORGET

_____

_____

_____

TIME	PLANS & SCHEDULE
6:00 am	
6:30 am	
7:00 am	
7:30 am	
8:00 am	
8:30 am	
9:00 am	
9:30 am	
10:00 am	
10:30 am	
11:00 am	
11:30 am	
12:00 pm	
12:30 pm	
1:00 pm	
1:30 pm	
2:00 pm	
2:30 pm	
3:00 pm	
3:30 pm	
4:00 pm	
4:30 pm	
5:00 pm	
5:30 pm	
6:00 pm	
6:30 pm	
7:00 pm	
7:30 pm	
8:00 pm	
8:30 pm	
9:00 pm	
9:30 pm	
10:00 pm	

DAILY PLANNER

JUNE 21, 2024

Friday

TODAY'S AFFIRMATION

WEATHER

MOOD

TOP 3 PRIORITIES

1 _____

_____

2 _____

_____

3 _____

_____

TO-DO LIST

- _____
- _____
- _____
- _____
- _____
- _____
- _____
- _____

DON'T FORGET

_____

_____

_____

TIME	PLANS & SCHEDULE
6:00 am	
6:30 am	
7:00 am	
7:30 am	
8:00 am	
8:30 am	
9:00 am	
9:30 am	
10:00 am	
10:30 am	
11:00 am	
11:30 am	
12:00 pm	
12:30 pm	
1:00 pm	
1:30 pm	
2:00 pm	
2:30 pm	
3:00 pm	
3:30 pm	
4:00 pm	
4:30 pm	
5:00 pm	
5:30 pm	
6:00 pm	
6:30 pm	
7:00 pm	
7:30 pm	
8:00 pm	
8:30 pm	
9:00 pm	
9:30 pm	
10:00 pm	

DAILY PLANNER

JUNE 22, 2024

Saturday

TODAY'S AFFIRMATION

TOP 3 PRIORITIES

1 _____

_____

2 _____

_____

3 _____

_____

TO-DO LIST

- _____
- _____
- _____
- _____
- _____
- _____
- _____
- _____

DON'T FORGET

_____

_____

_____

WEATHER

MOOD

TIME	PLANS & SCHEDULE
6:00 am	
6:30 am	
7:00 am	
7:30 am	
8:00 am	
8:30 am	
9:00 am	
9:30 am	
10:00 am	
10:30 am	
11:00 am	
11:30 am	
12:00 pm	
12:30 pm	
1:00 pm	
1:30 pm	
2:00 pm	
2:30 pm	
3:00 pm	
3:30 pm	
4:00 pm	
4:30 pm	
5:00 pm	
5:30 pm	
6:00 pm	
6:30 pm	
7:00 pm	
7:30 pm	
8:00 pm	
8:30 pm	
9:00 pm	
9:30 pm	
10:00 pm	

DAILY PLANNER

JUNE 23, 2024

Sunday

TODAY'S AFFIRMATION

WEATHER

MOOD

TOP 3 PRIORITIES

1 _____
_____

2 _____
_____

3 _____
_____

TO-DO LIST

- _____
- _____
- _____
- _____
- _____
- _____
- _____
- _____

DON'T FORGET

_____
_____
_____

TIME	PLANS & SCHEDULE
6:00 am	
6:30 am	
7:00 am	
7:30 am	
8:00 am	
8:30 am	
9:00 am	
9:30 am	
10:00 am	
10:30 am	
11:00 am	
11:30 am	
12:00 pm	
12:30 pm	
1:00 pm	
1:30 pm	
2:00 pm	
2:30 pm	
3:00 pm	
3:30 pm	
4:00 pm	
4:30 pm	
5:00 pm	
5:30 pm	
6:00 pm	
6:30 pm	
7:00 pm	
7:30 pm	
8:00 pm	
8:30 pm	
9:00 pm	
9:30 pm	
10:00 pm	

DAILY PLANNER

JUNE 24, 2024

Monday

TODAY'S AFFIRMATION

WEATHER

MOOD

TOP 3 PRIORITIES

1 _____
_____

2 _____
_____

3 _____
_____

TO-DO LIST

☐ _____
☐ _____
☐ _____
☐ _____
☐ _____
☐ _____
☐ _____
☐ _____

DON'T FORGET

_____
_____
_____

TIME	PLANS & SCHEDULE
6:00 am	
6:30 am	
7:00 am	
7:30 am	
8:00 am	
8:30 am	
9:00 am	
9:30 am	
10:00 am	
10:30 am	
11:00 am	
11:30 am	
12:00 pm	
12:30 pm	
1:00 pm	
1:30 pm	
2:00 pm	
2:30 pm	
3:00 pm	
3:30 pm	
4:00 pm	
4:30 pm	
5:00 pm	
5:30 pm	
6:00 pm	
6:30 pm	
7:00 pm	
7:30 pm	
8:00 pm	
8:30 pm	
9:00 pm	
9:30 pm	
10:00 pm	

DAILY PLANNER

JUNE 25, 2024

Tuesday

TODAY'S AFFIRMATION

WEATHER

MOOD

TOP 3 PRIORITIES

1 _____

2 _____

3 _____

TO-DO LIST

☐ _____

☐ _____

☐ _____

☐ _____

☐ _____

☐ _____

☐ _____

☐ _____

DON'T FORGET

_____

_____

_____

TIME	PLANS & SCHEDULE
6:00 am	
6:30 am	
7:00 am	
7:30 am	
8:00 am	
8:30 am	
9:00 am	
9:30 am	
10:00 am	
10:30 am	
11:00 am	
11:30 am	
12:00 pm	
12:30 pm	
1:00 pm	
1:30 pm	
2:00 pm	
2:30 pm	
3:00 pm	
3:30 pm	
4:00 pm	
4:30 pm	
5:00 pm	
5:30 pm	
6:00 pm	
6:30 pm	
7:00 pm	
7:30 pm	
8:00 pm	
8:30 pm	
9:00 pm	
9:30 pm	
10:00 pm	

DAILY PLANNER

JUNE 26, 2024

Wednesday

TODAY'S AFFIRMATION

WEATHER

MOOD

TOP 3 PRIORITIES

1 _____
_____

2 _____
_____

3 _____
_____

TO-DO LIST

☐ _____

☐ _____

☐ _____

☐ _____

☐ _____

☐ _____

☐ _____

☐ _____

DON'T FORGET

_____

_____

_____

TIME	PLANS & SCHEDULE
6:00 am	
6:30 am	
7:00 am	
7:30 am	
8:00 am	
8:30 am	
9:00 am	
9:30 am	
10:00 am	
10:30 am	
11:00 am	
11:30 am	
12:00 pm	
12:30 pm	
1:00 pm	
1:30 pm	
2:00 pm	
2:30 pm	
3:00 pm	
3:30 pm	
4:00 pm	
4:30 pm	
5:00 pm	
5:30 pm	
6:00 pm	
6:30 pm	
7:00 pm	
7:30 pm	
8:00 pm	
8:30 pm	
9:00 pm	
9:30 pm	
10:00 pm	

DAILY PLANNER

JUNE 27, 2024

Thursday

TODAY'S AFFIRMATION

WEATHER

MOOD

TOP 3 PRIORITIES

1 _____
_____

2 _____
_____

3 _____
_____

TO-DO LIST

☐ _____
☐ _____
☐ _____
☐ _____
☐ _____
☐ _____
☐ _____
☐ _____

DON'T FORGET

_____
_____
_____

TIME	PLANS & SCHEDULE
6:00 am	
6:30 am	
7:00 am	
7:30 am	
8:00 am	
8:30 am	
9:00 am	
9:30 am	
10:00 am	
10:30 am	
11:00 am	
11:30 am	
12:00 pm	
12:30 pm	
1:00 pm	
1:30 pm	
2:00 pm	
2:30 pm	
3:00 pm	
3:30 pm	
4:00 pm	
4:30 pm	
5:00 pm	
5:30 pm	
6:00 pm	
6:30 pm	
7:00 pm	
7:30 pm	
8:00 pm	
8:30 pm	
9:00 pm	
9:30 pm	
10:00 pm	

DAILY PLANNER

JUNE 28, 2024

Friday

TODAY'S AFFIRMATION

WEATHER

MOOD

TOP 3 PRIORITIES

1 _____
_____

2 _____
_____

3 _____
_____

TO-DO LIST

☐ _____

☐ _____

☐ _____

☐ _____

☐ _____

☐ _____

☐ _____

☐ _____

DON'T FORGET

_____

_____

_____

TIME	PLANS & SCHEDULE
6:00 am	
6:30 am	
7:00 am	
7:30 am	
8:00 am	
8:30 am	
9:00 am	
9:30 am	
10:00 am	
10:30 am	
11:00 am	
11:30 am	
12:00 pm	
12:30 pm	
1:00 pm	
1:30 pm	
2:00 pm	
2:30 pm	
3:00 pm	
3:30 pm	
4:00 pm	
4:30 pm	
5:00 pm	
5:30 pm	
6:00 pm	
6:30 pm	
7:00 pm	
7:30 pm	
8:00 pm	
8:30 pm	
9:00 pm	
9:30 pm	
10:00 pm	

DAILY PLANNER

JUNE 29, 2024

Saturday

TODAY'S AFFIRMATION

WEATHER

MOOD

TIME	PLANS & SCHEDULE
6:00 am	
6:30 am	
7:00 am	
7:30 am	
8:00 am	
8:30 am	
9:00 am	
9:30 am	
10:00 am	
10:30 am	
11:00 am	
11:30 am	
12:00 pm	
12:30 pm	
1:00 pm	
1:30 pm	
2:00 pm	
2:30 pm	
3:00 pm	
3:30 pm	
4:00 pm	
4:30 pm	
5:00 pm	
5:30 pm	
6:00 pm	
6:30 pm	
7:00 pm	
7:30 pm	
8:00 pm	
8:30 pm	
9:00 pm	
9:30 pm	
10:00 pm	

TOP 3 PRIORITIES

1 _____

2 _____

3 _____

TO-DO LIST

- _____
- _____
- _____
- _____
- _____
- _____
- _____
- _____

DON'T FORGET

DAILY PLANNER

JUNE 30, 2024

Sunday

TODAY'S AFFIRMATION

WEATHER

MOOD

TOP 3 PRIORITIES

1 _____
_____

2 _____
_____

3 _____
_____

TO-DO LIST

- _____
- _____
- _____
- _____
- _____
- _____
- _____
- _____

DON'T FORGET

_____
_____
_____

TIME	PLANS & SCHEDULE
6:00 am	
6:30 am	
7:00 am	
7:30 am	
8:00 am	
8:30 am	
9:00 am	
9:30 am	
10:00 am	
10:30 am	
11:00 am	
11:30 am	
12:00 pm	
12:30 pm	
1:00 pm	
1:30 pm	
2:00 pm	
2:30 pm	
3:00 pm	
3:30 pm	
4:00 pm	
4:30 pm	
5:00 pm	
5:30 pm	
6:00 pm	
6:30 pm	
7:00 pm	
7:30 pm	
8:00 pm	
8:30 pm	
9:00 pm	
9:30 pm	
10:00 pm	

MONTHLY BUDGET PLANNER

Budget Goal: _____   Month: _____

Income

Date	Description	Amount
Total		

Fixed Expenses

Date	Description	Amount
Total		

Other Expenses

Date	Description	Amount
Total		

Bills

Date	Description	Amount
Total		

Recap

	Goal	Actual	Difference
Earnt			
Spent			
Debt			
Saved			

Notes

Date:

☐
☐
☐
☐
☐

GRATITUDE JOURNAL

DATE: _____   S M T W T F S

TODAY I'M GRATEFUL FOR

● _____

● _____

● _____

WATER INTAKE

◊ ◊ ◊ ◊   ◊ ◊ ◊ ◊   ◊ ◊
       1L   2L   3L

WEATHER

TODAY'S AFFIRMATION

● _____

● _____

● _____

● _____

NOTES / REMINDERS

SOMETHING I'M PROUD OF

● _____

● _____

● _____

● _____

TOMORROW I LOOK FORWARD TO

● _____

● _____

● _____

● _____

30 DAY
Self-Care Challenge

DAY 1	DAY 2	DAY 3	DAY 4	DAY 5
Start a gratitude journal	Learn to meditate	Spend the day social media free	Call someone you love	Take a 15 minute walk outdoors
DAY 6	**DAY 7**	**DAY 8**	**DAY 9**	**DAY 10**
Listen to a podcast	Learn to cook a new recipe	Stretch for 10-15 minutes	Listen to your favorite song	Practice deep breathing
DAY 11	**DAY 12**	**DAY 13**	**DAY 14**	**DAY 15**
Try a free online workout	Read a book for 15 minutes	Write a list of short-term goals	De-clutter a room or desk	Go to bed 30 minutes earlier
DAY 16	**DAY 17**	**DAY 18**	**DAY 19**	**DAY 20**
Have a game night	Wake up 15 minutes earlier	Make your favorite meal	Buy yourself something nice	Create a bucket list
DAY 21	**DAY 22**	**DAY 23**	**DAY 24**	**DAY 25**
Watch a movie or series	Write down your thoughts	Take a long shower or bath	Have a home spa day	Read inspirational quotes
DAY 26	**DAY 27**	**DAY 28**	**DAY 29**	**DAY 30**
Create a vision board	Spend some time outside	Do a hair mask	Write it all down in a journal	Take a power nap

JULY 2024

Sunday	Monday	Tuesday	Wednesday
	01	02	03
07	08	09	10
14	15	16	17
21	22	23	24
28	29	30	31

JULY 2024

Thursday	Friday	Saturday	Notes
04	05	06	....
11	12	13	....
18	19	20	....
25	26	27	....
			....

JULY

Goal

Action Plan

Date

....

....

....

....

....

....

....

....

....

....

Grateful For

....

....

....

....

....

To Improve

....

....

....

....

Notes

....

....

....

....

DAILY PLANNER

JULY 1, 2024

Monday

TODAY'S AFFIRMATION

WEATHER

MOOD

TOP 3 PRIORITIES

1 _____
_____

2 _____
_____

3 _____
_____

TO-DO LIST

☐ _____

☐ _____

☐ _____

☐ _____

☐ _____

☐ _____

☐ _____

☐ _____

DON'T FORGET

_____
_____
_____

TIME	PLANS & SCHEDULE
6:00 am	
6:30 am	
7:00 am	
7:30 am	
8:00 am	
8:30 am	
9:00 am	
9:30 am	
10:00 am	
10:30 am	
11:00 am	
11:30 am	
12:00 pm	
12:30 pm	
1:00 pm	
1:30 pm	
2:00 pm	
2:30 pm	
3:00 pm	
3:30 pm	
4:00 pm	
4:30 pm	
5:00 pm	
5:30 pm	
6:00 pm	
6:30 pm	
7:00 pm	
7:30 pm	
8:00 pm	
8:30 pm	
9:00 pm	
9:30 pm	
10:00 pm	

DAILY PLANNER

JULY 2, 2024

Tuesday

TODAY'S AFFIRMATION

WEATHER

MOOD

TOP 3 PRIORITIES

1 _____
_____

2 _____
_____

3 _____
_____

TO-DO LIST

- ☐ _____
- ☐ _____
- ☐ _____
- ☐ _____
- ☐ _____
- ☐ _____
- ☐ _____
- ☐ _____

DON'T FORGET

_____
_____
_____

TIME	PLANS & SCHEDULE
6:00 am	
6:30 am	
7:00 am	
7:30 am	
8:00 am	
8:30 am	
9:00 am	
9:30 am	
10:00 am	
10:30 am	
11:00 am	
11:30 am	
12:00 pm	
12:30 pm	
1:00 pm	
1:30 pm	
2:00 pm	
2:30 pm	
3:00 pm	
3:30 pm	
4:00 pm	
4:30 pm	
5:00 pm	
5:30 pm	
6:00 pm	
6:30 pm	
7:00 pm	
7:30 pm	
8:00 pm	
8:30 pm	
9:00 pm	
9:30 pm	
10:00 pm	

DAILY PLANNER

JULY 3, 2024

Wednesday

TODAY'S AFFIRMATION

WEATHER

MOOD

TOP 3 PRIORITIES

1 _____

2 _____

3 _____

TO-DO LIST

☐ _____

☐ _____

☐ _____

☐ _____

☐ _____

☐ _____

☐ _____

☐ _____

DON'T FORGET

_____

_____

_____

TIME	PLANS & SCHEDULE
6:00 am	
6:30 am	
7:00 am	
7:30 am	
8:00 am	
8:30 am	
9:00 am	
9:30 am	
10:00 am	
10:30 am	
11:00 am	
11:30 am	
12:00 pm	
12:30 pm	
1:00 pm	
1:30 pm	
2:00 pm	
2:30 pm	
3:00 pm	
3:30 pm	
4:00 pm	
4:30 pm	
5:00 pm	
5:30 pm	
6:00 pm	
6:30 pm	
7:00 pm	
7:30 pm	
8:00 pm	
8:30 pm	
9:00 pm	
9:30 pm	
10:00 pm	

DAILY PLANNER

JULY 4, 2024

Thursday

TODAY'S AFFIRMATION

WEATHER

MOOD

TOP 3 PRIORITIES

1 _____

_____

2 _____

_____

3 _____

_____

TO-DO LIST

☐ _____

☐ _____

☐ _____

☐ _____

☐ _____

☐ _____

☐ _____

☐ _____

DON'T FORGET

_____

_____

_____

TIME	PLANS & SCHEDULE
6:00 am	
6:30 am	
7:00 am	
7:30 am	
8:00 am	
8:30 am	
9:00 am	
9:30 am	
10:00 am	
10:30 am	
11:00 am	
11:30 am	
12:00 pm	
12:30 pm	
1:00 pm	
1:30 pm	
2:00 pm	
2:30 pm	
3:00 pm	
3:30 pm	
4:00 pm	
4:30 pm	
5:00 pm	
5:30 pm	
6:00 pm	
6:30 pm	
7:00 pm	
7:30 pm	
8:00 pm	
8:30 pm	
9:00 pm	
9:30 pm	
10:00 pm	

DAILY PLANNER

JULY 5, 2024

Friday

TODAY'S AFFIRMATION

WEATHER

MOOD

TOP 3 PRIORITIES

1 _____
_____

2 _____
_____

3 _____
_____

TO-DO LIST

☐ _____

☐ _____

☐ _____

☐ _____

☐ _____

☐ _____

☐ _____

☐ _____

DON'T FORGET

_____
_____
_____

TIME	PLANS & SCHEDULE
6:00 am	
6:30 am	
7:00 am	
7:30 am	
8:00 am	
8:30 am	
9:00 am	
9:30 am	
10:00 am	
10:30 am	
11:00 am	
11:30 am	
12:00 pm	
12:30 pm	
1:00 pm	
1:30 pm	
2:00 pm	
2:30 pm	
3:00 pm	
3:30 pm	
4:00 pm	
4:30 pm	
5:00 pm	
5:30 pm	
6:00 pm	
6:30 pm	
7:00 pm	
7:30 pm	
8:00 pm	
8:30 pm	
9:00 pm	
9:30 pm	
10:00 pm	

DAILY PLANNER

JULY 6, 2024

Saturday

TODAY'S AFFIRMATION

WEATHER

MOOD

TOP 3 PRIORITIES

1 _____

_____

2 _____

_____

3 _____

_____

TO-DO LIST

☐ _____

☐ _____

☐ _____

☐ _____

☐ _____

☐ _____

☐ _____

☐ _____

DON'T FORGET

_____

_____

_____

TIME	PLANS & SCHEDULE
6:00 am	
6:30 am	
7:00 am	
7:30 am	
8:00 am	
8:30 am	
9:00 am	
9:30 am	
10:00 am	
10:30 am	
11:00 am	
11:30 am	
12:00 pm	
12:30 pm	
1:00 pm	
1:30 pm	
2:00 pm	
2:30 pm	
3:00 pm	
3:30 pm	
4:00 pm	
4:30 pm	
5:00 pm	
5:30 pm	
6:00 pm	
6:30 pm	
7:00 pm	
7:30 pm	
8:00 pm	
8:30 pm	
9:00 pm	
9:30 pm	
10:00 pm	

DAILY PLANNER

JULY 7, 2024

Sunday

TODAY'S AFFIRMATION

WEATHER

MOOD

TOP 3 PRIORITIES

1 _____

_____

2 _____

_____

3 _____

_____

TO-DO LIST

- _____
- _____
- _____
- _____
- _____
- _____
- _____
- _____

DON'T FORGET

_____

_____

_____

TIME	PLANS & SCHEDULE
6:00 am	
6:30 am	
7:00 am	
7:30 am	
8:00 am	
8:30 am	
9:00 am	
9:30 am	
10:00 am	
10:30 am	
11:00 am	
11:30 am	
12:00 pm	
12:30 pm	
1:00 pm	
1:30 pm	
2:00 pm	
2:30 pm	
3:00 pm	
3:30 pm	
4:00 pm	
4:30 pm	
5:00 pm	
5:30 pm	
6:00 pm	
6:30 pm	
7:00 pm	
7:30 pm	
8:00 pm	
8:30 pm	
9:00 pm	
9:30 pm	
10:00 pm	

DAILY PLANNER

JULY 8, 2024

Monday

TODAY'S AFFIRMATION

WEATHER

MOOD

TOP 3 PRIORITIES

1 _____
_____

2 _____
_____

3 _____
_____

TO-DO LIST

☐ _____
☐ _____
☐ _____
☐ _____
☐ _____
☐ _____
☐ _____
☐ _____

DON'T FORGET

_____
_____
_____

TIME	PLANS & SCHEDULE
6:00 am	
6:30 am	
7:00 am	
7:30 am	
8:00 am	
8:30 am	
9:00 am	
9:30 am	
10:00 am	
10:30 am	
11:00 am	
11:30 am	
12:00 pm	
12:30 pm	
1:00 pm	
1:30 pm	
2:00 pm	
2:30 pm	
3:00 pm	
3:30 pm	
4:00 pm	
4:30 pm	
5:00 pm	
5:30 pm	
6:00 pm	
6:30 pm	
7:00 pm	
7:30 pm	
8:00 pm	
8:30 pm	
9:00 pm	
9:30 pm	
10:00 pm	

DAILY PLANNER

JULY 9, 2024

Tuesday

TODAY'S AFFIRMATION

WEATHER

MOOD

TOP 3 PRIORITIES

1 _____

_____

2 _____

_____

3 _____

_____

TO-DO LIST

- ☐ _____
- ☐ _____
- ☐ _____
- ☐ _____
- ☐ _____
- ☐ _____
- ☐ _____
- ☐ _____

DON'T FORGET

_____

_____

_____

TIME	PLANS & SCHEDULE
6:00 am	
6:30 am	
7:00 am	
7:30 am	
8:00 am	
8:30 am	
9:00 am	
9:30 am	
10:00 am	
10:30 am	
11:00 am	
11:30 am	
12:00 pm	
12:30 pm	
1:00 pm	
1:30 pm	
2:00 pm	
2:30 pm	
3:00 pm	
3:30 pm	
4:00 pm	
4:30 pm	
5:00 pm	
5:30 pm	
6:00 pm	
6:30 pm	
7:00 pm	
7:30 pm	
8:00 pm	
8:30 pm	
9:00 pm	
9:30 pm	
10:00 pm	

DAILY PLANNER

JULY 10, 2024

Wednesday

TODAY'S AFFIRMATION

WEATHER

MOOD

TOP 3 PRIORITIES

1 _____
_____

2 _____
_____

3 _____
_____

TO-DO LIST

- _____
- _____
- _____
- _____
- _____
- _____
- _____
- _____

DON'T FORGET

_____
_____
_____

TIME	PLANS & SCHEDULE
6:00 am	
6:30 am	
7:00 am	
7:30 am	
8:00 am	
8:30 am	
9:00 am	
9:30 am	
10:00 am	
10:30 am	
11:00 am	
11:30 am	
12:00 pm	
12:30 pm	
1:00 pm	
1:30 pm	
2:00 pm	
2:30 pm	
3:00 pm	
3:30 pm	
4:00 pm	
4:30 pm	
5:00 pm	
5:30 pm	
6:00 pm	
6:30 pm	
7:00 pm	
7:30 pm	
8:00 pm	
8:30 pm	
9:00 pm	
9:30 pm	
10:00 pm	

DAILY PLANNER

JULY 11, 2024

Thursday

TODAY'S AFFIRMATION

WEATHER

MOOD

TOP 3 PRIORITIES

1 _____
_____

2 _____
_____

3 _____
_____

TO-DO LIST

☐ _____

☐ _____

☐ _____

☐ _____

☐ _____

☐ _____

☐ _____

☐ _____

DON'T FORGET

_____

_____

_____

TIME	PLANS & SCHEDULE
6:00 am	
6:30 am	
7:00 am	
7:30 am	
8:00 am	
8:30 am	
9:00 am	
9:30 am	
10:00 am	
10:30 am	
11:00 am	
11:30 am	
12:00 pm	
12:30 pm	
1:00 pm	
1:30 pm	
2:00 pm	
2:30 pm	
3:00 pm	
3:30 pm	
4:00 pm	
4:30 pm	
5:00 pm	
5:30 pm	
6:00 pm	
6:30 pm	
7:00 pm	
7:30 pm	
8:00 pm	
8:30 pm	
9:00 pm	
9:30 pm	
10:00 pm	

DAILY PLANNER

JULY 12, 2024

Friday

TODAY'S AFFIRMATION

WEATHER	
MOOD	

TOP 3 PRIORITIES

1 _____

_____

2 _____

_____

3 _____

_____

TO-DO LIST

- _____
- _____
- _____
- _____
- _____
- _____
- _____
- _____

DON'T FORGET

_____

_____

_____

TIME	PLANS & SCHEDULE
6:00 am	
6:30 am	
7:00 am	
7:30 am	
8:00 am	
8:30 am	
9:00 am	
9:30 am	
10:00 am	
10:30 am	
11:00 am	
11:30 am	
12:00 pm	
12:30 pm	
1:00 pm	
1:30 pm	
2:00 pm	
2:30 pm	
3:00 pm	
3:30 pm	
4:00 pm	
4:30 pm	
5:00 pm	
5:30 pm	
6:00 pm	
6:30 pm	
7:00 pm	
7:30 pm	
8:00 pm	
8:30 pm	
9:00 pm	
9:30 pm	
10:00 pm	

DAILY PLANNER

JULY 13, 2024

Saturday

TODAY'S AFFIRMATION

WEATHER

MOOD

TOP 3 PRIORITIES

1 _____
_____

2 _____
_____

3 _____
_____

TO-DO LIST

- _____
- _____
- _____
- _____
- _____
- _____
- _____
- _____

DON'T FORGET

_____
_____
_____

TIME	PLANS & SCHEDULE
6:00 am	
6:30 am	
7:00 am	
7:30 am	
8:00 am	
8:30 am	
9:00 am	
9:30 am	
10:00 am	
10:30 am	
11:00 am	
11:30 am	
12:00 pm	
12:30 pm	
1:00 pm	
1:30 pm	
2:00 pm	
2:30 pm	
3:00 pm	
3:30 pm	
4:00 pm	
4:30 pm	
5:00 pm	
5:30 pm	
6:00 pm	
6:30 pm	
7:00 pm	
7:30 pm	
8:00 pm	
8:30 pm	
9:00 pm	
9:30 pm	
10:00 pm	

DAILY PLANNER

JULY 14, 2024

Sunday

TODAY'S AFFIRMATION

WEATHER

MOOD

TOP 3 PRIORITIES

1 _____

_____

2 _____

_____

3 _____

_____

TO-DO LIST

☐ _____

☐ _____

☐ _____

☐ _____

☐ _____

☐ _____

☐ _____

☐ _____

DON'T FORGET

_____

_____

_____

TIME	PLANS & SCHEDULE
6:00 am	
6:30 am	
7:00 am	
7:30 am	
8:00 am	
8:30 am	
9:00 am	
9:30 am	
10:00 am	
10:30 am	
11:00 am	
11:30 am	
12:00 pm	
12:30 pm	
1:00 pm	
1:30 pm	
2:00 pm	
2:30 pm	
3:00 pm	
3:30 pm	
4:00 pm	
4:30 pm	
5:00 pm	
5:30 pm	
6:00 pm	
6:30 pm	
7:00 pm	
7:30 pm	
8:00 pm	
8:30 pm	
9:00 pm	
9:30 pm	
10:00 pm	

DAILY PLANNER

JULY 15, 2024

Monday

TODAY'S AFFIRMATION

WEATHER

MOOD

TOP 3 PRIORITIES

1 _____

2 _____

3 _____

TO-DO LIST

☐ _____

☐ _____

☐ _____

☐ _____

☐ _____

☐ _____

☐ _____

☐ _____

DON'T FORGET

_____

_____

_____

TIME	PLANS & SCHEDULE
6:00 am	
6:30 am	
7:00 am	
7:30 am	
8:00 am	
8:30 am	
9:00 am	
9:30 am	
10:00 am	
10:30 am	
11:00 am	
11:30 am	
12:00 pm	
12:30 pm	
1:00 pm	
1:30 pm	
2:00 pm	
2:30 pm	
3:00 pm	
3:30 pm	
4:00 pm	
4:30 pm	
5:00 pm	
5:30 pm	
6:00 pm	
6:30 pm	
7:00 pm	
7:30 pm	
8:00 pm	
8:30 pm	
9:00 pm	
9:30 pm	
10:00 pm	

DAILY PLANNER

JULY 16, 2024

Tuesday

TODAY'S AFFIRMATION

WEATHER

MOOD

TOP 3 PRIORITIES

1. _____
   _____
2. _____
   _____
3. _____
   _____

TO-DO LIST

- ☐ _____
- ☐ _____
- ☐ _____
- ☐ _____
- ☐ _____
- ☐ _____
- ☐ _____
- ☐ _____

DON'T FORGET

_____
_____
_____

TIME	PLANS & SCHEDULE
6:00 am	
6:30 am	
7:00 am	
7:30 am	
8:00 am	
8:30 am	
9:00 am	
9:30 am	
10:00 am	
10:30 am	
11:00 am	
11:30 am	
12:00 pm	
12:30 pm	
1:00 pm	
1:30 pm	
2:00 pm	
2:30 pm	
3:00 pm	
3:30 pm	
4:00 pm	
4:30 pm	
5:00 pm	
5:30 pm	
6:00 pm	
6:30 pm	
7:00 pm	
7:30 pm	
8:00 pm	
8:30 pm	
9:00 pm	
9:30 pm	
10:00 pm	

JULY 17, 2024

Wednesday

TODAY'S AFFIRMATION

WEATHER

MOOD

TOP 3 PRIORITIES

1 _____
_____

2 _____
_____

3 _____
_____

TO-DO LIST

- _____
- _____
- _____
- _____
- _____
- _____
- _____
- _____

DON'T FORGET

_____
_____
_____

TIME	PLANS & SCHEDULE
6:00 am	
6:30 am	
7:00 am	
7:30 am	
8:00 am	
8:30 am	
9:00 am	
9:30 am	
10:00 am	
10:30 am	
11:00 am	
11:30 am	
12:00 pm	
12:30 pm	
1:00 pm	
1:30 pm	
2:00 pm	
2:30 pm	
3:00 pm	
3:30 pm	
4:00 pm	
4:30 pm	
5:00 pm	
5:30 pm	
6:00 pm	
6:30 pm	
7:00 pm	
7:30 pm	
8:00 pm	
8:30 pm	
9:00 pm	
9:30 pm	
10:00 pm	

DAILY PLANNER

JULY 18, 2024

Thursday

TODAY'S AFFIRMATION

WEATHER

MOOD

TOP 3 PRIORITIES

1 _____
_____

2 _____
_____

3 _____
_____

TO-DO LIST

- ☐ _____
- ☐ _____
- ☐ _____
- ☐ _____
- ☐ _____
- ☐ _____
- ☐ _____
- ☐ _____

DON'T FORGET

_____
_____
_____

TIME	PLANS & SCHEDULE
6:00 am	
6:30 am	
7:00 am	
7:30 am	
8:00 am	
8:30 am	
9:00 am	
9:30 am	
10:00 am	
10:30 am	
11:00 am	
11:30 am	
12:00 pm	
12:30 pm	
1:00 pm	
1:30 pm	
2:00 pm	
2:30 pm	
3:00 pm	
3:30 pm	
4:00 pm	
4:30 pm	
5:00 pm	
5:30 pm	
6:00 pm	
6:30 pm	
7:00 pm	
7:30 pm	
8:00 pm	
8:30 pm	
9:00 pm	
9:30 pm	
10:00 pm	

DAILY PLANNER

JULY 19, 2024

Friday

TODAY'S AFFIRMATION

WEATHER

MOOD

TOP 3 PRIORITIES

1 _____
_____

2 _____
_____

3 _____
_____

TO-DO LIST

- _____
- _____
- _____
- _____
- _____
- _____
- _____
- _____

DON'T FORGET

_____
_____
_____

TIME	PLANS & SCHEDULE
6:00 am	
6:30 am	
7:00 am	
7:30 am	
8:00 am	
8:30 am	
9:00 am	
9:30 am	
10:00 am	
10:30 am	
11:00 am	
11:30 am	
12:00 pm	
12:30 pm	
1:00 pm	
1:30 pm	
2:00 pm	
2:30 pm	
3:00 pm	
3:30 pm	
4:00 pm	
4:30 pm	
5:00 pm	
5:30 pm	
6:00 pm	
6:30 pm	
7:00 pm	
7:30 pm	
8:00 pm	
8:30 pm	
9:00 pm	
9:30 pm	
10:00 pm	

DAILY PLANNER

JULY 20, 2024

Saturday

TODAY'S AFFIRMATION

WEATHER

MOOD

TOP 3 PRIORITIES

1 _____
_____

2 _____
_____

3 _____
_____

TO-DO LIST

☐ _____
☐ _____
☐ _____
☐ _____
☐ _____
☐ _____
☐ _____
☐ _____

DON'T FORGET

_____
_____
_____

TIME	PLANS & SCHEDULE
6:00 am	
6:30 am	
7:00 am	
7:30 am	
8:00 am	
8:30 am	
9:00 am	
9:30 am	
10:00 am	
10:30 am	
11:00 am	
11:30 am	
12:00 pm	
12:30 pm	
1:00 pm	
1:30 pm	
2:00 pm	
2:30 pm	
3:00 pm	
3:30 pm	
4:00 pm	
4:30 pm	
5:00 pm	
5:30 pm	
6:00 pm	
6:30 pm	
7:00 pm	
7:30 pm	
8:00 pm	
8:30 pm	
9:00 pm	
9:30 pm	
10:00 pm	

DAILY PLANNER

JULY 21, 2024

Sunday

TODAY'S AFFIRMATION

WEATHER

MOOD

TIME	PLANS & SCHEDULE
6:00 am	
6:30 am	
7:00 am	
7:30 am	
8:00 am	
8:30 am	
9:00 am	
9:30 am	
10:00 am	
10:30 am	
11:00 am	
11:30 am	
12:00 pm	
12:30 pm	
1:00 pm	
1:30 pm	
2:00 pm	
2:30 pm	
3:00 pm	
3:30 pm	
4:00 pm	
4:30 pm	
5:00 pm	
5:30 pm	
6:00 pm	
6:30 pm	
7:00 pm	
7:30 pm	
8:00 pm	
8:30 pm	
9:00 pm	
9:30 pm	
10:00 pm	

TOP 3 PRIORITIES

1 _____

_____

2 _____

_____

3 _____

_____

TO-DO LIST

- _____
- _____
- _____
- _____
- _____
- _____
- _____
- _____

DON'T FORGET

_____

_____

_____

DAILY PLANNER

JULY 22, 2024

Monday

TODAY'S AFFIRMATION

WEATHER

MOOD

TOP 3 PRIORITIES

1 _____

2 _____

3 _____

TO-DO LIST

- _____
- _____
- _____
- _____
- _____
- _____
- _____
- _____

DON'T FORGET

_____

_____

_____

TIME	PLANS & SCHEDULE
6:00 am	
6:30 am	
7:00 am	
7:30 am	
8:00 am	
8:30 am	
9:00 am	
9:30 am	
10:00 am	
10:30 am	
11:00 am	
11:30 am	
12:00 pm	
12:30 pm	
1:00 pm	
1:30 pm	
2:00 pm	
2:30 pm	
3:00 pm	
3:30 pm	
4:00 pm	
4:30 pm	
5:00 pm	
5:30 pm	
6:00 pm	
6:30 pm	
7:00 pm	
7:30 pm	
8:00 pm	
8:30 pm	
9:00 pm	
9:30 pm	
10:00 pm	

DAILY PLANNER

JULY 23, 2024

Tuesday

TODAY'S AFFIRMATION

WEATHER

MOOD

TOP 3 PRIORITIES

1 _____

_____

2 _____

_____

3 _____

_____

TO-DO LIST

☑ _____

☑ _____

☑ _____

☑ _____

☑ _____

☑ _____

☑ _____

☑ _____

DON'T FORGET

_____

_____

_____

TIME	PLANS & SCHEDULE
6:00 am	
6:30 am	
7:00 am	
7:30 am	
8:00 am	
8:30 am	
9:00 am	
9:30 am	
10:00 am	
10:30 am	
11:00 am	
11:30 am	
12:00 pm	
12:30 pm	
1:00 pm	
1:30 pm	
2:00 pm	
2:30 pm	
3:00 pm	
3:30 pm	
4:00 pm	
4:30 pm	
5:00 pm	
5:30 pm	
6:00 pm	
6:30 pm	
7:00 pm	
7:30 pm	
8:00 pm	
8:30 pm	
9:00 pm	
9:30 pm	
10:00 pm	

DAILY PLANNER

JULY 24, 2024

Wednesday

TODAY'S AFFIRMATION

WEATHER

MOOD

TOP 3 PRIORITIES

1 _____
_____

2 _____
_____

3 _____
_____

TO-DO LIST

- _____
- _____
- _____
- _____
- _____
- _____
- _____
- _____

DON'T FORGET

_____
_____
_____

TIME	PLANS & SCHEDULE
6:00 am	
6:30 am	
7:00 am	
7:30 am	
8:00 am	
8:30 am	
9:00 am	
9:30 am	
10:00 am	
10:30 am	
11:00 am	
11:30 am	
12:00 pm	
12:30 pm	
1:00 pm	
1:30 pm	
2:00 pm	
2:30 pm	
3:00 pm	
3:30 pm	
4:00 pm	
4:30 pm	
5:00 pm	
5:30 pm	
6:00 pm	
6:30 pm	
7:00 pm	
7:30 pm	
8:00 pm	
8:30 pm	
9:00 pm	
9:30 pm	
10:00 pm	

DAILY PLANNER

JULY 25, 2024

Thursday

TODAY'S AFFIRMATION

WEATHER

MOOD

TOP 3 PRIORITIES

1 _____
_____

2 _____
_____

3 _____
_____

TO-DO LIST

☐ _____

☐ _____

☐ _____

☐ _____

☐ _____

☐ _____

☐ _____

☐ _____

DON'T FORGET

_____
_____
_____

TIME	PLANS & SCHEDULE
6:00 am	
6:30 am	
7:00 am	
7:30 am	
8:00 am	
8:30 am	
9:00 am	
9:30 am	
10:00 am	
10:30 am	
11:00 am	
11:30 am	
12:00 pm	
12:30 pm	
1:00 pm	
1:30 pm	
2:00 pm	
2:30 pm	
3:00 pm	
3:30 pm	
4:00 pm	
4:30 pm	
5:00 pm	
5:30 pm	
6:00 pm	
6:30 pm	
7:00 pm	
7:30 pm	
8:00 pm	
8:30 pm	
9:00 pm	
9:30 pm	
10:00 pm	

DAILY PLANNER

JULY 26, 2024

Friday

TODAY'S AFFIRMATION

WEATHER

MOOD

TOP 3 PRIORITIES

1 _____
_____

2 _____
_____

3 _____
_____

TO-DO LIST

☐ _____

☐ _____

☐ _____

☐ _____

☐ _____

☐ _____

☐ _____

☐ _____

DON'T FORGET

_____
_____
_____

TIME	PLANS & SCHEDULE
6:00 am	
6:30 am	
7:00 am	
7:30 am	
8:00 am	
8:30 am	
9:00 am	
9:30 am	
10:00 am	
10:30 am	
11:00 am	
11:30 am	
12:00 pm	
12:30 pm	
1:00 pm	
1:30 pm	
2:00 pm	
2:30 pm	
3:00 pm	
3:30 pm	
4:00 pm	
4:30 pm	
5:00 pm	
5:30 pm	
6:00 pm	
6:30 pm	
7:00 pm	
7:30 pm	
8:00 pm	
8:30 pm	
9:00 pm	
9:30 pm	
10:00 pm	

DAILY PLANNER

JULY 27, 2024

Saturday

TODAY'S AFFIRMATION

WEATHER

MOOD

TOP 3 PRIORITIES

1 _____
_____

2 _____
_____

3 _____
_____

TO-DO LIST

☐ _____

☐ _____

☐ _____

☐ _____

☐ _____

☐ _____

☐ _____

☐ _____

DON'T FORGET

_____

_____

_____

TIME	PLANS & SCHEDULE
6:00 am	
6:30 am	
7:00 am	
7:30 am	
8:00 am	
8:30 am	
9:00 am	
9:30 am	
10:00 am	
10:30 am	
11:00 am	
11:30 am	
12:00 pm	
12:30 pm	
1:00 pm	
1:30 pm	
2:00 pm	
2:30 pm	
3:00 pm	
3:30 pm	
4:00 pm	
4:30 pm	
5:00 pm	
5:30 pm	
6:00 pm	
6:30 pm	
7:00 pm	
7:30 pm	
8:00 pm	
8:30 pm	
9:00 pm	
9:30 pm	
10:00 pm	

DAILY PLANNER

JULY 28, 2024

Sunday

TODAY'S AFFIRMATION

WEATHER

MOOD

TOP 3 PRIORITIES

1 _____
_____

2 _____
_____

3 _____
_____

TO-DO LIST

- _____
- _____
- _____
- _____
- _____
- _____
- _____
- _____

DON'T FORGET

_____
_____
_____

TIME	PLANS & SCHEDULE
6:00 am	
6:30 am	
7:00 am	
7:30 am	
8:00 am	
8:30 am	
9:00 am	
9:30 am	
10:00 am	
10:30 am	
11:00 am	
11:30 am	
12:00 pm	
12:30 pm	
1:00 pm	
1:30 pm	
2:00 pm	
2:30 pm	
3:00 pm	
3:30 pm	
4:00 pm	
4:30 pm	
5:00 pm	
5:30 pm	
6:00 pm	
6:30 pm	
7:00 pm	
7:30 pm	
8:00 pm	
8:30 pm	
9:00 pm	
9:30 pm	
10:00 pm	

DAILY PLANNER

JULY 29, 2024

Monday

TODAY'S AFFIRMATION

WEATHER

MOOD

TOP 3 PRIORITIES

1 _____

_____

2 _____

_____

3 _____

_____

TO-DO LIST

☐ _____

☐ _____

☐ _____

☐ _____

☐ _____

☐ _____

☐ _____

☐ _____

DON'T FORGET

_____

_____

_____

TIME	PLANS & SCHEDULE
6:00 am	
6:30 am	
7:00 am	
7:30 am	
8:00 am	
8:30 am	
9:00 am	
9:30 am	
10:00 am	
10:30 am	
11:00 am	
11:30 am	
12:00 pm	
12:30 pm	
1:00 pm	
1:30 pm	
2:00 pm	
2:30 pm	
3:00 pm	
3:30 pm	
4:00 pm	
4:30 pm	
5:00 pm	
5:30 pm	
6:00 pm	
6:30 pm	
7:00 pm	
7:30 pm	
8:00 pm	
8:30 pm	
9:00 pm	
9:30 pm	
10:00 pm	

DAILY PLANNER

JULY 30, 2024

Tuesday

TODAY'S AFFIRMATION

WEATHER

MOOD

TOP 3 PRIORITIES

1 _____
_____

2 _____
_____

3 _____
_____

TO-DO LIST

- _____
- _____
- _____
- _____
- _____
- _____
- _____
- _____

DON'T FORGET

_____
_____
_____

TIME	PLANS & SCHEDULE
6:00 am	
6:30 am	
7:00 am	
7:30 am	
8:00 am	
8:30 am	
9:00 am	
9:30 am	
10:00 am	
10:30 am	
11:00 am	
11:30 am	
12:00 pm	
12:30 pm	
1:00 pm	
1:30 pm	
2:00 pm	
2:30 pm	
3:00 pm	
3:30 pm	
4:00 pm	
4:30 pm	
5:00 pm	
5:30 pm	
6:00 pm	
6:30 pm	
7:00 pm	
7:30 pm	
8:00 pm	
8:30 pm	
9:00 pm	
9:30 pm	
10:00 pm	

DAILY PLANNER

JULY 31, 2024

Wednesday

TODAY'S AFFIRMATION

WEATHER

MOOD

TIME	PLANS & SCHEDULE
6:00 am	
6:30 am	
7:00 am	
7:30 am	
8:00 am	
8:30 am	
9:00 am	
9:30 am	
10:00 am	
10:30 am	
11:00 am	
11:30 am	
12:00 pm	
12:30 pm	
1:00 pm	
1:30 pm	
2:00 pm	
2:30 pm	
3:00 pm	
3:30 pm	
4:00 pm	
4:30 pm	
5:00 pm	
5:30 pm	
6:00 pm	
6:30 pm	
7:00 pm	
7:30 pm	
8:00 pm	
8:30 pm	
9:00 pm	
9:30 pm	
10:00 pm	

TOP 3 PRIORITIES

1

2

3

TO-DO LIST

DON'T FORGET

MONTHLY BUDGET PLANNER

Budget Goal: _____   Month: _____

Income

Date	Description	Amount
Total		

Fixed Expenses

Date	Description	Amount
Total		

Other Expenses

Date	Description	Amount
Total		

Bills

Date	Description	Amount
Total		

Recap

	Goal	Actual	Difference
Earnt			
Spent			
Debt			
Saved			

Notes

Date:

GRATITUDE JOURNAL

DATE: _____   S M T W T F S

TODAY I'M GRATEFUL FOR

- _____
- _____
- _____

WATER INTAKE

○ ○ ○ ○   ○ ○ ○ ○   ○ ○
    1L   2L   3L

WEATHER

TODAY'S AFFIRMATION

- _____
- _____
- _____
- _____

NOTES / REMINDERS

SOMETHING I'M PROUD OF

- _____
- _____
- _____
- _____

TOMORROW I LOOK FORWARD TO

- _____
- _____
- _____
- _____

30 DAY
Self-Care Challenge

DAY 1	DAY 2	DAY 3	DAY 4	DAY 5
Start a gratitude journal	Learn to meditate	Spend the day social media free	Call someone you love	Take a 15 minute walk outdoors
DAY 6	**DAY 7**	**DAY 8**	**DAY 9**	**DAY 10**
Listen to a podcast	Learn to cook a new recipe	Stretch for 10-15 minutes	Listen to your favorite song	Practice deep breathing
DAY 11	**DAY 12**	**DAY 13**	**DAY 14**	**DAY 15**
Try a free online workout	Read a book for 15 minutes	Write a list of short-term goals	De-clutter a room or desk	Go to bed 30 minutes earlier
DAY 16	**DAY 17**	**DAY 18**	**DAY 19**	**DAY 20**
Have a game night	Wake up 15 minutes earlier	Make your favorite meal	Buy yourself something nice	Create a bucket list
DAY 21	**DAY 22**	**DAY 23**	**DAY 24**	**DAY 25**
Watch a movie or series	Write down your thoughts	Take a long shower or bath	Have a home spa day	Read inspirational quotes
DAY 26	**DAY 27**	**DAY 28**	**DAY 29**	**DAY 30**
Create a vision board	Spend some time outside	Do a hair mask	Write it all down in a journal	Take a power nap

AUGUST 2024

Sunday	Monday	Tuesday	Wednesday
04	05	06	07
11	12	13	14
18	19	20	21
25	26	27	28

AUGUST 2024

Thursday	Friday	Saturday	Notes
01	02	03	....
08	09	10	....
15	16	17	....
22	23	24	....
29	30	31	....

AUGUST

Goal

Action Plan

Date

Grateful For

To Improve

Notes

DAILY PLANNER

AUGUST 1, 2024

Thursday

TODAY'S AFFIRMATION

WEATHER

MOOD

TOP 3 PRIORITIES

1 _____
_____

2 _____
_____

3 _____
_____

TO-DO LIST

☐ _____

☐ _____

☐ _____

☐ _____

☐ _____

☐ _____

☐ _____

☐ _____

DON'T FORGET

_____

_____

_____

TIME	PLANS & SCHEDULE
6:00 am	
6:30 am	
7:00 am	
7:30 am	
8:00 am	
8:30 am	
9:00 am	
9:30 am	
10:00 am	
10:30 am	
11:00 am	
11:30 am	
12:00 pm	
12:30 pm	
1:00 pm	
1:30 pm	
2:00 pm	
2:30 pm	
3:00 pm	
3:30 pm	
4:00 pm	
4:30 pm	
5:00 pm	
5:30 pm	
6:00 pm	
6:30 pm	
7:00 pm	
7:30 pm	
8:00 pm	
8:30 pm	
9:00 pm	
9:30 pm	
10:00 pm	

DAILY PLANNER

AUGUST 2, 2024

Friday

TODAY'S AFFIRMATION

WEATHER

MOOD

TOP 3 PRIORITIES

1 _____

2 _____

3 _____

TO-DO LIST

- _____
- _____
- _____
- _____
- _____
- _____
- _____
- _____

DON'T FORGET

_____
_____
_____

TIME	PLANS & SCHEDULE
6:00 am	
6:30 am	
7:00 am	
7:30 am	
8:00 am	
8:30 am	
9:00 am	
9:30 am	
10:00 am	
10:30 am	
11:00 am	
11:30 am	
12:00 pm	
12:30 pm	
1:00 pm	
1:30 pm	
2:00 pm	
2:30 pm	
3:00 pm	
3:30 pm	
4:00 pm	
4:30 pm	
5:00 pm	
5:30 pm	
6:00 pm	
6:30 pm	
7:00 pm	
7:30 pm	
8:00 pm	
8:30 pm	
9:00 pm	
9:30 pm	
10:00 pm	

DAILY PLANNER

AUGUST 3, 2024

Saturday

TODAY'S AFFIRMATION

WEATHER

MOOD

TOP 3 PRIORITIES

1 _____
_____

2 _____
_____

3 _____
_____

TO-DO LIST

- _____
- _____
- _____
- _____
- _____
- _____
- _____
- _____

DON'T FORGET

_____
_____
_____

TIME	PLANS & SCHEDULE
6:00 am	
6:30 am	
7:00 am	
7:30 am	
8:00 am	
8:30 am	
9:00 am	
9:30 am	
10:00 am	
10:30 am	
11:00 am	
11:30 am	
12:00 pm	
12:30 pm	
1:00 pm	
1:30 pm	
2:00 pm	
2:30 pm	
3:00 pm	
3:30 pm	
4:00 pm	
4:30 pm	
5:00 pm	
5:30 pm	
6:00 pm	
6:30 pm	
7:00 pm	
7:30 pm	
8:00 pm	
8:30 pm	
9:00 pm	
9:30 pm	
10:00 pm	

DAILY PLANNER

AUGUST 4, 2024

Sunday

TODAY'S AFFIRMATION

WEATHER

MOOD

TOP 3 PRIORITIES

1 _____

_____

2 _____

_____

3 _____

_____

TO-DO LIST

☐ _____

☐ _____

☐ _____

☐ _____

☐ _____

☐ _____

☐ _____

☐ _____

DON'T FORGET

_____

_____

_____

TIME	PLANS & SCHEDULE
6:00 am	
6:30 am	
7:00 am	
7:30 am	
8:00 am	
8:30 am	
9:00 am	
9:30 am	
10:00 am	
10:30 am	
11:00 am	
11:30 am	
12:00 pm	
12:30 pm	
1:00 pm	
1:30 pm	
2:00 pm	
2:30 pm	
3:00 pm	
3:30 pm	
4:00 pm	
4:30 pm	
5:00 pm	
5:30 pm	
6:00 pm	
6:30 pm	
7:00 pm	
7:30 pm	
8:00 pm	
8:30 pm	
9:00 pm	
9:30 pm	
10:00 pm	

DAILY PLANNER

AUGUST 5, 2024

Monday

TODAY'S AFFIRMATION

WEATHER

MOOD

TOP 3 PRIORITIES

1 _____

2 _____

3 _____

TO-DO LIST

- _____
- _____
- _____
- _____
- _____
- _____
- _____
- _____

DON'T FORGET

_____

_____

_____

TIME	PLANS & SCHEDULE
6:00 am	
6:30 am	
7:00 am	
7:30 am	
8:00 am	
8:30 am	
9:00 am	
9:30 am	
10:00 am	
10:30 am	
11:00 am	
11:30 am	
12:00 pm	
12:30 pm	
1:00 pm	
1:30 pm	
2:00 pm	
2:30 pm	
3:00 pm	
3:30 pm	
4:00 pm	
4:30 pm	
5:00 pm	
5:30 pm	
6:00 pm	
6:30 pm	
7:00 pm	
7:30 pm	
8:00 pm	
8:30 pm	
9:00 pm	
9:30 pm	
10:00 pm	

DAILY PLANNER

AUGUST 6, 2024

Tuesday

TODAY'S AFFIRMATION

WEATHER

MOOD

TOP 3 PRIORITIES

1 _____
_____

2 _____
_____

3 _____
_____

TO-DO LIST

☐ _____

☐ _____

☐ _____

☐ _____

☐ _____

☐ _____

☐ _____

☐ _____

DON'T FORGET

_____

_____

_____

TIME	PLANS & SCHEDULE
6:00 am	
6:30 am	
7:00 am	
7:30 am	
8:00 am	
8:30 am	
9:00 am	
9:30 am	
10:00 am	
10:30 am	
11:00 am	
11:30 am	
12:00 pm	
12:30 pm	
1:00 pm	
1:30 pm	
2:00 pm	
2:30 pm	
3:00 pm	
3:30 pm	
4:00 pm	
4:30 pm	
5:00 pm	
5:30 pm	
6:00 pm	
6:30 pm	
7:00 pm	
7:30 pm	
8:00 pm	
8:30 pm	
9:00 pm	
9:30 pm	
10:00 pm	

DAILY PLANNER

AUGUST 7, 2024

Wednesday

TODAY'S AFFIRMATION

WEATHER

MOOD

TOP 3 PRIORITIES

1 _____
_____

2 _____
_____

3 _____
_____

TO-DO LIST

- _____
- _____
- _____
- _____
- _____
- _____
- _____
- _____

DON'T FORGET

_____

_____

_____

TIME	PLANS & SCHEDULE
6:00 am	
6:30 am	
7:00 am	
7:30 am	
8:00 am	
8:30 am	
9:00 am	
9:30 am	
10:00 am	
10:30 am	
11:00 am	
11:30 am	
12:00 pm	
12:30 pm	
1:00 pm	
1:30 pm	
2:00 pm	
2:30 pm	
3:00 pm	
3:30 pm	
4:00 pm	
4:30 pm	
5:00 pm	
5:30 pm	
6:00 pm	
6:30 pm	
7:00 pm	
7:30 pm	
8:00 pm	
8:30 pm	
9:00 pm	
9:30 pm	
10:00 pm	

DAILY PLANNER

AUGUST 8, 2024

Thursday

TODAY'S AFFIRMATION

WEATHER

MOOD

TOP 3 PRIORITIES

1 _____
_____

2 _____
_____

3 _____
_____

TO-DO LIST

- _____
- _____
- _____
- _____
- _____
- _____
- _____
- _____

DON'T FORGET

_____
_____
_____

TIME	PLANS & SCHEDULE
6:00 am	
6:30 am	
7:00 am	
7:30 am	
8:00 am	
8:30 am	
9:00 am	
9:30 am	
10:00 am	
10:30 am	
11:00 am	
11:30 am	
12:00 pm	
12:30 pm	
1:00 pm	
1:30 pm	
2:00 pm	
2:30 pm	
3:00 pm	
3:30 pm	
4:00 pm	
4:30 pm	
5:00 pm	
5:30 pm	
6:00 pm	
6:30 pm	
7:00 pm	
7:30 pm	
8:00 pm	
8:30 pm	
9:00 pm	
9:30 pm	
10:00 pm	

DAILY PLANNER

AUGUST 9, 2024

Friday

TODAY'S AFFIRMATION

WEATHER

MOOD

TOP 3 PRIORITIES

1 _____
_____

2 _____
_____

3 _____
_____

TO-DO LIST

☐ _____

☐ _____

☐ _____

☐ _____

☐ _____

☐ _____

☐ _____

☐ _____

DON'T FORGET

_____
_____
_____

TIME	PLANS & SCHEDULE
6:00 am	
6:30 am	
7:00 am	
7:30 am	
8:00 am	
8:30 am	
9:00 am	
9:30 am	
10:00 am	
10:30 am	
11:00 am	
11:30 am	
12:00 pm	
12:30 pm	
1:00 pm	
1:30 pm	
2:00 pm	
2:30 pm	
3:00 pm	
3:30 pm	
4:00 pm	
4:30 pm	
5:00 pm	
5:30 pm	
6:00 pm	
6:30 pm	
7:00 pm	
7:30 pm	
8:00 pm	
8:30 pm	
9:00 pm	
9:30 pm	
10:00 pm	

DAILY PLANNER

AUGUST 10, 2024

Saturday

TODAY'S AFFIRMATION

WEATHER

MOOD

TOP 3 PRIORITIES

1 _____

_____

2 _____

_____

3 _____

_____

TO-DO LIST

- _____
- _____
- _____
- _____
- _____
- _____
- _____
- _____

DON'T FORGET

_____

_____

_____

TIME	PLANS & SCHEDULE
6:00 am	
6:30 am	
7:00 am	
7:30 am	
8:00 am	
8:30 am	
9:00 am	
9:30 am	
10:00 am	
10:30 am	
11:00 am	
11:30 am	
12:00 pm	
12:30 pm	
1:00 pm	
1:30 pm	
2:00 pm	
2:30 pm	
3:00 pm	
3:30 pm	
4:00 pm	
4:30 pm	
5:00 pm	
5:30 pm	
6:00 pm	
6:30 pm	
7:00 pm	
7:30 pm	
8:00 pm	
8:30 pm	
9:00 pm	
9:30 pm	
10:00 pm	

DAILY PLANNER

AUGUST 11, 2024

Sunday

TODAY'S AFFIRMATION

WEATHER

MOOD

TOP 3 PRIORITIES

1 _____

_____

2 _____

_____

3 _____

_____

TO-DO LIST

☐ _____

☐ _____

☐ _____

☐ _____

☐ _____

☐ _____

☐ _____

☐ _____

DON'T FORGET

_____

_____

_____

TIME	PLANS & SCHEDULE
6:00 am	
6:30 am	
7:00 am	
7:30 am	
8:00 am	
8:30 am	
9:00 am	
9:30 am	
10:00 am	
10:30 am	
11:00 am	
11:30 am	
12:00 pm	
12:30 pm	
1:00 pm	
1:30 pm	
2:00 pm	
2:30 pm	
3:00 pm	
3:30 pm	
4:00 pm	
4:30 pm	
5:00 pm	
5:30 pm	
6:00 pm	
6:30 pm	
7:00 pm	
7:30 pm	
8:00 pm	
8:30 pm	
9:00 pm	
9:30 pm	
10:00 pm	

DAILY PLANNER

AUGUST 12, 2024

Monday

TODAY'S AFFIRMATION

WEATHER

MOOD

TOP 3 PRIORITIES

1 _____
_____

2 _____
_____

3 _____
_____

TO-DO LIST

☐ _____

☐ _____

☐ _____

☐ _____

☐ _____

☐ _____

☐ _____

☐ _____

DON'T FORGET

_____

_____

_____

TIME	PLANS & SCHEDULE
6:00 am	
6:30 am	
7:00 am	
7:30 am	
8:00 am	
8:30 am	
9:00 am	
9:30 am	
10:00 am	
10:30 am	
11:00 am	
11:30 am	
12:00 pm	
12:30 pm	
1:00 pm	
1:30 pm	
2:00 pm	
2:30 pm	
3:00 pm	
3:30 pm	
4:00 pm	
4:30 pm	
5:00 pm	
5:30 pm	
6:00 pm	
6:30 pm	
7:00 pm	
7:30 pm	
8:00 pm	
8:30 pm	
9:00 pm	
9:30 pm	
10:00 pm	

DAILY PLANNER

AUGUST 13, 2024

Tuesday

TODAY'S AFFIRMATION

WEATHER

MOOD

TOP 3 PRIORITIES

1 _____
_____

2 _____
_____

3 _____
_____

TO-DO LIST

- _____
- _____
- _____
- _____
- _____
- _____
- _____
- _____

DON'T FORGET

_____
_____
_____

TIME	PLANS & SCHEDULE
6:00 am	
6:30 am	
7:00 am	
7:30 am	
8:00 am	
8:30 am	
9:00 am	
9:30 am	
10:00 am	
10:30 am	
11:00 am	
11:30 am	
12:00 pm	
12:30 pm	
1:00 pm	
1:30 pm	
2:00 pm	
2:30 pm	
3:00 pm	
3:30 pm	
4:00 pm	
4:30 pm	
5:00 pm	
5:30 pm	
6:00 pm	
6:30 pm	
7:00 pm	
7:30 pm	
8:00 pm	
8:30 pm	
9:00 pm	
9:30 pm	
10:00 pm	

DAILY PLANNER

AUGUST 14, 2024

Wednesday

TODAY'S AFFIRMATION

WEATHER

MOOD

TOP 3 PRIORITIES

1 _____

2 _____

3 _____

TO-DO LIST

- ☐ _____
- ☐ _____
- ☐ _____
- ☐ _____
- ☐ _____
- ☐ _____
- ☐ _____
- ☐ _____

DON'T FORGET

_____

_____

_____

TIME	PLANS & SCHEDULE
6:00 am	
6:30 am	
7:00 am	
7:30 am	
8:00 am	
8:30 am	
9:00 am	
9:30 am	
10:00 am	
10:30 am	
11:00 am	
11:30 am	
12:00 pm	
12:30 pm	
1:00 pm	
1:30 pm	
2:00 pm	
2:30 pm	
3:00 pm	
3:30 pm	
4:00 pm	
4:30 pm	
5:00 pm	
5:30 pm	
6:00 pm	
6:30 pm	
7:00 pm	
7:30 pm	
8:00 pm	
8:30 pm	
9:00 pm	
9:30 pm	
10:00 pm	

DAILY PLANNER

AUGUST 15, 2024

Thursday

TODAY'S AFFIRMATION

WEATHER

MOOD

TOP 3 PRIORITIES

1 _____
_____

2 _____
_____

3 _____
_____

TO-DO LIST

- ■ _____
- ■ _____
- ■ _____
- ■ _____
- ■ _____
- ■ _____
- ■ _____
- ■ _____

DON'T FORGET

_____
_____
_____

TIME	PLANS & SCHEDULE
6:00 am	
6:30 am	
7:00 am	
7:30 am	
8:00 am	
8:30 am	
9:00 am	
9:30 am	
10:00 am	
10:30 am	
11:00 am	
11:30 am	
12:00 pm	
12:30 pm	
1:00 pm	
1:30 pm	
2:00 pm	
2:30 pm	
3:00 pm	
3:30 pm	
4:00 pm	
4:30 pm	
5:00 pm	
5:30 pm	
6:00 pm	
6:30 pm	
7:00 pm	
7:30 pm	
8:00 pm	
8:30 pm	
9:00 pm	
9:30 pm	
10:00 pm	

DAILY PLANNER

AUGUST 16, 2024

Friday

TODAY'S AFFIRMATION

WEATHER	

MOOD	

TOP 3 PRIORITIES

1 _____

2 _____

3 _____

TO-DO LIST

- ◼ _____
- ◼ _____
- ◼ _____
- ◼ _____
- ◼ _____
- ◼ _____
- ◼ _____
- ◼ _____

DON'T FORGET

_____

_____

_____

TIME	PLANS & SCHEDULE
6:00 am	
6:30 am	
7:00 am	
7:30 am	
8:00 am	
8:30 am	
9:00 am	
9:30 am	
10:00 am	
10:30 am	
11:00 am	
11:30 am	
12:00 pm	
12:30 pm	
1:00 pm	
1:30 pm	
2:00 pm	
2:30 pm	
3:00 pm	
3:30 pm	
4:00 pm	
4:30 pm	
5:00 pm	
5:30 pm	
6:00 pm	
6:30 pm	
7:00 pm	
7:30 pm	
8:00 pm	
8:30 pm	
9:00 pm	
9:30 pm	
10:00 pm	

DAILY PLANNER

AUGUST 17, 2024

Saturday

TODAY'S AFFIRMATION

TOP 3 PRIORITIES

1 _____

2 _____

3 _____

TO-DO LIST

- _____
- _____
- _____
- _____
- _____
- _____
- _____
- _____

DON'T FORGET

_____

_____

_____

WEATHER

MOOD

TIME	PLANS & SCHEDULE
6:00 am	
6:30 am	
7:00 am	
7:30 am	
8:00 am	
8:30 am	
9:00 am	
9:30 am	
10:00 am	
10:30 am	
11:00 am	
11:30 am	
12:00 pm	
12:30 pm	
1:00 pm	
1:30 pm	
2:00 pm	
2:30 pm	
3:00 pm	
3:30 pm	
4:00 pm	
4:30 pm	
5:00 pm	
5:30 pm	
6:00 pm	
6:30 pm	
7:00 pm	
7:30 pm	
8:00 pm	
8:30 pm	
9:00 pm	
9:30 pm	
10:00 pm	

DAILY PLANNER

AUGUST 18, 2024

Sunday

TODAY'S AFFIRMATION

WEATHER

MOOD

TOP 3 PRIORITIES

1 _____

_____

2 _____

_____

3 _____

_____

TO-DO LIST

- ◼ _____
- ◼ _____
- ◼ _____
- ◼ _____
- ◼ _____
- ◼ _____
- ◼ _____
- ◼ _____

DON'T FORGET

_____

_____

_____

TIME	PLANS & SCHEDULE
6:00 am	
6:30 am	
7:00 am	
7:30 am	
8:00 am	
8:30 am	
9:00 am	
9:30 am	
10:00 am	
10:30 am	
11:00 am	
11:30 am	
12:00 pm	
12:30 pm	
1:00 pm	
1:30 pm	
2:00 pm	
2:30 pm	
3:00 pm	
3:30 pm	
4:00 pm	
4:30 pm	
5:00 pm	
5:30 pm	
6:00 pm	
6:30 pm	
7:00 pm	
7:30 pm	
8:00 pm	
8:30 pm	
9:00 pm	
9:30 pm	
10:00 pm	

DAILY PLANNER

AUGUST 19, 2024

Monday

TODAY'S AFFIRMATION

WEATHER

MOOD

TOP 3 PRIORITIES

1
2
3

TO-DO LIST

- ▪
- ▪
- ▪
- ▪
- ▪
- ▪
- ▪
- ▪

DON'T FORGET

TIME	PLANS & SCHEDULE
6:00 am	
6:30 am	
7:00 am	
7:30 am	
8:00 am	
8:30 am	
9:00 am	
9:30 am	
10:00 am	
10:30 am	
11:00 am	
11:30 am	
12:00 pm	
12:30 pm	
1:00 pm	
1:30 pm	
2:00 pm	
2:30 pm	
3:00 pm	
3:30 pm	
4:00 pm	
4:30 pm	
5:00 pm	
5:30 pm	
6:00 pm	
6:30 pm	
7:00 pm	
7:30 pm	
8:00 pm	
8:30 pm	
9:00 pm	
9:30 pm	
10:00 pm	

DAILY PLANNER

AUGUST 20, 2024

Tuesday

TODAY'S AFFIRMATION

WEATHER

MOOD

TOP 3 PRIORITIES

1 _____
_____

2 _____
_____

3 _____
_____

TO-DO LIST

- ◼ _____
- ◼ _____
- ◼ _____
- ◼ _____
- ◼ _____
- ◼ _____
- ◼ _____
- ◼ _____

DON'T FORGET

_____
_____
_____

TIME	PLANS & SCHEDULE
6:00 am	
6:30 am	
7:00 am	
7:30 am	
8:00 am	
8:30 am	
9:00 am	
9:30 am	
10:00 am	
10:30 am	
11:00 am	
11:30 am	
12:00 pm	
12:30 pm	
1:00 pm	
1:30 pm	
2:00 pm	
2:30 pm	
3:00 pm	
3:30 pm	
4:00 pm	
4:30 pm	
5:00 pm	
5:30 pm	
6:00 pm	
6:30 pm	
7:00 pm	
7:30 pm	
8:00 pm	
8:30 pm	
9:00 pm	
9:30 pm	
10:00 pm	

DAILY PLANNER

AUGUST 21, 2024

Wednesday

TODAY'S AFFIRMATION

WEATHER

MOOD

TOP 3 PRIORITIES

1 _____
_____

2 _____
_____

3 _____
_____

TO-DO LIST

- _____
- _____
- _____
- _____
- _____
- _____
- _____
- _____

DON'T FORGET

_____
_____
_____

TIME	PLANS & SCHEDULE
6:00 am	
6:30 am	
7:00 am	
7:30 am	
8:00 am	
8:30 am	
9:00 am	
9:30 am	
10:00 am	
10:30 am	
11:00 am	
11:30 am	
12:00 pm	
12:30 pm	
1:00 pm	
1:30 pm	
2:00 pm	
2:30 pm	
3:00 pm	
3:30 pm	
4:00 pm	
4:30 pm	
5:00 pm	
5:30 pm	
6:00 pm	
6:30 pm	
7:00 pm	
7:30 pm	
8:00 pm	
8:30 pm	
9:00 pm	
9:30 pm	
10:00 pm	

DAILY PLANNER

AUGUST 22, 2024

Thursday

TODAY'S AFFIRMATION

WEATHER	

MOOD	

TOP 3 PRIORITIES

1 _____
_____

2 _____
_____

3 _____
_____

TO-DO LIST

■ _____

■ _____

■ _____

■ _____

■ _____

■ _____

■ _____

■ _____

DON'T FORGET

_____

_____

_____

TIME	PLANS & SCHEDULE
6:00 am	
6:30 am	
7:00 am	
7:30 am	
8:00 am	
8:30 am	
9:00 am	
9:30 am	
10:00 am	
10:30 am	
11:00 am	
11:30 am	
12:00 pm	
12:30 pm	
1:00 pm	
1:30 pm	
2:00 pm	
2:30 pm	
3:00 pm	
3:30 pm	
4:00 pm	
4:30 pm	
5:00 pm	
5:30 pm	
6:00 pm	
6:30 pm	
7:00 pm	
7:30 pm	
8:00 pm	
8:30 pm	
9:00 pm	
9:30 pm	
10:00 pm	

DAILY PLANNER

AUGUST 23, 2024

Friday

TODAY'S AFFIRMATION

TOP 3 PRIORITIES

1 _____
_____

2 _____
_____

3 _____
_____

TO-DO LIST

■ _____

■ _____

■ _____

■ _____

■ _____

■ _____

■ _____

■ _____

DON'T FORGET

_____

_____

_____

WEATHER

MOOD

TIME	PLANS & SCHEDULE
6:00 am	
6:30 am	
7:00 am	
7:30 am	
8:00 am	
8:30 am	
9:00 am	
9:30 am	
10:00 am	
10:30 am	
11:00 am	
11:30 am	
12:00 pm	
12:30 pm	
1:00 pm	
1:30 pm	
2:00 pm	
2:30 pm	
3:00 pm	
3:30 pm	
4:00 pm	
4:30 pm	
5:00 pm	
5:30 pm	
6:00 pm	
6:30 pm	
7:00 pm	
7:30 pm	
8:00 pm	
8:30 pm	
9:00 pm	
9:30 pm	
10:00 pm	

DAILY PLANNER

AUGUST 24, 2024

Saturday

TODAY'S AFFIRMATION

TOP 3 PRIORITIES

1 _____
_____

2 _____
_____

3 _____
_____

TO-DO LIST

- ◼ _____
- ◼ _____
- ◼ _____
- ◼ _____
- ◼ _____
- ◼ _____
- ◼ _____
- ◼ _____

DON'T FORGET

_____
_____
_____

WEATHER

MOOD

TIME	PLANS & SCHEDULE
6:00 am	
6:30 am	
7:00 am	
7:30 am	
8:00 am	
8:30 am	
9:00 am	
9:30 am	
10:00 am	
10:30 am	
11:00 am	
11:30 am	
12:00 pm	
12:30 pm	
1:00 pm	
1:30 pm	
2:00 pm	
2:30 pm	
3:00 pm	
3:30 pm	
4:00 pm	
4:30 pm	
5:00 pm	
5:30 pm	
6:00 pm	
6:30 pm	
7:00 pm	
7:30 pm	
8:00 pm	
8:30 pm	
9:00 pm	
9:30 pm	
10:00 pm	

DAILY PLANNER

AUGUST 25, 2024

Sunday

TODAY'S AFFIRMATION

WEATHER

MOOD

TOP 3 PRIORITIES

1 _____

2 _____

3 _____

TO-DO LIST

- ☐ _____
- ☐ _____
- ☐ _____
- ☐ _____
- ☐ _____
- ☐ _____
- ☐ _____
- ☐ _____

DON'T FORGET

_____

_____

_____

TIME	PLANS & SCHEDULE
6:00 am	
6:30 am	
7:00 am	
7:30 am	
8:00 am	
8:30 am	
9:00 am	
9:30 am	
10:00 am	
10:30 am	
11:00 am	
11:30 am	
12:00 pm	
12:30 pm	
1:00 pm	
1:30 pm	
2:00 pm	
2:30 pm	
3:00 pm	
3:30 pm	
4:00 pm	
4:30 pm	
5:00 pm	
5:30 pm	
6:00 pm	
6:30 pm	
7:00 pm	
7:30 pm	
8:00 pm	
8:30 pm	
9:00 pm	
9:30 pm	
10:00 pm	

DAILY PLANNER

AUGUST 26, 2024

Monday

TODAY'S AFFIRMATION

WEATHER

MOOD

TOP 3 PRIORITIES

1 _____
_____

2 _____
_____

3 _____
_____

TO-DO LIST

- ◾ _____
- ◾ _____
- ◾ _____
- ◾ _____
- ◾ _____
- ◾ _____
- ◾ _____
- ◾ _____

DON'T FORGET

_____
_____
_____

TIME	PLANS & SCHEDULE
6:00 am	
6:30 am	
7:00 am	
7:30 am	
8:00 am	
8:30 am	
9:00 am	
9:30 am	
10:00 am	
10:30 am	
11:00 am	
11:30 am	
12:00 pm	
12:30 pm	
1:00 pm	
1:30 pm	
2:00 pm	
2:30 pm	
3:00 pm	
3:30 pm	
4:00 pm	
4:30 pm	
5:00 pm	
5:30 pm	
6:00 pm	
6:30 pm	
7:00 pm	
7:30 pm	
8:00 pm	
8:30 pm	
9:00 pm	
9:30 pm	
10:00 pm	

DAILY PLANNER

AUGUST 27, 2024

Tuesday

TODAY'S AFFIRMATION

TOP 3 PRIORITIES

1 _____

_____

2 _____

_____

3 _____

_____

TO-DO LIST

- _____
- _____
- _____
- _____
- _____
- _____
- _____
- _____

DON'T FORGET

_____

_____

_____

WEATHER

MOOD

TIME	PLANS & SCHEDULE
6:00 am	
6:30 am	
7:00 am	
7:30 am	
8:00 am	
8:30 am	
9:00 am	
9:30 am	
10:00 am	
10:30 am	
11:00 am	
11:30 am	
12:00 pm	
12:30 pm	
1:00 pm	
1:30 pm	
2:00 pm	
2:30 pm	
3:00 pm	
3:30 pm	
4:00 pm	
4:30 pm	
5:00 pm	
5:30 pm	
6:00 pm	
6:30 pm	
7:00 pm	
7:30 pm	
8:00 pm	
8:30 pm	
9:00 pm	
9:30 pm	
10:00 pm	

DAILY PLANNER

AUGUST 28, 2024

Wednesday

TODAY'S AFFIRMATION

| WEATHER |  |
| MOOD |  |

TOP 3 PRIORITIES

1 _____
_____

2 _____
_____

3 _____
_____

TO-DO LIST

- _____
- _____
- _____
- _____
- _____
- _____
- _____
- _____

DON'T FORGET

_____
_____
_____

TIME	PLANS & SCHEDULE
6:00 am	
6:30 am	
7:00 am	
7:30 am	
8:00 am	
8:30 am	
9:00 am	
9:30 am	
10:00 am	
10:30 am	
11:00 am	
11:30 am	
12:00 pm	
12:30 pm	
1:00 pm	
1:30 pm	
2:00 pm	
2:30 pm	
3:00 pm	
3:30 pm	
4:00 pm	
4:30 pm	
5:00 pm	
5:30 pm	
6:00 pm	
6:30 pm	
7:00 pm	
7:30 pm	
8:00 pm	
8:30 pm	
9:00 pm	
9:30 pm	
10:00 pm	

DAILY PLANNER

AUGUST 29, 2024

Thursday

TODAY'S AFFIRMATION

WEATHER

MOOD

TOP 3 PRIORITIES

1 _____

_____

2 _____

_____

3 _____

_____

TO-DO LIST

- _____
- _____
- _____
- _____
- _____
- _____
- _____
- _____

DON'T FORGET

_____

_____

_____

TIME	PLANS & SCHEDULE
6:00 am	
6:30 am	
7:00 am	
7:30 am	
8:00 am	
8:30 am	
9:00 am	
9:30 am	
10:00 am	
10:30 am	
11:00 am	
11:30 am	
12:00 pm	
12:30 pm	
1:00 pm	
1:30 pm	
2:00 pm	
2:30 pm	
3:00 pm	
3:30 pm	
4:00 pm	
4:30 pm	
5:00 pm	
5:30 pm	
6:00 pm	
6:30 pm	
7:00 pm	
7:30 pm	
8:00 pm	
8:30 pm	
9:00 pm	
9:30 pm	
10:00 pm	

DAILY PLANNER

AUGUST 30, 2024

Friday

TODAY'S AFFIRMATION

WEATHER	

MOOD	

TOP 3 PRIORITIES

1 _____
_____

2 _____
_____

3 _____
_____

TO-DO LIST

- ☐ _____
- ☐ _____
- ☐ _____
- ☐ _____
- ☐ _____
- ☐ _____
- ☐ _____
- ☐ _____

DON'T FORGET

_____
_____
_____

TIME	PLANS & SCHEDULE
6:00 am	
6:30 am	
7:00 am	
7:30 am	
8:00 am	
8:30 am	
9:00 am	
9:30 am	
10:00 am	
10:30 am	
11:00 am	
11:30 am	
12:00 pm	
12:30 pm	
1:00 pm	
1:30 pm	
2:00 pm	
2:30 pm	
3:00 pm	
3:30 pm	
4:00 pm	
4:30 pm	
5:00 pm	
5:30 pm	
6:00 pm	
6:30 pm	
7:00 pm	
7:30 pm	
8:00 pm	
8:30 pm	
9:00 pm	
9:30 pm	
10:00 pm	

DAILY PLANNER

AUGUST 31, 2024

Saturday

TODAY'S AFFIRMATION

WEATHER

MOOD

TOP 3 PRIORITIES

1

2

3

TO-DO LIST

-
-
-
-
-
-
-
-

DON'T FORGET

TIME	PLANS & SCHEDULE
6:00 am	
6:30 am	
7:00 am	
7:30 am	
8:00 am	
8:30 am	
9:00 am	
9:30 am	
10:00 am	
10:30 am	
11:00 am	
11:30 am	
12:00 pm	
12:30 pm	
1:00 pm	
1:30 pm	
2:00 pm	
2:30 pm	
3:00 pm	
3:30 pm	
4:00 pm	
4:30 pm	
5:00 pm	
5:30 pm	
6:00 pm	
6:30 pm	
7:00 pm	
7:30 pm	
8:00 pm	
8:30 pm	
9:00 pm	
9:30 pm	
10:00 pm	

MONTHLY BUDGET PLANNER

Budget Goal: _____   Month: _____

Income

Date	Description	Amount
Total		

Fixed Expenses

Date	Description	Amount
Total		

Other Expenses

Date	Description	Amount
Total		

Bills

Date	Description	Amount
Total		

Recap

	Goal	Actual	Difference
Earnt			
Spent			
Debt			
Saved			

Notes

Date:

GRATITUDE JOURNAL

DATE: _____   S M T W T F S

TODAY I'M GRATEFUL FOR

- _____
- _____
- _____

WATER INTAKE

      1L   2L   3L

WEATHER

TODAY'S AFFIRMATION

- _____
- _____
- _____
- _____

NOTES / REMINDERS

SOMETHING I'M PROUD OF

- _____
- _____
- _____
- _____

TOMORROW I LOOK FORWARD TO

- _____
- _____
- _____
- _____

30 DAY
Self-Care Challenge

DAY 1	DAY 2	DAY 3	DAY 4	DAY 5
Start a gratitude journal	Learn to meditate	Spend the day social media free	Call someone you love	Take a 15 minute walk outdoors
DAY 6	**DAY 7**	**DAY 8**	**DAY 9**	**DAY 10**
Listen to a podcast	Learn to cook a new recipe	Stretch for 10-15 minutes	Listen to your favorite song	Practice deep breathing
DAY 11	**DAY 12**	**DAY 13**	**DAY 14**	**DAY 15**
Try a free online workout	Read a book for 15 minutes	Write a list of short-term goals	De-clutter a room or desk	Go to bed 30 minutes earlier
DAY 16	**DAY 17**	**DAY 18**	**DAY 19**	**DAY 20**
Have a game night	Wake up 15 minutes earlier	Make your favorite meal	Buy yourself something nice	Create a bucket list
DAY 21	**DAY 22**	**DAY 23**	**DAY 24**	**DAY 25**
Watch a movie or series	Write down your thoughts	Take a long shower or bath	Have a home spa day	Read inspirational quotes
DAY 26	**DAY 27**	**DAY 28**	**DAY 29**	**DAY 30**
Create a vision board	Spend some time outside	Do a hair mask	Write it all down in a journal	Take a power nap

SEPTEMBER 2024

Sunday	Monday	Tuesday	Wednesday
01	02	03	04
08	09	10	11
15	16	17	18
22	23	24	25
29	30		

SEPTEMBER 2024

Thursday	Friday	Saturday	Notes
05	06	07	....
12	13	14	....
19	20	21	....
16	27	28	....
			....

SEPTEMBER

Goal

Action Plan

Date

....

....

....

....

....

....

....

....

Grateful For

To Improve

....

....

....

....

....

....

Notes

....

....

....

DAILY PLANNER

SEPTEMBER 1, 2024

Sunday

TODAY'S AFFIRMATION

WEATHER

MOOD

TOP 3 PRIORITIES

1 _____

_____

2 _____

_____

3 _____

_____

TO-DO LIST

- ▪ _____
- ▪ _____
- ▪ _____
- ▪ _____
- ▪ _____
- ▪ _____
- ▪ _____
- ▪ _____

DON'T FORGET

_____

_____

_____

TIME	PLANS & SCHEDULE
6:00 am	
6:30 am	
7:00 am	
7:30 am	
8:00 am	
8:30 am	
9:00 am	
9:30 am	
10:00 am	
10:30 am	
11:00 am	
11:30 am	
12:00 pm	
12:30 pm	
1:00 pm	
1:30 pm	
2:00 pm	
2:30 pm	
3:00 pm	
3:30 pm	
4:00 pm	
4:30 pm	
5:00 pm	
5:30 pm	
6:00 pm	
6:30 pm	
7:00 pm	
7:30 pm	
8:00 pm	
8:30 pm	
9:00 pm	
9:30 pm	
10:00 pm	

DAILY PLANNER

SEPTEMBER 2, 2024

Monday

TODAY'S AFFIRMATION

TOP 3 PRIORITIES

1 _____

2 _____

3 _____

TO-DO LIST

- ☐ _____
- ☐ _____
- ☐ _____
- ☐ _____
- ☐ _____
- ☐ _____
- ☐ _____
- ☐ _____

DON'T FORGET

_____
_____
_____

WEATHER

MOOD

TIME	PLANS & SCHEDULE
6:00 am	
6:30 am	
7:00 am	
7:30 am	
8:00 am	
8:30 am	
9:00 am	
9:30 am	
10:00 am	
10:30 am	
11:00 am	
11:30 am	
12:00 pm	
12:30 pm	
1:00 pm	
1:30 pm	
2:00 pm	
2:30 pm	
3:00 pm	
3:30 pm	
4:00 pm	
4:30 pm	
5:00 pm	
5:30 pm	
6:00 pm	
6:30 pm	
7:00 pm	
7:30 pm	
8:00 pm	
8:30 pm	
9:00 pm	
9:30 pm	
10:00 pm	

DAILY PLANNER

SEPTEMBER 3, 2024

Tuesday

TODAY'S AFFIRMATION

TOP 3 PRIORITIES

1 _____
_____

2 _____
_____

3 _____
_____

TO-DO LIST

- _____
- _____
- _____
- _____
- _____
- _____
- _____
- _____

DON'T FORGET

_____
_____
_____

WEATHER

MOOD

TIME	PLANS & SCHEDULE
6:00 am	
6:30 am	
7:00 am	
7:30 am	
8:00 am	
8:30 am	
9:00 am	
9:30 am	
10:00 am	
10:30 am	
11:00 am	
11:30 am	
12:00 pm	
12:30 pm	
1:00 pm	
1:30 pm	
2:00 pm	
2:30 pm	
3:00 pm	
3:30 pm	
4:00 pm	
4:30 pm	
5:00 pm	
5:30 pm	
6:00 pm	
6:30 pm	
7:00 pm	
7:30 pm	
8:00 pm	
8:30 pm	
9:00 pm	
9:30 pm	
10:00 pm	

DAILY PLANNER

SEPTEMBER 4, 2024

Wednesday

TODAY'S AFFIRMATION

WEATHER

MOOD

TOP 3 PRIORITIES

1 _____

2 _____

3 _____

TO-DO LIST

-
-
-
-
-
-
-
-

DON'T FORGET

TIME	PLANS & SCHEDULE
6:00 am	
6:30 am	
7:00 am	
7:30 am	
8:00 am	
8:30 am	
9:00 am	
9:30 am	
10:00 am	
10:30 am	
11:00 am	
11:30 am	
12:00 pm	
12:30 pm	
1:00 pm	
1:30 pm	
2:00 pm	
2:30 pm	
3:00 pm	
3:30 pm	
4:00 pm	
4:30 pm	
5:00 pm	
5:30 pm	
6:00 pm	
6:30 pm	
7:00 pm	
7:30 pm	
8:00 pm	
8:30 pm	
9:00 pm	
9:30 pm	
10:00 pm	

DAILY PLANNER

SEPTEMBER 5, 2024

Thursday

TODAY'S AFFIRMATION

WEATHER	

MOOD	

TOP 3 PRIORITIES

1 _____

_____

2 _____

_____

3 _____

_____

TO-DO LIST

■ _____

■ _____

■ _____

■ _____

■ _____

■ _____

■ _____

■ _____

DON'T FORGET

_____

_____

_____

TIME	PLANS & SCHEDULE
6:00 am	
6:30 am	
7:00 am	
7:30 am	
8:00 am	
8:30 am	
9:00 am	
9:30 am	
10:00 am	
10:30 am	
11:00 am	
11:30 am	
12:00 pm	
12:30 pm	
1:00 pm	
1:30 pm	
2:00 pm	
2:30 pm	
3:00 pm	
3:30 pm	
4:00 pm	
4:30 pm	
5:00 pm	
5:30 pm	
6:00 pm	
6:30 pm	
7:00 pm	
7:30 pm	
8:00 pm	
8:30 pm	
9:00 pm	
9:30 pm	
10:00 pm	

DAILY PLANNER

SEPTEMBER 6, 2024

Friday

TODAY'S AFFIRMATION

WEATHER

MOOD

TOP 3 PRIORITIES

1. _____
_____

2. _____
_____

3. _____
_____

TO-DO LIST

- ☐ _____
- ☐ _____
- ☐ _____
- ☐ _____
- ☐ _____
- ☐ _____
- ☐ _____
- ☐ _____

DON'T FORGET

_____
_____
_____

TIME	PLANS & SCHEDULE
6:00 am	
6:30 am	
7:00 am	
7:30 am	
8:00 am	
8:30 am	
9:00 am	
9:30 am	
10:00 am	
10:30 am	
11:00 am	
11:30 am	
12:00 pm	
12:30 pm	
1:00 pm	
1:30 pm	
2:00 pm	
2:30 pm	
3:00 pm	
3:30 pm	
4:00 pm	
4:30 pm	
5:00 pm	
5:30 pm	
6:00 pm	
6:30 pm	
7:00 pm	
7:30 pm	
8:00 pm	
8:30 pm	
9:00 pm	
9:30 pm	
10:00 pm	

DAILY PLANNER

SEPTEMBER 7, 2024

Saturday

TODAY'S AFFIRMATION

WEATHER

MOOD

TOP 3 PRIORITIES

1 _____
_____

2 _____
_____

3 _____
_____

TO-DO LIST

☑ _____

☑ _____

☑ _____

☑ _____

☑ _____

☑ _____

☑ _____

☑ _____

DON'T FORGET

_____
_____
_____

TIME	PLANS & SCHEDULE
6:00 am	
6:30 am	
7:00 am	
7:30 am	
8:00 am	
8:30 am	
9:00 am	
9:30 am	
10:00 am	
10:30 am	
11:00 am	
11:30 am	
12:00 pm	
12:30 pm	
1:00 pm	
1:30 pm	
2:00 pm	
2:30 pm	
3:00 pm	
3:30 pm	
4:00 pm	
4:30 pm	
5:00 pm	
5:30 pm	
6:00 pm	
6:30 pm	
7:00 pm	
7:30 pm	
8:00 pm	
8:30 pm	
9:00 pm	
9:30 pm	
10:00 pm	

DAILY PLANNER

SEPTEMBER 8, 2024

Sunday

TODAY'S AFFIRMATION

WEATHER

MOOD

TOP 3 PRIORITIES

1 _____

2 _____

3 _____

TO-DO LIST

- ▪
- ▪
- ▪
- ▪
- ▪
- ▪
- ▪
- ▪

DON'T FORGET

TIME	PLANS & SCHEDULE
6:00 am	
6:30 am	
7:00 am	
7:30 am	
8:00 am	
8:30 am	
9:00 am	
9:30 am	
10:00 am	
10:30 am	
11:00 am	
11:30 am	
12:00 pm	
12:30 pm	
1:00 pm	
1:30 pm	
2:00 pm	
2:30 pm	
3:00 pm	
3:30 pm	
4:00 pm	
4:30 pm	
5:00 pm	
5:30 pm	
6:00 pm	
6:30 pm	
7:00 pm	
7:30 pm	
8:00 pm	
8:30 pm	
9:00 pm	
9:30 pm	
10:00 pm	

DAILY PLANNER

SEPTEMBER 9, 2024

Monday

TODAY'S AFFIRMATION

WEATHER

MOOD

TOP 3 PRIORITIES

1 _____

_____

2 _____

_____

3 _____

_____

TO-DO LIST

- ▪ _____
- ▪ _____
- ▪ _____
- ▪ _____
- ▪ _____
- ▪ _____
- ▪ _____
- ▪ _____

DON'T FORGET

_____

_____

_____

TIME	PLANS & SCHEDULE
6:00 am	
6:30 am	
7:00 am	
7:30 am	
8:00 am	
8:30 am	
9:00 am	
9:30 am	
10:00 am	
10:30 am	
11:00 am	
11:30 am	
12:00 pm	
12:30 pm	
1:00 pm	
1:30 pm	
2:00 pm	
2:30 pm	
3:00 pm	
3:30 pm	
4:00 pm	
4:30 pm	
5:00 pm	
5:30 pm	
6:00 pm	
6:30 pm	
7:00 pm	
7:30 pm	
8:00 pm	
8:30 pm	
9:00 pm	
9:30 pm	
10:00 pm	

DAILY PLANNER

SEPTEMBER 10, 2024

Tuesday

TODAY'S AFFIRMATION

WEATHER

MOOD

TOP 3 PRIORITIES

1 _____

2 _____

3 _____

TO-DO LIST

- ▪
- ▪
- ▪
- ▪
- ▪
- ▪
- ▪
- ▪

DON'T FORGET

_____

_____

_____

TIME	PLANS & SCHEDULE
6:00 am	
6:30 am	
7:00 am	
7:30 am	
8:00 am	
8:30 am	
9:00 am	
9:30 am	
10:00 am	
10:30 am	
11:00 am	
11:30 am	
12:00 pm	
12:30 pm	
1:00 pm	
1:30 pm	
2:00 pm	
2:30 pm	
3:00 pm	
3:30 pm	
4:00 pm	
4:30 pm	
5:00 pm	
5:30 pm	
6:00 pm	
6:30 pm	
7:00 pm	
7:30 pm	
8:00 pm	
8:30 pm	
9:00 pm	
9:30 pm	
10:00 pm	

DAILY PLANNER

SEPTEMBER 11, 2024

Wednesday

TODAY'S AFFIRMATION

WEATHER

MOOD

TOP 3 PRIORITIES

1 _____

2 _____

3 _____

TO-DO LIST

- ☐ _____
- ☐ _____
- ☐ _____
- ☐ _____
- ☐ _____
- ☐ _____
- ☐ _____
- ☐ _____

DON'T FORGET

_____

_____

_____

TIME	PLANS & SCHEDULE
6:00 am	
6:30 am	
7:00 am	
7:30 am	
8:00 am	
8:30 am	
9:00 am	
9:30 am	
10:00 am	
10:30 am	
11:00 am	
11:30 am	
12:00 pm	
12:30 pm	
1:00 pm	
1:30 pm	
2:00 pm	
2:30 pm	
3:00 pm	
3:30 pm	
4:00 pm	
4:30 pm	
5:00 pm	
5:30 pm	
6:00 pm	
6:30 pm	
7:00 pm	
7:30 pm	
8:00 pm	
8:30 pm	
9:00 pm	
9:30 pm	
10:00 pm	

DAILY PLANNER

SEPTEMBER 12, 2024

Thursday

TODAY'S AFFIRMATION

WEATHER

MOOD

TOP 3 PRIORITIES

1 _____

2 _____

3 _____

TO-DO LIST

- _____
- _____
- _____
- _____
- _____
- _____
- _____
- _____

DON'T FORGET

_____

_____

_____

TIME	PLANS & SCHEDULE
6:00 am	
6:30 am	
7:00 am	
7:30 am	
8:00 am	
8:30 am	
9:00 am	
9:30 am	
10:00 am	
10:30 am	
11:00 am	
11:30 am	
12:00 pm	
12:30 pm	
1:00 pm	
1:30 pm	
2:00 pm	
2:30 pm	
3:00 pm	
3:30 pm	
4:00 pm	
4:30 pm	
5:00 pm	
5:30 pm	
6:00 pm	
6:30 pm	
7:00 pm	
7:30 pm	
8:00 pm	
8:30 pm	
9:00 pm	
9:30 pm	
10:00 pm	

DAILY PLANNER

SEPTEMBER 13, 2024

Friday

TODAY'S AFFIRMATION

WEATHER

MOOD

TOP 3 PRIORITIES

1 _____
_____

2 _____
_____

3 _____
_____

TO-DO LIST

- ☐ _____
- ☐ _____
- ☐ _____
- ☐ _____
- ☐ _____
- ☐ _____
- ☐ _____
- ☐ _____

DON'T FORGET

_____
_____
_____

TIME	PLANS & SCHEDULE
6:00 am	
6:30 am	
7:00 am	
7:30 am	
8:00 am	
8:30 am	
9:00 am	
9:30 am	
10:00 am	
10:30 am	
11:00 am	
11:30 am	
12:00 pm	
12:30 pm	
1:00 pm	
1:30 pm	
2:00 pm	
2:30 pm	
3:00 pm	
3:30 pm	
4:00 pm	
4:30 pm	
5:00 pm	
5:30 pm	
6:00 pm	
6:30 pm	
7:00 pm	
7:30 pm	
8:00 pm	
8:30 pm	
9:00 pm	
9:30 pm	
10:00 pm	

DAILY PLANNER

SEPTEMBER 14, 2024

Saturday

TODAY'S AFFIRMATION

WEATHER

MOOD

TOP 3 PRIORITIES

1 _____
_____

2 _____
_____

3 _____
_____

TO-DO LIST

- ▪ _____
- ▪ _____
- ▪ _____
- ▪ _____
- ▪ _____
- ▪ _____
- ▪ _____
- ▪ _____

DON'T FORGET

_____
_____
_____

TIME	PLANS & SCHEDULE
6:00 am	
6:30 am	
7:00 am	
7:30 am	
8:00 am	
8:30 am	
9:00 am	
9:30 am	
10:00 am	
10:30 am	
11:00 am	
11:30 am	
12:00 pm	
12:30 pm	
1:00 pm	
1:30 pm	
2:00 pm	
2:30 pm	
3:00 pm	
3:30 pm	
4:00 pm	
4:30 pm	
5:00 pm	
5:30 pm	
6:00 pm	
6:30 pm	
7:00 pm	
7:30 pm	
8:00 pm	
8:30 pm	
9:00 pm	
9:30 pm	
10:00 pm	

DAILY PLANNER

SEPTEMBER 15, 2024

Sunday

TODAY'S AFFIRMATION

WEATHER

MOOD

TOP 3 PRIORITIES

1 _____
_____

2 _____
_____

3 _____
_____

TO-DO LIST

- ☐ _____
- ☐ _____
- ☐ _____
- ☐ _____
- ☐ _____
- ☐ _____
- ☐ _____
- ☐ _____

DON'T FORGET

_____
_____
_____

TIME	PLANS & SCHEDULE
6:00 am	
6:30 am	
7:00 am	
7:30 am	
8:00 am	
8:30 am	
9:00 am	
9:30 am	
10:00 am	
10:30 am	
11:00 am	
11:30 am	
12:00 pm	
12:30 pm	
1:00 pm	
1:30 pm	
2:00 pm	
2:30 pm	
3:00 pm	
3:30 pm	
4:00 pm	
4:30 pm	
5:00 pm	
5:30 pm	
6:00 pm	
6:30 pm	
7:00 pm	
7:30 pm	
8:00 pm	
8:30 pm	
9:00 pm	
9:30 pm	
10:00 pm	

DAILY PLANNER

SEPTEMBER 16, 2024

Monday

TODAY'S AFFIRMATION

WEATHER

MOOD

TOP 3 PRIORITIES

1 _____

2 _____

3 _____

TO-DO LIST

- ▪ _____
- ▪ _____
- ▪ _____
- ▪ _____
- ▪ _____
- ▪ _____
- ▪ _____
- ▪ _____

DON'T FORGET

_____

_____

_____

TIME	PLANS & SCHEDULE
6:00 am	
6:30 am	
7:00 am	
7:30 am	
8:00 am	
8:30 am	
9:00 am	
9:30 am	
10:00 am	
10:30 am	
11:00 am	
11:30 am	
12:00 pm	
12:30 pm	
1:00 pm	
1:30 pm	
2:00 pm	
2:30 pm	
3:00 pm	
3:30 pm	
4:00 pm	
4:30 pm	
5:00 pm	
5:30 pm	
6:00 pm	
6:30 pm	
7:00 pm	
7:30 pm	
8:00 pm	
8:30 pm	
9:00 pm	
9:30 pm	
10:00 pm	

DAILY PLANNER

SEPTEMBER 17, 2024

Tuesday

TODAY'S AFFIRMATION

TOP 3 PRIORITIES

1 _____

_____

2 _____

_____

3 _____

_____

TO-DO LIST

■ _____

■ _____

■ _____

■ _____

■ _____

■ _____

■ _____

■ _____

DON'T FORGET

_____

_____

_____

WEATHER

MOOD

TIME	PLANS & SCHEDULE
6:00 am	
6:30 am	
7:00 am	
7:30 am	
8:00 am	
8:30 am	
9:00 am	
9:30 am	
10:00 am	
10:30 am	
11:00 am	
11:30 am	
12:00 pm	
12:30 pm	
1:00 pm	
1:30 pm	
2:00 pm	
2:30 pm	
3:00 pm	
3:30 pm	
4:00 pm	
4:30 pm	
5:00 pm	
5:30 pm	
6:00 pm	
6:30 pm	
7:00 pm	
7:30 pm	
8:00 pm	
8:30 pm	
9:00 pm	
9:30 pm	
10:00 pm	

DAILY PLANNER

SEPTEMBER 18, 2024

Wednesday

TODAY'S AFFIRMATION

WEATHER

MOOD

TOP 3 PRIORITIES

1

2

3

TO-DO LIST

-
-
-
-
-
-
-
-

DON'T FORGET

TIME	PLANS & SCHEDULE
6:00 am	
6:30 am	
7:00 am	
7:30 am	
8:00 am	
8:30 am	
9:00 am	
9:30 am	
10:00 am	
10:30 am	
11:00 am	
11:30 am	
12:00 pm	
12:30 pm	
1:00 pm	
1:30 pm	
2:00 pm	
2:30 pm	
3:00 pm	
3:30 pm	
4:00 pm	
4:30 pm	
5:00 pm	
5:30 pm	
6:00 pm	
6:30 pm	
7:00 pm	
7:30 pm	
8:00 pm	
8:30 pm	
9:00 pm	
9:30 pm	
10:00 pm	

DAILY PLANNER

SEPTEMBER 19, 2024

Thursday

TODAY'S AFFIRMATION

WEATHER

MOOD

TOP 3 PRIORITIES

1 _____
_____

2 _____
_____

3 _____
_____

TO-DO LIST

- ☐ _____
- ☐ _____
- ☐ _____
- ☐ _____
- ☐ _____
- ☐ _____
- ☐ _____
- ☐ _____

DON'T FORGET

_____
_____
_____

TIME	PLANS & SCHEDULE
6:00 am	
6:30 am	
7:00 am	
7:30 am	
8:00 am	
8:30 am	
9:00 am	
9:30 am	
10:00 am	
10:30 am	
11:00 am	
11:30 am	
12:00 pm	
12:30 pm	
1:00 pm	
1:30 pm	
2:00 pm	
2:30 pm	
3:00 pm	
3:30 pm	
4:00 pm	
4:30 pm	
5:00 pm	
5:30 pm	
6:00 pm	
6:30 pm	
7:00 pm	
7:30 pm	
8:00 pm	
8:30 pm	
9:00 pm	
9:30 pm	
10:00 pm	

DAILY PLANNER

SEPTEMBER 20, 2024

Friday

TODAY'S AFFIRMATION

WEATHER

MOOD

TOP 3 PRIORITIES

1 _____

_____

2 _____

_____

3 _____

_____

TO-DO LIST

- ☐ _____
- ☐ _____
- ☐ _____
- ☐ _____
- ☐ _____
- ☐ _____
- ☐ _____
- ☐ _____

DON'T FORGET

_____

_____

_____

TIME	PLANS & SCHEDULE
6:00 am	
6:30 am	
7:00 am	
7:30 am	
8:00 am	
8:30 am	
9:00 am	
9:30 am	
10:00 am	
10:30 am	
11:00 am	
11:30 am	
12:00 pm	
12:30 pm	
1:00 pm	
1:30 pm	
2:00 pm	
2:30 pm	
3:00 pm	
3:30 pm	
4:00 pm	
4:30 pm	
5:00 pm	
5:30 pm	
6:00 pm	
6:30 pm	
7:00 pm	
7:30 pm	
8:00 pm	
8:30 pm	
9:00 pm	
9:30 pm	
10:00 pm	

DAILY PLANNER

SEPTEMBER 21, 2024

Saturday

TODAY'S AFFIRMATION

WEATHER

MOOD

TOP 3 PRIORITIES

1 _____
_____

2 _____
_____

3 _____
_____

TO-DO LIST

- _____
- _____
- _____
- _____
- _____
- _____
- _____
- _____

DON'T FORGET

_____
_____
_____

TIME	PLANS & SCHEDULE
6:00 am	
6:30 am	
7:00 am	
7:30 am	
8:00 am	
8:30 am	
9:00 am	
9:30 am	
10:00 am	
10:30 am	
11:00 am	
11:30 am	
12:00 pm	
12:30 pm	
1:00 pm	
1:30 pm	
2:00 pm	
2:30 pm	
3:00 pm	
3:30 pm	
4:00 pm	
4:30 pm	
5:00 pm	
5:30 pm	
6:00 pm	
6:30 pm	
7:00 pm	
7:30 pm	
8:00 pm	
8:30 pm	
9:00 pm	
9:30 pm	
10:00 pm	

DAILY PLANNER

SEPTEMBER 22, 2024

Sunday

TODAY'S AFFIRMATION

TOP 3 PRIORITIES

1 _____

2 _____

3 _____

TO-DO LIST

- ☐ _____
- ☐ _____
- ☐ _____
- ☐ _____
- ☐ _____
- ☐ _____
- ☐ _____
- ☐ _____

DON'T FORGET

_____

_____

_____

WEATHER

MOOD

TIME	PLANS & SCHEDULE
6:00 am	
6:30 am	
7:00 am	
7:30 am	
8:00 am	
8:30 am	
9:00 am	
9:30 am	
10:00 am	
10:30 am	
11:00 am	
11:30 am	
12:00 pm	
12:30 pm	
1:00 pm	
1:30 pm	
2:00 pm	
2:30 pm	
3:00 pm	
3:30 pm	
4:00 pm	
4:30 pm	
5:00 pm	
5:30 pm	
6:00 pm	
6:30 pm	
7:00 pm	
7:30 pm	
8:00 pm	
8:30 pm	
9:00 pm	
9:30 pm	
10:00 pm	

DAILY PLANNER

SEPTEMBER 23, 2024

Monday

TODAY'S AFFIRMATION

WEATHER

MOOD

TOP 3 PRIORITIES

1 _____

_____

2 _____

_____

3 _____

_____

TO-DO LIST

- ▪ _____
- ▪ _____
- ▪ _____
- ▪ _____
- ▪ _____
- ▪ _____
- ▪ _____
- ▪ _____

DON'T FORGET

_____

_____

_____

TIME	PLANS & SCHEDULE
6:00 am	
6:30 am	
7:00 am	
7:30 am	
8:00 am	
8:30 am	
9:00 am	
9:30 am	
10:00 am	
10:30 am	
11:00 am	
11:30 am	
12:00 pm	
12:30 pm	
1:00 pm	
1:30 pm	
2:00 pm	
2:30 pm	
3:00 pm	
3:30 pm	
4:00 pm	
4:30 pm	
5:00 pm	
5:30 pm	
6:00 pm	
6:30 pm	
7:00 pm	
7:30 pm	
8:00 pm	
8:30 pm	
9:00 pm	
9:30 pm	
10:00 pm	

DAILY PLANNER

SEPTEMBER 24, 2024

Tuesday

TODAY'S AFFIRMATION

WEATHER

MOOD

TOP 3 PRIORITIES

1 _____
_____

2 _____
_____

3 _____
_____

TO-DO LIST

- _____
- _____
- _____
- _____
- _____
- _____
- _____
- _____

DON'T FORGET

_____
_____
_____

TIME	PLANS & SCHEDULE
6:00 am	
6:30 am	
7:00 am	
7:30 am	
8:00 am	
8:30 am	
9:00 am	
9:30 am	
10:00 am	
10:30 am	
11:00 am	
11:30 am	
12:00 pm	
12:30 pm	
1:00 pm	
1:30 pm	
2:00 pm	
2:30 pm	
3:00 pm	
3:30 pm	
4:00 pm	
4:30 pm	
5:00 pm	
5:30 pm	
6:00 pm	
6:30 pm	
7:00 pm	
7:30 pm	
8:00 pm	
8:30 pm	
9:00 pm	
9:30 pm	
10:00 pm	

DAILY PLANNER

SEPTEMBER 25, 2024

Wednesday

TODAY'S AFFIRMATION

WEATHER

MOOD

TOP 3 PRIORITIES

1 _____

_____

2 _____

_____

3 _____

_____

TO-DO LIST

- ■ _____
- ■ _____
- ■ _____
- ■ _____
- ■ _____
- ■ _____
- ■ _____
- ■ _____

DON'T FORGET

_____

_____

_____

TIME	PLANS & SCHEDULE
6:00 am	
6:30 am	
7:00 am	
7:30 am	
8:00 am	
8:30 am	
9:00 am	
9:30 am	
10:00 am	
10:30 am	
11:00 am	
11:30 am	
12:00 pm	
12:30 pm	
1:00 pm	
1:30 pm	
2:00 pm	
2:30 pm	
3:00 pm	
3:30 pm	
4:00 pm	
4:30 pm	
5:00 pm	
5:30 pm	
6:00 pm	
6:30 pm	
7:00 pm	
7:30 pm	
8:00 pm	
8:30 pm	
9:00 pm	
9:30 pm	
10:00 pm	

DAILY PLANNER

SEPTEMBER 26, 2024

Thursday

TODAY'S AFFIRMATION

WEATHER

MOOD

TOP 3 PRIORITIES

1 _____

2 _____

3 _____

TO-DO LIST

- _____
- _____
- _____
- _____
- _____
- _____
- _____
- _____

DON'T FORGET

_____

_____

_____

TIME	PLANS & SCHEDULE
6:00 am	
6:30 am	
7:00 am	
7:30 am	
8:00 am	
8:30 am	
9:00 am	
9:30 am	
10:00 am	
10:30 am	
11:00 am	
11:30 am	
12:00 pm	
12:30 pm	
1:00 pm	
1:30 pm	
2:00 pm	
2:30 pm	
3:00 pm	
3:30 pm	
4:00 pm	
4:30 pm	
5:00 pm	
5:30 pm	
6:00 pm	
6:30 pm	
7:00 pm	
7:30 pm	
8:00 pm	
8:30 pm	
9:00 pm	
9:30 pm	
10:00 pm	

DAILY PLANNER

SEPTEMBER 27, 2024

Friday

TODAY'S AFFIRMATION

WEATHER

MOOD

TOP 3 PRIORITIES

1 _____

2 _____

3 _____

TO-DO LIST

- ☐ _____
- ☐ _____
- ☐ _____
- ☐ _____
- ☐ _____
- ☐ _____
- ☐ _____
- ☐ _____

DON'T FORGET

_____

_____

_____

TIME	PLANS & SCHEDULE
6:00 am	
6:30 am	
7:00 am	
7:30 am	
8:00 am	
8:30 am	
9:00 am	
9:30 am	
10:00 am	
10:30 am	
11:00 am	
11:30 am	
12:00 pm	
12:30 pm	
1:00 pm	
1:30 pm	
2:00 pm	
2:30 pm	
3:00 pm	
3:30 pm	
4:00 pm	
4:30 pm	
5:00 pm	
5:30 pm	
6:00 pm	
6:30 pm	
7:00 pm	
7:30 pm	
8:00 pm	
8:30 pm	
9:00 pm	
9:30 pm	
10:00 pm	

DAILY PLANNER

SEPTEMBER 28, 2024

Saturday

TODAY'S AFFIRMATION

TOP 3 PRIORITIES

1. _____
   _____

2. _____
   _____

3. _____
   _____

TO-DO LIST

- ▪ _____
- ▪ _____
- ▪ _____
- ▪ _____
- ▪ _____
- ▪ _____
- ▪ _____
- ▪ _____

DON'T FORGET

_____
_____
_____

TIME	PLANS & SCHEDULE
6:00 am	
6:30 am	
7:00 am	
7:30 am	
8:00 am	
8:30 am	
9:00 am	
9:30 am	
10:00 am	
10:30 am	
11:00 am	
11:30 am	
12:00 pm	
12:30 pm	
1:00 pm	
1:30 pm	
2:00 pm	
2:30 pm	
3:00 pm	
3:30 pm	
4:00 pm	
4:30 pm	
5:00 pm	
5:30 pm	
6:00 pm	
6:30 pm	
7:00 pm	
7:30 pm	
8:00 pm	
8:30 pm	
9:00 pm	
9:30 pm	
10:00 pm	

DAILY PLANNER

SEPTEMBER 29, 2024

Sunday

TODAY'S AFFIRMATION

WEATHER

MOOD

TOP 3 PRIORITIES

1 _____
_____

2 _____
_____

3 _____
_____

TO-DO LIST

- ◼ _____
- ◼ _____
- ◼ _____
- ◼ _____
- ◼ _____
- ◼ _____
- ◼ _____
- ◼ _____

DON'T FORGET

_____
_____
_____

TIME	PLANS & SCHEDULE
6:00 am	
6:30 am	
7:00 am	
7:30 am	
8:00 am	
8:30 am	
9:00 am	
9:30 am	
10:00 am	
10:30 am	
11:00 am	
11:30 am	
12:00 pm	
12:30 pm	
1:00 pm	
1:30 pm	
2:00 pm	
2:30 pm	
3:00 pm	
3:30 pm	
4:00 pm	
4:30 pm	
5:00 pm	
5:30 pm	
6:00 pm	
6:30 pm	
7:00 pm	
7:30 pm	
8:00 pm	
8:30 pm	
9:00 pm	
9:30 pm	
10:00 pm	

DAILY PLANNER

SEPTEMBER 30, 2024

Monday

TODAY'S AFFIRMATION

WEATHER

MOOD

TOP 3 PRIORITIES

1 _____
_____

2 _____
_____

3 _____
_____

TO-DO LIST

- ▪ _____
- ▪ _____
- ▪ _____
- ▪ _____
- ▪ _____
- ▪ _____
- ▪ _____
- ▪ _____

DON'T FORGET

_____
_____
_____

TIME	PLANS & SCHEDULE
6:00 am	
6:30 am	
7:00 am	
7:30 am	
8:00 am	
8:30 am	
9:00 am	
9:30 am	
10:00 am	
10:30 am	
11:00 am	
11:30 am	
12:00 pm	
12:30 pm	
1:00 pm	
1:30 pm	
2:00 pm	
2:30 pm	
3:00 pm	
3:30 pm	
4:00 pm	
4:30 pm	
5:00 pm	
5:30 pm	
6:00 pm	
6:30 pm	
7:00 pm	
7:30 pm	
8:00 pm	
8:30 pm	
9:00 pm	
9:30 pm	
10:00 pm	

MONTHLY BUDGET PLANNER

Budget Goal: _____   Month: _____

Income

Date	Description	Amount
Total		

Fixed Expenses

Date	Description	Amount
Total		

Other Expenses

Date	Description	Amount
Total		

Bills

Date	Description	Amount
Total		

Recap

	Goal	Actual	Difference
Earnt			
Spent			
Debt			
Saved			

Notes

Date:

GRATITUDE JOURNAL

DATE: _____ S M T W T F S

TODAY I'M GRATEFUL FOR

- _____
- _____
- _____

WATER INTAKE

◊ ◊ ◊ ◊   ◊ ◊ ◊ ◊   ◊ ◊
   1L   2L   3L

WEATHER

TODAY'S AFFIRMATION

- _____
- _____
- _____
- _____

NOTES / REMINDERS

SOMETHING I'M PROUD OF

- _____
- _____
- _____
- _____

TOMORROW I LOOK FORWARD TO

- _____
- _____
- _____
- _____

30 DAY
Self-Care Challenge

DAY 1	DAY 2	DAY 3	DAY 4	DAY 5
Start a gratitude journal	Learn to meditate	Spend the day social media free	Call someone you love	Take a 15 minute walk outdoors
DAY 6	**DAY 7**	**DAY 8**	**DAY 9**	**DAY 10**
Listen to a podcast	Learn to cook a new recipe	Stretch for 10-15 minutes	Listen to your favorite song	Practice deep breathing
DAY 11	**DAY 12**	**DAY 13**	**DAY 14**	**DAY 15**
Try a free online workout	Read a book for 15 minutes	Write a list of short-term goals	De-clutter a room or desk	Go to bed 30 minutes earlier
DAY 16	**DAY 17**	**DAY 18**	**DAY 19**	**DAY 20**
Have a game night	Wake up 15 minutes earlier	Make your favorite meal	Buy yourself something nice	Create a bucket list
DAY 21	**DAY 22**	**DAY 23**	**DAY 24**	**DAY 25**
Watch a movie or series	Write down your thoughts	Take a long shower or bath	Have a home spa day	Read inspirational quotes
DAY 26	**DAY 27**	**DAY 28**	**DAY 29**	**DAY 30**
Create a vision board	Spend some time outside	Do a hair mask	Write it all down in a journal	Take a power nap

OCTOBER 2024

Sunday	Monday	Tuesday	Wednesday
		01	02
06	07	08	09
13	14	15	16
20	21	22	23
27	28	29	30

OCTOBER 2024

Thursday	Friday	Saturday	Notes
03	04	05	
10	11	12	
17	18	19	
24	25	26	
31			

OCTOBER

Goal

Action Plan

Date

....

....

....

....

....

....

....

....

....

....

Grateful For

....

....

....

....

To Improve

....

....

....

....

Notes

....

....

....

DAILY PLANNER

OCTOBER 1, 2024

Tuesday

TODAY'S AFFIRMATION

WEATHER

MOOD

TOP 3 PRIORITIES

1 _____
_____

2 _____
_____

3 _____
_____

TO-DO LIST

- ☐ _____
- ☐ _____
- ☐ _____
- ☐ _____
- ☐ _____
- ☐ _____
- ☐ _____
- ☐ _____

DON'T FORGET

_____
_____
_____

TIME	PLANS & SCHEDULE
6:00 am	
6:30 am	
7:00 am	
7:30 am	
8:00 am	
8:30 am	
9:00 am	
9:30 am	
10:00 am	
10:30 am	
11:00 am	
11:30 am	
12:00 pm	
12:30 pm	
1:00 pm	
1:30 pm	
2:00 pm	
2:30 pm	
3:00 pm	
3:30 pm	
4:00 pm	
4:30 pm	
5:00 pm	
5:30 pm	
6:00 pm	
6:30 pm	
7:00 pm	
7:30 pm	
8:00 pm	
8:30 pm	
9:00 pm	
9:30 pm	
10:00 pm	

DAILY PLANNER

OCTOBER 2, 2024

Wednesday

TODAY'S AFFIRMATION

WEATHER

MOOD

TOP 3 PRIORITIES

1 _____

2 _____

3 _____

TO-DO LIST

- ☐
- ☐
- ☐
- ☐
- ☐
- ☐
- ☐
- ☐

DON'T FORGET

_____

_____

_____

TIME	PLANS & SCHEDULE
6:00 am	
6:30 am	
7:00 am	
7:30 am	
8:00 am	
8:30 am	
9:00 am	
9:30 am	
10:00 am	
10:30 am	
11:00 am	
11:30 am	
12:00 pm	
12:30 pm	
1:00 pm	
1:30 pm	
2:00 pm	
2:30 pm	
3:00 pm	
3:30 pm	
4:00 pm	
4:30 pm	
5:00 pm	
5:30 pm	
6:00 pm	
6:30 pm	
7:00 pm	
7:30 pm	
8:00 pm	
8:30 pm	
9:00 pm	
9:30 pm	
10:00 pm	

DAILY PLANNER

OCTOBER 3, 2024

Thursday

TODAY'S AFFIRMATION

WEATHER

MOOD

TOP 3 PRIORITIES

1 _____

_____

2 _____

_____

3 _____

_____

TO-DO LIST

- ■ _____
- ■ _____
- ■ _____
- ■ _____
- ■ _____
- ■ _____
- ■ _____
- ■ _____

DON'T FORGET

_____

_____

_____

TIME	PLANS & SCHEDULE
6:00 am	
6:30 am	
7:00 am	
7:30 am	
8:00 am	
8:30 am	
9:00 am	
9:30 am	
10:00 am	
10:30 am	
11:00 am	
11:30 am	
12:00 pm	
12:30 pm	
1:00 pm	
1:30 pm	
2:00 pm	
2:30 pm	
3:00 pm	
3:30 pm	
4:00 pm	
4:30 pm	
5:00 pm	
5:30 pm	
6:00 pm	
6:30 pm	
7:00 pm	
7:30 pm	
8:00 pm	
8:30 pm	
9:00 pm	
9:30 pm	
10:00 pm	

DAILY PLANNER

OCTOBER 4, 2024

Friday

TODAY'S AFFIRMATION

WEATHER

MOOD

TOP 3 PRIORITIES

1 _____

2 _____

3 _____

TO-DO LIST

- ☐ _____
- ☐ _____
- ☐ _____
- ☐ _____
- ☐ _____
- ☐ _____
- ☐ _____
- ☐ _____

DON'T FORGET

_____
_____
_____

TIME	PLANS & SCHEDULE
6:00 am	
6:30 am	
7:00 am	
7:30 am	
8:00 am	
8:30 am	
9:00 am	
9:30 am	
10:00 am	
10:30 am	
11:00 am	
11:30 am	
12:00 pm	
12:30 pm	
1:00 pm	
1:30 pm	
2:00 pm	
2:30 pm	
3:00 pm	
3:30 pm	
4:00 pm	
4:30 pm	
5:00 pm	
5:30 pm	
6:00 pm	
6:30 pm	
7:00 pm	
7:30 pm	
8:00 pm	
8:30 pm	
9:00 pm	
9:30 pm	
10:00 pm	

DAILY PLANNER

OCTOBER 5, 2024

Saturday

TODAY'S AFFIRMATION

WEATHER

MOOD

TOP 3 PRIORITIES

1 _____

_____

2 _____

_____

3 _____

_____

TO-DO LIST

- ◼ _____
- ◼ _____
- ◼ _____
- ◼ _____
- ◼ _____
- ◼ _____
- ◼ _____
- ◼ _____

DON'T FORGET

_____

_____

_____

TIME	PLANS & SCHEDULE
6:00 am	
6:30 am	
7:00 am	
7:30 am	
8:00 am	
8:30 am	
9:00 am	
9:30 am	
10:00 am	
10:30 am	
11:00 am	
11:30 am	
12:00 pm	
12:30 pm	
1:00 pm	
1:30 pm	
2:00 pm	
2:30 pm	
3:00 pm	
3:30 pm	
4:00 pm	
4:30 pm	
5:00 pm	
5:30 pm	
6:00 pm	
6:30 pm	
7:00 pm	
7:30 pm	
8:00 pm	
8:30 pm	
9:00 pm	
9:30 pm	
10:00 pm	

DAILY PLANNER

OCTOBER 6, 2024

Sunday

TODAY'S AFFIRMATION

WEATHER

MOOD

TOP 3 PRIORITIES

1 _____

2 _____

3 _____

TO-DO LIST

- _____
- _____
- _____
- _____
- _____
- _____
- _____
- _____

DON'T FORGET

_____

_____

_____

TIME	PLANS & SCHEDULE
6:00 am	
6:30 am	
7:00 am	
7:30 am	
8:00 am	
8:30 am	
9:00 am	
9:30 am	
10:00 am	
10:30 am	
11:00 am	
11:30 am	
12:00 pm	
12:30 pm	
1:00 pm	
1:30 pm	
2:00 pm	
2:30 pm	
3:00 pm	
3:30 pm	
4:00 pm	
4:30 pm	
5:00 pm	
5:30 pm	
6:00 pm	
6:30 pm	
7:00 pm	
7:30 pm	
8:00 pm	
8:30 pm	
9:00 pm	
9:30 pm	
10:00 pm	

DAILY PLANNER

OCTOBER 7, 2024

Monday

TODAY'S AFFIRMATION

WEATHER	
MOOD	

TOP 3 PRIORITIES

1 _____

_____

2 _____

_____

3 _____

_____

TO-DO LIST

- ▪ _____
- ▪ _____
- ▪ _____
- ▪ _____
- ▪ _____
- ▪ _____
- ▪ _____
- ▪ _____

DON'T FORGET

_____

_____

_____

TIME	PLANS & SCHEDULE
6:00 am	
6:30 am	
7:00 am	
7:30 am	
8:00 am	
8:30 am	
9:00 am	
9:30 am	
10:00 am	
10:30 am	
11:00 am	
11:30 am	
12:00 pm	
12:30 pm	
1:00 pm	
1:30 pm	
2:00 pm	
2:30 pm	
3:00 pm	
3:30 pm	
4:00 pm	
4:30 pm	
5:00 pm	
5:30 pm	
6:00 pm	
6:30 pm	
7:00 pm	
7:30 pm	
8:00 pm	
8:30 pm	
9:00 pm	
9:30 pm	
10:00 pm	

DAILY PLANNER

OCTOBER 8, 2024

Tuesday

TODAY'S AFFIRMATION

WEATHER

MOOD

TOP 3 PRIORITIES

1 _____

2 _____

3 _____

TO-DO LIST

- _____
- _____
- _____
- _____
- _____
- _____
- _____
- _____

DON'T FORGET

_____

_____

_____

TIME	PLANS & SCHEDULE
6:00 am	
6:30 am	
7:00 am	
7:30 am	
8:00 am	
8:30 am	
9:00 am	
9:30 am	
10:00 am	
10:30 am	
11:00 am	
11:30 am	
12:00 pm	
12:30 pm	
1:00 pm	
1:30 pm	
2:00 pm	
2:30 pm	
3:00 pm	
3:30 pm	
4:00 pm	
4:30 pm	
5:00 pm	
5:30 pm	
6:00 pm	
6:30 pm	
7:00 pm	
7:30 pm	
8:00 pm	
8:30 pm	
9:00 pm	
9:30 pm	
10:00 pm	

OCTOBER 9, 2024

Wednesday

TODAY'S AFFIRMATION

WEATHER	
MOOD	

TOP 3 PRIORITIES

1 _____
_____

2 _____
_____

3 _____
_____

TO-DO LIST

- ☐ _____
- ☐ _____
- ☐ _____
- ☐ _____
- ☐ _____
- ☐ _____
- ☐ _____
- ☐ _____

DON'T FORGET

_____
_____
_____

TIME	PLANS & SCHEDULE
6:00 am	
6:30 am	
7:00 am	
7:30 am	
8:00 am	
8:30 am	
9:00 am	
9:30 am	
10:00 am	
10:30 am	
11:00 am	
11:30 am	
12:00 pm	
12:30 pm	
1:00 pm	
1:30 pm	
2:00 pm	
2:30 pm	
3:00 pm	
3:30 pm	
4:00 pm	
4:30 pm	
5:00 pm	
5:30 pm	
6:00 pm	
6:30 pm	
7:00 pm	
7:30 pm	
8:00 pm	
8:30 pm	
9:00 pm	
9:30 pm	
10:00 pm	

DAILY PLANNER

OCTOBER 10, 2024

Thursday

TODAY'S AFFIRMATION

TOP 3 PRIORITIES

1 _____
_____

2 _____
_____

3 _____
_____

TO-DO LIST

- ■ _____
- ■ _____
- ■ _____
- ■ _____
- ■ _____
- ■ _____
- ■ _____
- ■ _____

DON'T FORGET

_____
_____
_____

WEATHER

MOOD

TIME	PLANS & SCHEDULE
6:00 am	
6:30 am	
7:00 am	
7:30 am	
8:00 am	
8:30 am	
9:00 am	
9:30 am	
10:00 am	
10:30 am	
11:00 am	
11:30 am	
12:00 pm	
12:30 pm	
1:00 pm	
1:30 pm	
2:00 pm	
2:30 pm	
3:00 pm	
3:30 pm	
4:00 pm	
4:30 pm	
5:00 pm	
5:30 pm	
6:00 pm	
6:30 pm	
7:00 pm	
7:30 pm	
8:00 pm	
8:30 pm	
9:00 pm	
9:30 pm	
10:00 pm	

DAILY PLANNER

OCTOBER 11, 2024

Friday

TODAY'S AFFIRMATION

WEATHER	

MOOD	

TOP 3 PRIORITIES

1 _____

2 _____

3 _____

TO-DO LIST

- ▪ _____
- ▪ _____
- ▪ _____
- ▪ _____
- ▪ _____
- ▪ _____
- ▪ _____
- ▪ _____

DON'T FORGET

TIME	PLANS & SCHEDULE
6:00 am	
6:30 am	
7:00 am	
7:30 am	
8:00 am	
8:30 am	
9:00 am	
9:30 am	
10:00 am	
10:30 am	
11:00 am	
11:30 am	
12:00 pm	
12:30 pm	
1:00 pm	
1:30 pm	
2:00 pm	
2:30 pm	
3:00 pm	
3:30 pm	
4:00 pm	
4:30 pm	
5:00 pm	
5:30 pm	
6:00 pm	
6:30 pm	
7:00 pm	
7:30 pm	
8:00 pm	
8:30 pm	
9:00 pm	
9:30 pm	
10:00 pm	

DAILY PLANNER

OCTOBER 12, 2024

Saturday

TODAY'S AFFIRMATION

WEATHER

MOOD

TOP 3 PRIORITIES

1 _____
_____

2 _____
_____

3 _____
_____

TO-DO LIST

- ☐ _____
- ☐ _____
- ☐ _____
- ☐ _____
- ☐ _____
- ☐ _____
- ☐ _____
- ☐ _____

DON'T FORGET

_____
_____
_____

TIME	PLANS & SCHEDULE
6:00 am	
6:30 am	
7:00 am	
7:30 am	
8:00 am	
8:30 am	
9:00 am	
9:30 am	
10:00 am	
10:30 am	
11:00 am	
11:30 am	
12:00 pm	
12:30 pm	
1:00 pm	
1:30 pm	
2:00 pm	
2:30 pm	
3:00 pm	
3:30 pm	
4:00 pm	
4:30 pm	
5:00 pm	
5:30 pm	
6:00 pm	
6:30 pm	
7:00 pm	
7:30 pm	
8:00 pm	
8:30 pm	
9:00 pm	
9:30 pm	
10:00 pm	

DAILY PLANNER

OCTOBER 13, 2024

Sunday

TODAY'S AFFIRMATION

WEATHER	

MOOD	

TOP 3 PRIORITIES

1 _____

_____

2 _____

_____

3 _____

_____

TO-DO LIST

■ _____

■ _____

■ _____

■ _____

■ _____

■ _____

■ _____

■ _____

DON'T FORGET

_____

_____

_____

TIME	PLANS & SCHEDULE
6:00 am	
6:30 am	
7:00 am	
7:30 am	
8:00 am	
8:30 am	
9:00 am	
9:30 am	
10:00 am	
10:30 am	
11:00 am	
11:30 am	
12:00 pm	
12:30 pm	
1:00 pm	
1:30 pm	
2:00 pm	
2:30 pm	
3:00 pm	
3:30 pm	
4:00 pm	
4:30 pm	
5:00 pm	
5:30 pm	
6:00 pm	
6:30 pm	
7:00 pm	
7:30 pm	
8:00 pm	
8:30 pm	
9:00 pm	
9:30 pm	
10:00 pm	

DAILY PLANNER

OCTOBER 14, 2024

Monday

TODAY'S AFFIRMATION

WEATHER

MOOD

TOP 3 PRIORITIES

1. _____
_____

2. _____
_____

3. _____
_____

TO-DO LIST

- ☐ _____
- ☐ _____
- ☐ _____
- ☐ _____
- ☐ _____
- ☐ _____
- ☐ _____
- ☐ _____

DON'T FORGET

_____
_____
_____

TIME	PLANS & SCHEDULE
6:00 am	
6:30 am	
7:00 am	
7:30 am	
8:00 am	
8:30 am	
9:00 am	
9:30 am	
10:00 am	
10:30 am	
11:00 am	
11:30 am	
12:00 pm	
12:30 pm	
1:00 pm	
1:30 pm	
2:00 pm	
2:30 pm	
3:00 pm	
3:30 pm	
4:00 pm	
4:30 pm	
5:00 pm	
5:30 pm	
6:00 pm	
6:30 pm	
7:00 pm	
7:30 pm	
8:00 pm	
8:30 pm	
9:00 pm	
9:30 pm	
10:00 pm	

DAILY PLANNER

OCTOBER 15, 2024

Tuesday

TODAY'S AFFIRMATION

WEATHER

MOOD

TOP 3 PRIORITIES

1 _____

_____

2 _____

_____

3 _____

_____

TO-DO LIST

- ☐ _____
- ☐ _____
- ☐ _____
- ☐ _____
- ☐ _____
- ☐ _____
- ☐ _____
- ☐ _____

DON'T FORGET

_____

_____

_____

TIME	PLANS & SCHEDULE
6:00 am	
6:30 am	
7:00 am	
7:30 am	
8:00 am	
8:30 am	
9:00 am	
9:30 am	
10:00 am	
10:30 am	
11:00 am	
11:30 am	
12:00 pm	
12:30 pm	
1:00 pm	
1:30 pm	
2:00 pm	
2:30 pm	
3:00 pm	
3:30 pm	
4:00 pm	
4:30 pm	
5:00 pm	
5:30 pm	
6:00 pm	
6:30 pm	
7:00 pm	
7:30 pm	
8:00 pm	
8:30 pm	
9:00 pm	
9:30 pm	
10:00 pm	

DAILY PLANNER

OCTOBER 16, 2024

Wednesday

TODAY'S AFFIRMATION

WEATHER

MOOD

TOP 3 PRIORITIES

1 _____
_____

2 _____
_____

3 _____
_____

TO-DO LIST

- _____
- _____
- _____
- _____
- _____
- _____
- _____
- _____

DON'T FORGET

_____
_____
_____

TIME	PLANS & SCHEDULE
6:00 am	
6:30 am	
7:00 am	
7:30 am	
8:00 am	
8:30 am	
9:00 am	
9:30 am	
10:00 am	
10:30 am	
11:00 am	
11:30 am	
12:00 pm	
12:30 pm	
1:00 pm	
1:30 pm	
2:00 pm	
2:30 pm	
3:00 pm	
3:30 pm	
4:00 pm	
4:30 pm	
5:00 pm	
5:30 pm	
6:00 pm	
6:30 pm	
7:00 pm	
7:30 pm	
8:00 pm	
8:30 pm	
9:00 pm	
9:30 pm	
10:00 pm	

DAILY PLANNER

OCTOBER 17, 2024

Thursday

TODAY'S AFFIRMATION

WEATHER

MOOD

TOP 3 PRIORITIES

1 _____
_____

2 _____
_____

3 _____
_____

TO-DO LIST

- ■ _____
- ■ _____
- ■ _____
- ■ _____
- ■ _____
- ■ _____
- ■ _____
- ■ _____

DON'T FORGET

_____
_____
_____

TIME	PLANS & SCHEDULE
6:00 am	
6:30 am	
7:00 am	
7:30 am	
8:00 am	
8:30 am	
9:00 am	
9:30 am	
10:00 am	
10:30 am	
11:00 am	
11:30 am	
12:00 pm	
12:30 pm	
1:00 pm	
1:30 pm	
2:00 pm	
2:30 pm	
3:00 pm	
3:30 pm	
4:00 pm	
4:30 pm	
5:00 pm	
5:30 pm	
6:00 pm	
6:30 pm	
7:00 pm	
7:30 pm	
8:00 pm	
8:30 pm	
9:00 pm	
9:30 pm	
10:00 pm	

DAILY PLANNER

OCTOBER 18, 2024

Friday

TODAY'S AFFIRMATION

MOOD

TOP 3 PRIORITIES

1 _____

2 _____

3 _____

TO-DO LIST

- ■ _____
- ■ _____
- ■ _____
- ■ _____
- ■ _____
- ■ _____
- ■ _____
- ■ _____

DON'T FORGET

_____
_____
_____

TIME	PLANS & SCHEDULE
6:00 am	
6:30 am	
7:00 am	
7:30 am	
8:00 am	
8:30 am	
9:00 am	
9:30 am	
10:00 am	
10:30 am	
11:00 am	
11:30 am	
12:00 pm	
12:30 pm	
1:00 pm	
1:30 pm	
2:00 pm	
2:30 pm	
3:00 pm	
3:30 pm	
4:00 pm	
4:30 pm	
5:00 pm	
5:30 pm	
6:00 pm	
6:30 pm	
7:00 pm	
7:30 pm	
8:00 pm	
8:30 pm	
9:00 pm	
9:30 pm	
10:00 pm	

DAILY PLANNER

OCTOBER 19, 2024

Saturday

TODAY'S AFFIRMATION

WEATHER

MOOD

TOP 3 PRIORITIES

1 _____
_____

2 _____
_____

3 _____
_____

TO-DO LIST

- ◾ _____
- ◾ _____
- ◾ _____
- ◾ _____
- ◾ _____
- ◾ _____
- ◾ _____
- ◾ _____

DON'T FORGET

_____
_____
_____

TIME	PLANS & SCHEDULE
6:00 am	
6:30 am	
7:00 am	
7:30 am	
8:00 am	
8:30 am	
9:00 am	
9:30 am	
10:00 am	
10:30 am	
11:00 am	
11:30 am	
12:00 pm	
12:30 pm	
1:00 pm	
1:30 pm	
2:00 pm	
2:30 pm	
3:00 pm	
3:30 pm	
4:00 pm	
4:30 pm	
5:00 pm	
5:30 pm	
6:00 pm	
6:30 pm	
7:00 pm	
7:30 pm	
8:00 pm	
8:30 pm	
9:00 pm	
9:30 pm	
10:00 pm	

DAILY PLANNER

OCTOBER 20, 2024

Sunday

TODAY'S AFFIRMATION

WEATHER

MOOD

TOP 3 PRIORITIES

1 _____

2 _____

3 _____

TO-DO LIST

- ▪ _____
- ▪ _____
- ▪ _____
- ▪ _____
- ▪ _____
- ▪ _____
- ▪ _____
- ▪ _____

DON'T FORGET

_____

_____

_____

TIME	PLANS & SCHEDULE
6:00 am	
6:30 am	
7:00 am	
7:30 am	
8:00 am	
8:30 am	
9:00 am	
9:30 am	
10:00 am	
10:30 am	
11:00 am	
11:30 am	
12:00 pm	
12:30 pm	
1:00 pm	
1:30 pm	
2:00 pm	
2:30 pm	
3:00 pm	
3:30 pm	
4:00 pm	
4:30 pm	
5:00 pm	
5:30 pm	
6:00 pm	
6:30 pm	
7:00 pm	
7:30 pm	
8:00 pm	
8:30 pm	
9:00 pm	
9:30 pm	
10:00 pm	

DAILY PLANNER

OCTOBER 21, 2024

Monday

TODAY'S AFFIRMATION

WEATHER	
MOOD	

TOP 3 PRIORITIES

1 _____

_____

2 _____

_____

3 _____

_____

TO-DO LIST

- _____
- _____
- _____
- _____
- _____
- _____
- _____
- _____

DON'T FORGET

_____

_____

_____

TIME	PLANS & SCHEDULE
6:00 am	
6:30 am	
7:00 am	
7:30 am	
8:00 am	
8:30 am	
9:00 am	
9:30 am	
10:00 am	
10:30 am	
11:00 am	
11:30 am	
12:00 pm	
12:30 pm	
1:00 pm	
1:30 pm	
2:00 pm	
2:30 pm	
3:00 pm	
3:30 pm	
4:00 pm	
4:30 pm	
5:00 pm	
5:30 pm	
6:00 pm	
6:30 pm	
7:00 pm	
7:30 pm	
8:00 pm	
8:30 pm	
9:00 pm	
9:30 pm	
10:00 pm	

DAILY PLANNER

OCTOBER 22, 2024

Tuesday

TODAY'S AFFIRMATION

WEATHER

MOOD

TOP 3 PRIORITIES

1 _____

2 _____

3 _____

TO-DO LIST

- ▪ _____
- ▪ _____
- ▪ _____
- ▪ _____
- ▪ _____
- ▪ _____
- ▪ _____
- ▪ _____

DON'T FORGET

_____

_____

_____

TIME	PLANS & SCHEDULE
6:00 am	
6:30 am	
7:00 am	
7:30 am	
8:00 am	
8:30 am	
9:00 am	
9:30 am	
10:00 am	
10:30 am	
11:00 am	
11:30 am	
12:00 pm	
12:30 pm	
1:00 pm	
1:30 pm	
2:00 pm	
2:30 pm	
3:00 pm	
3:30 pm	
4:00 pm	
4:30 pm	
5:00 pm	
5:30 pm	
6:00 pm	
6:30 pm	
7:00 pm	
7:30 pm	
8:00 pm	
8:30 pm	
9:00 pm	
9:30 pm	
10:00 pm	

DAILY PLANNER

OCTOBER 23, 2024

Wednesday

TODAY'S AFFIRMATION

WEATHER

MOOD

TOP 3 PRIORITIES

1 _____

_____

2 _____

_____

3 _____

_____

TO-DO LIST

- ■ _____
- ■ _____
- ■ _____
- ■ _____
- ■ _____
- ■ _____
- ■ _____
- ■ _____

DON'T FORGET

_____

_____

_____

TIME	PLANS & SCHEDULE
6:00 am	
6:30 am	
7:00 am	
7:30 am	
8:00 am	
8:30 am	
9:00 am	
9:30 am	
10:00 am	
10:30 am	
11:00 am	
11:30 am	
12:00 pm	
12:30 pm	
1:00 pm	
1:30 pm	
2:00 pm	
2:30 pm	
3:00 pm	
3:30 pm	
4:00 pm	
4:30 pm	
5:00 pm	
5:30 pm	
6:00 pm	
6:30 pm	
7:00 pm	
7:30 pm	
8:00 pm	
8:30 pm	
9:00 pm	
9:30 pm	
10:00 pm	

OCTOBER 24, 2024

Thursday

TODAY'S AFFIRMATION

WEATHER

MOOD

TOP 3 PRIORITIES

1 _____
_____

2 _____
_____

3 _____
_____

TO-DO LIST

- ▪ _____
- ▪ _____
- ▪ _____
- ▪ _____
- ▪ _____
- ▪ _____
- ▪ _____
- ▪ _____

DON'T FORGET

_____
_____
_____

TIME	PLANS & SCHEDULE
6:00 am	
6:30 am	
7:00 am	
7:30 am	
8:00 am	
8:30 am	
9:00 am	
9:30 am	
10:00 am	
10:30 am	
11:00 am	
11:30 am	
12:00 pm	
12:30 pm	
1:00 pm	
1:30 pm	
2:00 pm	
2:30 pm	
3:00 pm	
3:30 pm	
4:00 pm	
4:30 pm	
5:00 pm	
5:30 pm	
6:00 pm	
6:30 pm	
7:00 pm	
7:30 pm	
8:00 pm	
8:30 pm	
9:00 pm	
9:30 pm	
10:00 pm	

DAILY PLANNER

OCTOBER 25, 2024

Friday

TODAY'S AFFIRMATION

WEATHER

MOOD

TOP 3 PRIORITIES

1 _____

_____

2 _____

_____

3 _____

_____

TO-DO LIST

- ■ _____
- ■ _____
- ■ _____
- ■ _____
- ■ _____
- ■ _____
- ■ _____
- ■ _____

DON'T FORGET

_____

_____

_____

TIME	PLANS & SCHEDULE
6:00 am	
6:30 am	
7:00 am	
7:30 am	
8:00 am	
8:30 am	
9:00 am	
9:30 am	
10:00 am	
10:30 am	
11:00 am	
11:30 am	
12:00 pm	
12:30 pm	
1:00 pm	
1:30 pm	
2:00 pm	
2:30 pm	
3:00 pm	
3:30 pm	
4:00 pm	
4:30 pm	
5:00 pm	
5:30 pm	
6:00 pm	
6:30 pm	
7:00 pm	
7:30 pm	
8:00 pm	
8:30 pm	
9:00 pm	
9:30 pm	
10:00 pm	

DAILY PLANNER

OCTOBER 26, 2024

Saturday

TODAY'S AFFIRMATION

WEATHER

MOOD

TOP 3 PRIORITIES

1 _____

2 _____

3 _____

TO-DO LIST

- ■ _____
- ■ _____
- ■ _____
- ■ _____
- ■ _____
- ■ _____
- ■ _____
- ■ _____

DON'T FORGET

TIME	PLANS & SCHEDULE
6:00 am	
6:30 am	
7:00 am	
7:30 am	
8:00 am	
8:30 am	
9:00 am	
9:30 am	
10:00 am	
10:30 am	
11:00 am	
11:30 am	
12:00 pm	
12:30 pm	
1:00 pm	
1:30 pm	
2:00 pm	
2:30 pm	
3:00 pm	
3:30 pm	
4:00 pm	
4:30 pm	
5:00 pm	
5:30 pm	
6:00 pm	
6:30 pm	
7:00 pm	
7:30 pm	
8:00 pm	
8:30 pm	
9:00 pm	
9:30 pm	
10:00 pm	

OCTOBER 27, 2024

Sunday

TODAY'S AFFIRMATION

WEATHER

MOOD

TOP 3 PRIORITIES

1 _____
_____

2 _____
_____

3 _____
_____

TO-DO LIST

- ■ _____
- ■ _____
- ■ _____
- ■ _____
- ■ _____
- ■ _____
- ■ _____
- ■ _____

DON'T FORGET

_____
_____
_____

TIME	PLANS & SCHEDULE
6:00 am	
6:30 am	
7:00 am	
7:30 am	
8:00 am	
8:30 am	
9:00 am	
9:30 am	
10:00 am	
10:30 am	
11:00 am	
11:30 am	
12:00 pm	
12:30 pm	
1:00 pm	
1:30 pm	
2:00 pm	
2:30 pm	
3:00 pm	
3:30 pm	
4:00 pm	
4:30 pm	
5:00 pm	
5:30 pm	
6:00 pm	
6:30 pm	
7:00 pm	
7:30 pm	
8:00 pm	
8:30 pm	
9:00 pm	
9:30 pm	
10:00 pm	

DAILY PLANNER

OCTOBER 28, 2024

Monday

TODAY'S AFFIRMATION

WEATHER

MOOD

TOP 3 PRIORITIES

1 _____
_____

2 _____
_____

3 _____
_____

TO-DO LIST

■ _____

■ _____

■ _____

■ _____

■ _____

■ _____

■ _____

■ _____

DON'T FORGET

_____
_____
_____

TIME	PLANS & SCHEDULE
6:00 am	
6:30 am	
7:00 am	
7:30 am	
8:00 am	
8:30 am	
9:00 am	
9:30 am	
10:00 am	
10:30 am	
11:00 am	
11:30 am	
12:00 pm	
12:30 pm	
1:00 pm	
1:30 pm	
2:00 pm	
2:30 pm	
3:00 pm	
3:30 pm	
4:00 pm	
4:30 pm	
5:00 pm	
5:30 pm	
6:00 pm	
6:30 pm	
7:00 pm	
7:30 pm	
8:00 pm	
8:30 pm	
9:00 pm	
9:30 pm	
10:00 pm	

DAILY PLANNER

OCTOBER 29, 2024

Tuesday

TODAY'S AFFIRMATION

WEATHER

MOOD

TOP 3 PRIORITIES

1 _____

_____

2 _____

_____

3 _____

_____

TO-DO LIST

- ▪ _____
- ▪ _____
- ▪ _____
- ▪ _____
- ▪ _____
- ▪ _____
- ▪ _____
- ▪ _____

DON'T FORGET

_____

_____

_____

TIME	PLANS & SCHEDULE
6:00 am	
6:30 am	
7:00 am	
7:30 am	
8:00 am	
8:30 am	
9:00 am	
9:30 am	
10:00 am	
10:30 am	
11:00 am	
11:30 am	
12:00 pm	
12:30 pm	
1:00 pm	
1:30 pm	
2:00 pm	
2:30 pm	
3:00 pm	
3:30 pm	
4:00 pm	
4:30 pm	
5:00 pm	
5:30 pm	
6:00 pm	
6:30 pm	
7:00 pm	
7:30 pm	
8:00 pm	
8:30 pm	
9:00 pm	
9:30 pm	
10:00 pm	

DAILY PLANNER

OCTOBER 30, 2024

Wednesday

TODAY'S AFFIRMATION

WEATHER

MOOD

TOP 3 PRIORITIES

1 _____
_____

2 _____
_____

3 _____

TO-DO LIST

- ▪ _____
- ▪ _____
- ▪ _____
- ▪ _____
- ▪ _____
- ▪ _____
- ▪ _____
- ▪ _____

DON'T FORGET

TIME	PLANS & SCHEDULE
6:00 am	
6:30 am	
7:00 am	
7:30 am	
8:00 am	
8:30 am	
9:00 am	
9:30 am	
10:00 am	
10:30 am	
11:00 am	
11:30 am	
12:00 pm	
12:30 pm	
1:00 pm	
1:30 pm	
2:00 pm	
2:30 pm	
3:00 pm	
3:30 pm	
4:00 pm	
4:30 pm	
5:00 pm	
5:30 pm	
6:00 pm	
6:30 pm	
7:00 pm	
7:30 pm	
8:00 pm	
8:30 pm	
9:00 pm	
9:30 pm	
10:00 pm	

DAILY PLANNER

OCTOBER 31, 2024

Thursday

TODAY'S AFFIRMATION

WEATHER

MOOD

TOP 3 PRIORITIES

1 _____

2 _____

3 _____

TO-DO LIST

- ■ _____
- ■ _____
- ■ _____
- ■ _____
- ■ _____
- ■ _____
- ■ _____
- ■ _____

DON'T FORGET

_____

_____

_____

TIME	PLANS & SCHEDULE
6:00 am	
6:30 am	
7:00 am	
7:30 am	
8:00 am	
8:30 am	
9:00 am	
9:30 am	
10:00 am	
10:30 am	
11:00 am	
11:30 am	
12:00 pm	
12:30 pm	
1:00 pm	
1:30 pm	
2:00 pm	
2:30 pm	
3:00 pm	
3:30 pm	
4:00 pm	
4:30 pm	
5:00 pm	
5:30 pm	
6:00 pm	
6:30 pm	
7:00 pm	
7:30 pm	
8:00 pm	
8:30 pm	
9:00 pm	
9:30 pm	
10:00 pm	

MONTHLY BUDGET PLANNER

Budget Goal: _____   Month: _____

Income

Date	Description	Amount
Total		

Fixed Expenses

Date	Description	Amount
Total		

Other Expenses

Date	Description	Amount
Total		

Bills

Date	Description	Amount
Total		

Recap

	Goal	Actual	Difference
Earnt			
Spent			
Debt			
Saved			

Notes

Date:

GRATITUDE JOURNAL

DATE: _____   S M T W T F S

TODAY I'M GRATEFUL FOR

- _____
- _____
- _____

WATER INTAKE

◊ ◊ ◊ ◊   ◊ ◊ ◊ ◊   ◊ ◊
     1L   2L   3L

WEATHER

TODAY'S AFFIRMATION

- _____
- _____
- _____
- _____

NOTES / REMINDERS

SOMETHING I'M PROUD OF

- _____
- _____
- _____
- _____

TOMORROW I LOOK FORWARD TO

- _____
- _____
- _____
- _____

30 DAY
Self-Care Challenge

DAY 1	DAY 2	DAY 3	DAY 4	DAY 5
Start a gratitude journal	Learn to meditate	Spend the day social media free	Call someone you love	Take a 15 minute walk outdoors
DAY 6	**DAY 7**	**DAY 8**	**DAY 9**	**DAY 10**
Listen to a podcast	Learn to cook a new recipe	Stretch for 10-15 minutes	Listen to your favorite song	Practice deep breathing
DAY 11	**DAY 12**	**DAY 13**	**DAY 14**	**DAY 15**
Try a free online workout	Read a book for 15 minutes	Write a list of short-term goals	De-clutter a room or desk	Go to bed 30 minutes earlier
DAY 16	**DAY 17**	**DAY 18**	**DAY 19**	**DAY 20**
Have a game night	Wake up 15 minutes earlier	Make your favorite meal	Buy yourself something nice	Create a bucket list
DAY 21	**DAY 22**	**DAY 23**	**DAY 24**	**DAY 25**
Watch a movie or series	Write down your thoughts	Take a long shower or bath	Have a home spa day	Read inspirational quotes
DAY 26	**DAY 27**	**DAY 28**	**DAY 29**	**DAY 30**
Create a vision board	Spend some time outside	Do a hair mask	Write it all down in a journal	Take a power nap

NOVEMBER 2024

Sunday	Monday	Tuesday	Wednesday
03	04	05	06
10	11	12	13
17	18	19	20
24	25	26	27

NOVEMBER 2024

Thursday	Friday	Saturday	Notes
	01	02	....
07	08	09	....
14	15	16	....
21	22	23	....
28	29	30	....

NOVEMBER

Goal

Action Plan

Date

....

....

....

....

Grateful For

....

....

....

....

To Improve

....

....

....

....

Notes

....

....

....

DAILY PLANNER

NOVEMBER 1, 2024

Friday

TODAY'S AFFIRMATION

WEATHER

MOOD

TOP 3 PRIORITIES

1 _____
_____

2 _____
_____

3 _____
_____

TO-DO LIST

- ▪ _____
- ▪ _____
- ▪ _____
- ▪ _____
- ▪ _____
- ▪ _____
- ▪ _____
- ▪ _____

DON'T FORGET

_____
_____
_____

TIME	PLANS & SCHEDULE
6:00 am	
6:30 am	
7:00 am	
7:30 am	
8:00 am	
8:30 am	
9:00 am	
9:30 am	
10:00 am	
10:30 am	
11:00 am	
11:30 am	
12:00 pm	
12:30 pm	
1:00 pm	
1:30 pm	
2:00 pm	
2:30 pm	
3:00 pm	
3:30 pm	
4:00 pm	
4:30 pm	
5:00 pm	
5:30 pm	
6:00 pm	
6:30 pm	
7:00 pm	
7:30 pm	
8:00 pm	
8:30 pm	
9:00 pm	
9:30 pm	
10:00 pm	

DAILY PLANNER

NOVEMBER 2, 2024

Saturday

TODAY'S AFFIRMATION

WEATHER

MOOD

TOP 3 PRIORITIES

1 _____
_____

2 _____
_____

3 _____
_____

TO-DO LIST

- _____
- _____
- _____
- _____
- _____
- _____
- _____
- _____

DON'T FORGET

_____
_____
_____

TIME	PLANS & SCHEDULE
6:00 am	
6:30 am	
7:00 am	
7:30 am	
8:00 am	
8:30 am	
9:00 am	
9:30 am	
10:00 am	
10:30 am	
11:00 am	
11:30 am	
12:00 pm	
12:30 pm	
1:00 pm	
1:30 pm	
2:00 pm	
2:30 pm	
3:00 pm	
3:30 pm	
4:00 pm	
4:30 pm	
5:00 pm	
5:30 pm	
6:00 pm	
6:30 pm	
7:00 pm	
7:30 pm	
8:00 pm	
8:30 pm	
9:00 pm	
9:30 pm	
10:00 pm	

DAILY PLANNER

NOVEMBER 3, 2024

Sunday

TODAY'S AFFIRMATION

WEATHER

MOOD

TOP 3 PRIORITIES

1 _____
  _____

2 _____
  _____

3 _____
  _____

TO-DO LIST

- _____
- _____
- _____
- _____
- _____
- _____
- _____
- _____

DON'T FORGET

_____
_____
_____

TIME	PLANS & SCHEDULE
6:00 am	
6:30 am	
7:00 am	
7:30 am	
8:00 am	
8:30 am	
9:00 am	
9:30 am	
10:00 am	
10:30 am	
11:00 am	
11:30 am	
12:00 pm	
12:30 pm	
1:00 pm	
1:30 pm	
2:00 pm	
2:30 pm	
3:00 pm	
3:30 pm	
4:00 pm	
4:30 pm	
5:00 pm	
5:30 pm	
6:00 pm	
6:30 pm	
7:00 pm	
7:30 pm	
8:00 pm	
8:30 pm	
9:00 pm	
9:30 pm	
10:00 pm	

DAILY PLANNER

NOVEMBER 4, 2024

Monday

TODAY'S AFFIRMATION

WEATHER

MOOD

TOP 3 PRIORITIES

1 _____
_____

2 _____
_____

3 _____
_____

TO-DO LIST

- _____
- _____
- _____
- _____
- _____
- _____
- _____
- _____

DON'T FORGET

_____
_____
_____

TIME	PLANS & SCHEDULE
6:00 am	
6:30 am	
7:00 am	
7:30 am	
8:00 am	
8:30 am	
9:00 am	
9:30 am	
10:00 am	
10:30 am	
11:00 am	
11:30 am	
12:00 pm	
12:30 pm	
1:00 pm	
1:30 pm	
2:00 pm	
2:30 pm	
3:00 pm	
3:30 pm	
4:00 pm	
4:30 pm	
5:00 pm	
5:30 pm	
6:00 pm	
6:30 pm	
7:00 pm	
7:30 pm	
8:00 pm	
8:30 pm	
9:00 pm	
9:30 pm	
10:00 pm	

DAILY PLANNER

NOVEMBER 5, 2024

Tuesday

TODAY'S AFFIRMATION

WEATHER

MOOD

TOP 3 PRIORITIES

1 _____
_____

2 _____
_____

3 _____
_____

TO-DO LIST

- ▪ _____
- ▪ _____
- ▪ _____
- ▪ _____
- ▪ _____
- ▪ _____
- ▪ _____
- ▪ _____

DON'T FORGET

_____
_____
_____

TIME	PLANS & SCHEDULE
6:00 am	
6:30 am	
7:00 am	
7:30 am	
8:00 am	
8:30 am	
9:00 am	
9:30 am	
10:00 am	
10:30 am	
11:00 am	
11:30 am	
12:00 pm	
12:30 pm	
1:00 pm	
1:30 pm	
2:00 pm	
2:30 pm	
3:00 pm	
3:30 pm	
4:00 pm	
4:30 pm	
5:00 pm	
5:30 pm	
6:00 pm	
6:30 pm	
7:00 pm	
7:30 pm	
8:00 pm	
8:30 pm	
9:00 pm	
9:30 pm	
10:00 pm	

DAILY PLANNER

NOVEMBER 6, 2024

Wednesday

TODAY'S AFFIRMATION

WEATHER

MOOD

TOP 3 PRIORITIES

1 _____
_____

2 _____
_____

3 _____
_____

TO-DO LIST

☐ _____
☐ _____
☐ _____
☐ _____
☐ _____
☐ _____
☐ _____
☐ _____

DON'T FORGET

_____
_____
_____

TIME	PLANS & SCHEDULE
6:00 am	
6:30 am	
7:00 am	
7:30 am	
8:00 am	
8:30 am	
9:00 am	
9:30 am	
10:00 am	
10:30 am	
11:00 am	
11:30 am	
12:00 pm	
12:30 pm	
1:00 pm	
1:30 pm	
2:00 pm	
2:30 pm	
3:00 pm	
3:30 pm	
4:00 pm	
4:30 pm	
5:00 pm	
5:30 pm	
6:00 pm	
6:30 pm	
7:00 pm	
7:30 pm	
8:00 pm	
8:30 pm	
9:00 pm	
9:30 pm	
10:00 pm	

DAILY PLANNER

NOVEMBER 7, 2024

Thursday

TODAY'S AFFIRMATION

WEATHER

MOOD

TOP 3 PRIORITIES

1 _____
_____

2 _____
_____

3 _____
_____

TO-DO LIST

- ▪ _____
- ▪ _____
- ▪ _____
- ▪ _____
- ▪ _____
- ▪ _____
- ▪ _____
- ▪ _____

DON'T FORGET

_____
_____
_____

TIME	PLANS & SCHEDULE
6:00 am	
6:30 am	
7:00 am	
7:30 am	
8:00 am	
8:30 am	
9:00 am	
9:30 am	
10:00 am	
10:30 am	
11:00 am	
11:30 am	
12:00 pm	
12:30 pm	
1:00 pm	
1:30 pm	
2:00 pm	
2:30 pm	
3:00 pm	
3:30 pm	
4:00 pm	
4:30 pm	
5:00 pm	
5:30 pm	
6:00 pm	
6:30 pm	
7:00 pm	
7:30 pm	
8:00 pm	
8:30 pm	
9:00 pm	
9:30 pm	
10:00 pm	

DAILY PLANNER

NOVEMBER 8, 2024

Friday

TODAY'S AFFIRMATION

WEATHER

MOOD

TOP 3 PRIORITIES

1 _____

2 _____

3 _____

TO-DO LIST

- ☐ _____
- ☐ _____
- ☐ _____
- ☐ _____
- ☐ _____
- ☐ _____
- ☐ _____
- ☐ _____

DON'T FORGET

_____
_____
_____

TIME	PLANS & SCHEDULE
6:00 am	
6:30 am	
7:00 am	
7:30 am	
8:00 am	
8:30 am	
9:00 am	
9:30 am	
10:00 am	
10:30 am	
11:00 am	
11:30 am	
12:00 pm	
12:30 pm	
1:00 pm	
1:30 pm	
2:00 pm	
2:30 pm	
3:00 pm	
3:30 pm	
4:00 pm	
4:30 pm	
5:00 pm	
5:30 pm	
6:00 pm	
6:30 pm	
7:00 pm	
7:30 pm	
8:00 pm	
8:30 pm	
9:00 pm	
9:30 pm	
10:00 pm	

DAILY PLANNER

NOVEMBER 9, 2024

Saturday

TODAY'S AFFIRMATION

WEATHER

MOOD

TOP 3 PRIORITIES

1 _____
  _____

2 _____
  _____

3 _____
  _____

TO-DO LIST

- ▪ _____
- ▪ _____
- ▪ _____
- ▪ _____
- ▪ _____
- ▪ _____
- ▪ _____
- ▪ _____

DON'T FORGET

_____
_____
_____

TIME	PLANS & SCHEDULE
6:00 am	
6:30 am	
7:00 am	
7:30 am	
8:00 am	
8:30 am	
9:00 am	
9:30 am	
10:00 am	
10:30 am	
11:00 am	
11:30 am	
12:00 pm	
12:30 pm	
1:00 pm	
1:30 pm	
2:00 pm	
2:30 pm	
3:00 pm	
3:30 pm	
4:00 pm	
4:30 pm	
5:00 pm	
5:30 pm	
6:00 pm	
6:30 pm	
7:00 pm	
7:30 pm	
8:00 pm	
8:30 pm	
9:00 pm	
9:30 pm	
10:00 pm	

DAILY PLANNER

NOVEMBER 10, 2024

Sunday

TODAY'S AFFIRMATION

WEATHER

MOOD

TOP 3 PRIORITIES

1 _____

2 _____

3 _____

TO-DO LIST

- _____
- _____
- _____
- _____
- _____
- _____
- _____
- _____

DON'T FORGET

_____

_____

_____

TIME	PLANS & SCHEDULE
6:00 am	
6:30 am	
7:00 am	
7:30 am	
8:00 am	
8:30 am	
9:00 am	
9:30 am	
10:00 am	
10:30 am	
11:00 am	
11:30 am	
12:00 pm	
12:30 pm	
1:00 pm	
1:30 pm	
2:00 pm	
2:30 pm	
3:00 pm	
3:30 pm	
4:00 pm	
4:30 pm	
5:00 pm	
5:30 pm	
6:00 pm	
6:30 pm	
7:00 pm	
7:30 pm	
8:00 pm	
8:30 pm	
9:00 pm	
9:30 pm	
10:00 pm	

NOVEMBER 11, 2024

Monday

TODAY'S AFFIRMATION

WEATHER	
MOOD	

TOP 3 PRIORITIES

1 _____

_____

2 _____

_____

3 _____

_____

TO-DO LIST

■ _____

■ _____

■ _____

■ _____

■ _____

■ _____

■ _____

■ _____

DON'T FORGET

_____

_____

_____

TIME	PLANS & SCHEDULE
6:00 am	
6:30 am	
7:00 am	
7:30 am	
8:00 am	
8:30 am	
9:00 am	
9:30 am	
10:00 am	
10:30 am	
11:00 am	
11:30 am	
12:00 pm	
12:30 pm	
1:00 pm	
1:30 pm	
2:00 pm	
2:30 pm	
3:00 pm	
3:30 pm	
4:00 pm	
4:30 pm	
5:00 pm	
5:30 pm	
6:00 pm	
6:30 pm	
7:00 pm	
7:30 pm	
8:00 pm	
8:30 pm	
9:00 pm	
9:30 pm	
10:00 pm	

DAILY PLANNER

NOVEMBER 12, 2024

Tuesday

TODAY'S AFFIRMATION

WEATHER

MOOD

TOP 3 PRIORITIES

1

2

3

TO-DO LIST

-
-
-
-
-
-
-
-

DON'T FORGET

TIME	PLANS & SCHEDULE
6:00 am	
6:30 am	
7:00 am	
7:30 am	
8:00 am	
8:30 am	
9:00 am	
9:30 am	
10:00 am	
10:30 am	
11:00 am	
11:30 am	
12:00 pm	
12:30 pm	
1:00 pm	
1:30 pm	
2:00 pm	
2:30 pm	
3:00 pm	
3:30 pm	
4:00 pm	
4:30 pm	
5:00 pm	
5:30 pm	
6:00 pm	
6:30 pm	
7:00 pm	
7:30 pm	
8:00 pm	
8:30 pm	
9:00 pm	
9:30 pm	
10:00 pm	

DAILY PLANNER

NOVEMBER 13, 2024

Wednesday

TODAY'S AFFIRMATION

WEATHER

MOOD

TOP 3 PRIORITIES

1 _____
_____

2 _____
_____

3 _____
_____

TO-DO LIST

- ☐ _____
- ☐ _____
- ☐ _____
- ☐ _____
- ☐ _____
- ☐ _____
- ☐ _____
- ☐ _____

DON'T FORGET

_____
_____
_____

TIME	PLANS & SCHEDULE
6:00 am	
6:30 am	
7:00 am	
7:30 am	
8:00 am	
8:30 am	
9:00 am	
9:30 am	
10:00 am	
10:30 am	
11:00 am	
11:30 am	
12:00 pm	
12:30 pm	
1:00 pm	
1:30 pm	
2:00 pm	
2:30 pm	
3:00 pm	
3:30 pm	
4:00 pm	
4:30 pm	
5:00 pm	
5:30 pm	
6:00 pm	
6:30 pm	
7:00 pm	
7:30 pm	
8:00 pm	
8:30 pm	
9:00 pm	
9:30 pm	
10:00 pm	

DAILY PLANNER

NOVEMBER 14, 2024

Thursday

TODAY'S AFFIRMATION

WEATHER

MOOD

TOP 3 PRIORITIES

1 _____

_____

2 _____

_____

3 _____

_____

TO-DO LIST

- ▪ _____
- ▪ _____
- ▪ _____
- ▪ _____
- ▪ _____
- ▪ _____
- ▪ _____
- ▪ _____

DON'T FORGET

_____

_____

_____

TIME	PLANS & SCHEDULE
6:00 am	
6:30 am	
7:00 am	
7:30 am	
8:00 am	
8:30 am	
9:00 am	
9:30 am	
10:00 am	
10:30 am	
11:00 am	
11:30 am	
12:00 pm	
12:30 pm	
1:00 pm	
1:30 pm	
2:00 pm	
2:30 pm	
3:00 pm	
3:30 pm	
4:00 pm	
4:30 pm	
5:00 pm	
5:30 pm	
6:00 pm	
6:30 pm	
7:00 pm	
7:30 pm	
8:00 pm	
8:30 pm	
9:00 pm	
9:30 pm	
10:00 pm	

DAILY PLANNER

NOVEMBER 15, 2024

Friday

TODAY'S AFFIRMATION

WEATHER	
MOOD	

TOP 3 PRIORITIES

1 _____

_____

2 _____

_____

3 _____

_____

TO-DO LIST

■ _____

■ _____

■ _____

■ _____

■ _____

■ _____

■ _____

■ _____

DON'T FORGET

_____

_____

_____

TIME	PLANS & SCHEDULE
6:00 am	
6:30 am	
7:00 am	
7:30 am	
8:00 am	
8:30 am	
9:00 am	
9:30 am	
10:00 am	
10:30 am	
11:00 am	
11:30 am	
12:00 pm	
12:30 pm	
1:00 pm	
1:30 pm	
2:00 pm	
2:30 pm	
3:00 pm	
3:30 pm	
4:00 pm	
4:30 pm	
5:00 pm	
5:30 pm	
6:00 pm	
6:30 pm	
7:00 pm	
7:30 pm	
8:00 pm	
8:30 pm	
9:00 pm	
9:30 pm	
10:00 pm	

DAILY PLANNER

NOVEMBER 16, 2024

Saturday

TODAY'S AFFIRMATION

TOP 3 PRIORITIES

1 _____
_____

2 _____
_____

3 _____
_____

TO-DO LIST

- _____
- _____
- _____
- _____
- _____
- _____
- _____
- _____

DON'T FORGET

_____
_____
_____

WEATHER

MOOD

TIME	PLANS & SCHEDULE
6:00 am	
6:30 am	
7:00 am	
7:30 am	
8:00 am	
8:30 am	
9:00 am	
9:30 am	
10:00 am	
10:30 am	
11:00 am	
11:30 am	
12:00 pm	
12:30 pm	
1:00 pm	
1:30 pm	
2:00 pm	
2:30 pm	
3:00 pm	
3:30 pm	
4:00 pm	
4:30 pm	
5:00 pm	
5:30 pm	
6:00 pm	
6:30 pm	
7:00 pm	
7:30 pm	
8:00 pm	
8:30 pm	
9:00 pm	
9:30 pm	
10:00 pm	

DAILY PLANNER

NOVEMBER 17, 2024

Sunday

WEATHER

MOOD

TOP 3 PRIORITIES

1 _____

_____

2 _____

_____

3 _____

_____

TO-DO LIST

- _____
- _____
- _____
- _____
- _____
- _____
- _____
- _____

DON'T FORGET

_____

_____

_____

TIME	PLANS & SCHEDULE
6:00 am	
6:30 am	
7:00 am	
7:30 am	
8:00 am	
8:30 am	
9:00 am	
9:30 am	
10:00 am	
10:30 am	
11:00 am	
11:30 am	
12:00 pm	
12:30 pm	
1:00 pm	
1:30 pm	
2:00 pm	
2:30 pm	
3:00 pm	
3:30 pm	
4:00 pm	
4:30 pm	
5:00 pm	
5:30 pm	
6:00 pm	
6:30 pm	
7:00 pm	
7:30 pm	
8:00 pm	
8:30 pm	
9:00 pm	
9:30 pm	
10:00 pm	

DAILY PLANNER

NOVEMBER 18, 2024

Monday

TODAY'S AFFIRMATION

WEATHER

MOOD

TOP 3 PRIORITIES

1 _____

_____

2 _____

_____

3 _____

_____

TO-DO LIST

- ▪ _____
- ▪ _____
- ▪ _____
- ▪ _____
- ▪ _____
- ▪ _____
- ▪ _____
- ▪ _____

DON'T FORGET

_____

_____

_____

TIME	PLANS & SCHEDULE
6:00 am	
6:30 am	
7:00 am	
7:30 am	
8:00 am	
8:30 am	
9:00 am	
9:30 am	
10:00 am	
10:30 am	
11:00 am	
11:30 am	
12:00 pm	
12:30 pm	
1:00 pm	
1:30 pm	
2:00 pm	
2:30 pm	
3:00 pm	
3:30 pm	
4:00 pm	
4:30 pm	
5:00 pm	
5:30 pm	
6:00 pm	
6:30 pm	
7:00 pm	
7:30 pm	
8:00 pm	
8:30 pm	
9:00 pm	
9:30 pm	
10:00 pm	

NOVEMBER 19, 2024

Tuesday

TODAY'S AFFIRMATION

WEATHER

MOOD

TOP 3 PRIORITIES

1 _____
_____

2 _____
_____

3 _____
_____

TO-DO LIST

- ☐ _____
- ☐ _____
- ☐ _____
- ☐ _____
- ☐ _____
- ☐ _____
- ☐ _____
- ☐ _____

DON'T FORGET

_____
_____
_____

TIME	PLANS & SCHEDULE
6:00 am	
6:30 am	
7:00 am	
7:30 am	
8:00 am	
8:30 am	
9:00 am	
9:30 am	
10:00 am	
10:30 am	
11:00 am	
11:30 am	
12:00 pm	
12:30 pm	
1:00 pm	
1:30 pm	
2:00 pm	
2:30 pm	
3:00 pm	
3:30 pm	
4:00 pm	
4:30 pm	
5:00 pm	
5:30 pm	
6:00 pm	
6:30 pm	
7:00 pm	
7:30 pm	
8:00 pm	
8:30 pm	
9:00 pm	
9:30 pm	
10:00 pm	

NOVEMBER 20, 2024

Wednesday

TODAY'S AFFIRMATION

WEATHER

MOOD

TOP 3 PRIORITIES

1 _____
_____

2 _____
_____

3 _____
_____

TO-DO LIST

- ▪ _____
- ▪ _____
- ▪ _____
- ▪ _____
- ▪ _____
- ▪ _____
- ▪ _____
- ▪ _____

DON'T FORGET

_____
_____
_____

TIME	PLANS & SCHEDULE
6:00 am	
6:30 am	
7:00 am	
7:30 am	
8:00 am	
8:30 am	
9:00 am	
9:30 am	
10:00 am	
10:30 am	
11:00 am	
11:30 am	
12:00 pm	
12:30 pm	
1:00 pm	
1:30 pm	
2:00 pm	
2:30 pm	
3:00 pm	
3:30 pm	
4:00 pm	
4:30 pm	
5:00 pm	
5:30 pm	
6:00 pm	
6:30 pm	
7:00 pm	
7:30 pm	
8:00 pm	
8:30 pm	
9:00 pm	
9:30 pm	
10:00 pm	

DAILY PLANNER

NOVEMBER 21, 2024

Thursday

TODAY'S AFFIRMATION

WEATHER

MOOD

TOP 3 PRIORITIES

1 _____
_____

2 _____
_____

3 _____
_____

TO-DO LIST

■ _____

■ _____

■ _____

■ _____

■ _____

■ _____

■ _____

■ _____

DON'T FORGET

_____
_____
_____

TIME	PLANS & SCHEDULE
6:00 am	
6:30 am	
7:00 am	
7:30 am	
8:00 am	
8:30 am	
9:00 am	
9:30 am	
10:00 am	
10:30 am	
11:00 am	
11:30 am	
12:00 pm	
12:30 pm	
1:00 pm	
1:30 pm	
2:00 pm	
2:30 pm	
3:00 pm	
3:30 pm	
4:00 pm	
4:30 pm	
5:00 pm	
5:30 pm	
6:00 pm	
6:30 pm	
7:00 pm	
7:30 pm	
8:00 pm	
8:30 pm	
9:00 pm	
9:30 pm	
10:00 pm	

DAILY PLANNER

NOVEMBER 22, 2024

Friday

TODAY'S AFFIRMATION

TOP 3 PRIORITIES

1 _____

2 _____

3 _____

TO-DO LIST

- ▪ _____
- ▪ _____
- ▪ _____
- ▪ _____
- ▪ _____
- ▪ _____
- ▪ _____
- ▪ _____

DON'T FORGET

_____

_____

_____

WEATHER

MOOD

TIME	PLANS & SCHEDULE
6:00 am	
6:30 am	
7:00 am	
7:30 am	
8:00 am	
8:30 am	
9:00 am	
9:30 am	
10:00 am	
10:30 am	
11:00 am	
11:30 am	
12:00 pm	
12:30 pm	
1:00 pm	
1:30 pm	
2:00 pm	
2:30 pm	
3:00 pm	
3:30 pm	
4:00 pm	
4:30 pm	
5:00 pm	
5:30 pm	
6:00 pm	
6:30 pm	
7:00 pm	
7:30 pm	
8:00 pm	
8:30 pm	
9:00 pm	
9:30 pm	
10:00 pm	

DAILY PLANNER

NOVEMBER 23, 2024

Saturday

TODAY'S AFFIRMATION

WEATHER

MOOD

TOP 3 PRIORITIES

1 _____

_____

2 _____

_____

3 _____

_____

TO-DO LIST

■ _____

■ _____

■ _____

■ _____

■ _____

■ _____

■ _____

■ _____

DON'T FORGET

_____

_____

_____

TIME	PLANS & SCHEDULE
6:00 am	
6:30 am	
7:00 am	
7:30 am	
8:00 am	
8:30 am	
9:00 am	
9:30 am	
10:00 am	
10:30 am	
11:00 am	
11:30 am	
12:00 pm	
12:30 pm	
1:00 pm	
1:30 pm	
2:00 pm	
2:30 pm	
3:00 pm	
3:30 pm	
4:00 pm	
4:30 pm	
5:00 pm	
5:30 pm	
6:00 pm	
6:30 pm	
7:00 pm	
7:30 pm	
8:00 pm	
8:30 pm	
9:00 pm	
9:30 pm	
10:00 pm	

DAILY PLANNER

NOVEMBER 24, 2024

Sunday

TODAY'S AFFIRMATION

WEATHER

MOOD

TOP 3 PRIORITIES

1 _____

_____

2 _____

_____

3 _____

_____

TO-DO LIST

- _____
- _____
- _____
- _____
- _____
- _____
- _____
- _____

DON'T FORGET

_____

_____

_____

TIME	PLANS & SCHEDULE
6:00 am	
6:30 am	
7:00 am	
7:30 am	
8:00 am	
8:30 am	
9:00 am	
9:30 am	
10:00 am	
10:30 am	
11:00 am	
11:30 am	
12:00 pm	
12:30 pm	
1:00 pm	
1:30 pm	
2:00 pm	
2:30 pm	
3:00 pm	
3:30 pm	
4:00 pm	
4:30 pm	
5:00 pm	
5:30 pm	
6:00 pm	
6:30 pm	
7:00 pm	
7:30 pm	
8:00 pm	
8:30 pm	
9:00 pm	
9:30 pm	
10:00 pm	

DAILY PLANNER

NOVEMBER 25, 2024

Monday

TODAY'S AFFIRMATION

WEATHER

MOOD

TOP 3 PRIORITIES

1 _____
_____

2 _____
_____

3 _____
_____

TO-DO LIST

- _____
- _____
- _____
- _____
- _____
- _____
- _____
- _____

DON'T FORGET

_____
_____
_____

TIME	PLANS & SCHEDULE
6:00 am	
6:30 am	
7:00 am	
7:30 am	
8:00 am	
8:30 am	
9:00 am	
9:30 am	
10:00 am	
10:30 am	
11:00 am	
11:30 am	
12:00 pm	
12:30 pm	
1:00 pm	
1:30 pm	
2:00 pm	
2:30 pm	
3:00 pm	
3:30 pm	
4:00 pm	
4:30 pm	
5:00 pm	
5:30 pm	
6:00 pm	
6:30 pm	
7:00 pm	
7:30 pm	
8:00 pm	
8:30 pm	
9:00 pm	
9:30 pm	
10:00 pm	

DAILY PLANNER

NOVEMBER 26, 2024

Tuesday

TODAY'S AFFIRMATION

WEATHER

MOOD

TOP 3 PRIORITIES

1 _____

2 _____

3 _____

TO-DO LIST

- _____
- _____
- _____
- _____
- _____
- _____
- _____
- _____

DON'T FORGET

_____

_____

_____

TIME	PLANS & SCHEDULE
6:00 am	
6:30 am	
7:00 am	
7:30 am	
8:00 am	
8:30 am	
9:00 am	
9:30 am	
10:00 am	
10:30 am	
11:00 am	
11:30 am	
12:00 pm	
12:30 pm	
1:00 pm	
1:30 pm	
2:00 pm	
2:30 pm	
3:00 pm	
3:30 pm	
4:00 pm	
4:30 pm	
5:00 pm	
5:30 pm	
6:00 pm	
6:30 pm	
7:00 pm	
7:30 pm	
8:00 pm	
8:30 pm	
9:00 pm	
9:30 pm	
10:00 pm	

NOVEMBER 27, 2024

Wednesday

TODAY'S AFFIRMATION

WEATHER

MOOD

TOP 3 PRIORITIES

1 _____

2 _____

3 _____

TO-DO LIST

- _____
- _____
- _____
- _____
- _____
- _____
- _____
- _____

DON'T FORGET

_____
_____
_____

TIME	PLANS & SCHEDULE
6:00 am	
6:30 am	
7:00 am	
7:30 am	
8:00 am	
8:30 am	
9:00 am	
9:30 am	
10:00 am	
10:30 am	
11:00 am	
11:30 am	
12:00 pm	
12:30 pm	
1:00 pm	
1:30 pm	
2:00 pm	
2:30 pm	
3:00 pm	
3:30 pm	
4:00 pm	
4:30 pm	
5:00 pm	
5:30 pm	
6:00 pm	
6:30 pm	
7:00 pm	
7:30 pm	
8:00 pm	
8:30 pm	
9:00 pm	
9:30 pm	
10:00 pm	

DAILY PLANNER

NOVEMBER 28, 2024

Thursday

TODAY'S AFFIRMATION

TOP 3 PRIORITIES

1 _____

2 _____

3 _____

TO-DO LIST

- ☐
- ☐
- ☐
- ☐
- ☐
- ☐
- ☐
- ☐

DON'T FORGET

WEATHER

MOOD

TIME	PLANS & SCHEDULE
6:00 am	
6:30 am	
7:00 am	
7:30 am	
8:00 am	
8:30 am	
9:00 am	
9:30 am	
10:00 am	
10:30 am	
11:00 am	
11:30 am	
12:00 pm	
12:30 pm	
1:00 pm	
1:30 pm	
2:00 pm	
2:30 pm	
3:00 pm	
3:30 pm	
4:00 pm	
4:30 pm	
5:00 pm	
5:30 pm	
6:00 pm	
6:30 pm	
7:00 pm	
7:30 pm	
8:00 pm	
8:30 pm	
9:00 pm	
9:30 pm	
10:00 pm	

DAILY PLANNER

NOVEMBER 29, 2024

Friday

TODAY'S AFFIRMATION

WEATHER	

MOOD	

TOP 3 PRIORITIES
1 _____
_____
2 _____
_____
3 _____
_____

TO-DO LIST
☐ _____
☐ _____
☐ _____
☐ _____
☐ _____
☐ _____
☐ _____
☐ _____

DON'T FORGET
_____
_____
_____

TIME	PLANS & SCHEDULE
6:00 am	
6:30 am	
7:00 am	
7:30 am	
8:00 am	
8:30 am	
9:00 am	
9:30 am	
10:00 am	
10:30 am	
11:00 am	
11:30 am	
12:00 pm	
12:30 pm	
1:00 pm	
1:30 pm	
2:00 pm	
2:30 pm	
3:00 pm	
3:30 pm	
4:00 pm	
4:30 pm	
5:00 pm	
5:30 pm	
6:00 pm	
6:30 pm	
7:00 pm	
7:30 pm	
8:00 pm	
8:30 pm	
9:00 pm	
9:30 pm	
10:00 pm	

DAILY PLANNER

NOVEMBER 30, 2024

Saturday

TODAY'S AFFIRMATION

WEATHER

MOOD

TOP 3 PRIORITIES

1 _____

2 _____

3 _____

TO-DO LIST

- ▪
- ▪
- ▪
- ▪
- ▪
- ▪
- ▪
- ▪

DON'T FORGET

_____

_____

TIME	PLANS & SCHEDULE
6:00 am	
6:30 am	
7:00 am	
7:30 am	
8:00 am	
8:30 am	
9:00 am	
9:30 am	
10:00 am	
10:30 am	
11:00 am	
11:30 am	
12:00 pm	
12:30 pm	
1:00 pm	
1:30 pm	
2:00 pm	
2:30 pm	
3:00 pm	
3:30 pm	
4:00 pm	
4:30 pm	
5:00 pm	
5:30 pm	
6:00 pm	
6:30 pm	
7:00 pm	
7:30 pm	
8:00 pm	
8:30 pm	
9:00 pm	
9:30 pm	
10:00 pm	

MONTHLY BUDGET PLANNER

Budget Goal: _____   Month: _____

Income

Date	Description	Amount
Total		

Fixed Expenses

Date	Description	Amount
Total		

Other Expenses

Date	Description	Amount
Total		

Bills

Date	Description	Amount
Total		

Recap

	Goal	Actual	Difference
Earnt			
Spent			
Debt			
Saved			

Notes

Date:

GRATITUDE JOURNAL

DATE: _____   S M T W T F S

TODAY I'M GRATEFUL FOR

- _____
- _____
- _____

WATER INTAKE

◊ ◊ ◊ ◊   ◊ ◊ ◊ ◊   ◊ ◊
　　1L　　　　2L　　3L

WEATHER

TODAY'S AFFIRMATION

- _____
- _____
- _____
- _____

NOTES / REMINDERS

SOMETHING I'M PROUD OF

- _____
- _____
- _____
- _____

TOMORROW I LOOK FORWARD TO

- _____
- _____
- _____
- _____

30 DAY
Self-Care Challenge

DAY 1	DAY 2	DAY 3	DAY 4	DAY 5
Start a gratitude journal	Learn to meditate	Spend the day social media free	Call someone you love	Take a 15 minute walk outdoors
DAY 6	**DAY 7**	**DAY 8**	**DAY 9**	**DAY 10**
Listen to a podcast	Learn to cook a new recipe	Stretch for 10-15 minutes	Listen to your favorite song	Practice deep breathing
DAY 11	**DAY 12**	**DAY 13**	**DAY 14**	**DAY 15**
Try a free online workout	Read a book for 15 minutes	Write a list of short-term goals	De-clutter a room or desk	Go to bed 30 minutes earlier
DAY 16	**DAY 17**	**DAY 18**	**DAY 19**	**DAY 20**
Have a game night	Wake up 15 minutes earlier	Make your favorite meal	Buy yourself something nice	Create a bucket list
DAY 21	**DAY 22**	**DAY 23**	**DAY 24**	**DAY 25**
Watch a movie or series	Write down your thoughts	Take a long shower or bath	Have a home spa day	Read inspirational quotes
DAY 26	**DAY 27**	**DAY 28**	**DAY 29**	**DAY 30**
Create a vision board	Spend some time outside	Do a hair mask	Write it all down in a journal	Take a power nap

DECEMBER 2024

Sunday	Monday	Tuesday	Wednesday
01	02	03	04
08	09	10	11
15	16	17	18
22	23	24	25
29	30	31	

DECEMBER 2024

Thursday	Friday	Saturday	Notes
05	06	07	
12	13	14	
19	20	21	
26	27	28	

DECEMBER

Goal

Action Plan

Date

....

....

....

....

....

Grateful For

....

....

....

....

....

To Improve

....

....

....

....

Notes

....

....

....

....

DAILY PLANNER

DECEMBER 1, 2024

Sunday

TODAY'S AFFIRMATION

WEATHER

MOOD

TOP 3 PRIORITIES

1.
2.
3.

TO-DO LIST

-
-
-
-
-
-
-
-

DON'T FORGET

TIME	PLANS & SCHEDULE
6:00 am	
6:30 am	
7:00 am	
7:30 am	
8:00 am	
8:30 am	
9:00 am	
9:30 am	
10:00 am	
10:30 am	
11:00 am	
11:30 am	
12:00 pm	
12:30 pm	
1:00 pm	
1:30 pm	
2:00 pm	
2:30 pm	
3:00 pm	
3:30 pm	
4:00 pm	
4:30 pm	
5:00 pm	
5:30 pm	
6:00 pm	
6:30 pm	
7:00 pm	
7:30 pm	
8:00 pm	
8:30 pm	
9:00 pm	
9:30 pm	
10:00 pm	

DAILY PLANNER

DECEMBER 2, 2024

Monday

TODAY'S AFFIRMATION

TOP 3 PRIORITIES

1

2

3

TO-DO LIST

- ▪
- ▪
- ▪
- ▪
- ▪
- ▪
- ▪
- ▪

DON'T FORGET

WEATHER

MOOD

TIME	PLANS & SCHEDULE
6:00 am	
6:30 am	
7:00 am	
7:30 am	
8:00 am	
8:30 am	
9:00 am	
9:30 am	
10:00 am	
10:30 am	
11:00 am	
11:30 am	
12:00 pm	
12:30 pm	
1:00 pm	
1:30 pm	
2:00 pm	
2:30 pm	
3:00 pm	
3:30 pm	
4:00 pm	
4:30 pm	
5:00 pm	
5:30 pm	
6:00 pm	
6:30 pm	
7:00 pm	
7:30 pm	
8:00 pm	
8:30 pm	
9:00 pm	
9:30 pm	
10:00 pm	

DAILY PLANNER

DECEMBER 3, 2024

Tuesday

TODAY'S AFFIRMATION

TOP 3 PRIORITIES

1
2
3

TO-DO LIST

- ■
- ■
- ■
- ■
- ■
- ■
- ■
- ■

DON'T FORGET

WEATHER

MOOD

TIME	PLANS & SCHEDULE
6:00 am	
6:30 am	
7:00 am	
7:30 am	
8:00 am	
8:30 am	
9:00 am	
9:30 am	
10:00 am	
10:30 am	
11:00 am	
11:30 am	
12:00 pm	
12:30 pm	
1:00 pm	
1:30 pm	
2:00 pm	
2:30 pm	
3:00 pm	
3:30 pm	
4:00 pm	
4:30 pm	
5:00 pm	
5:30 pm	
6:00 pm	
6:30 pm	
7:00 pm	
7:30 pm	
8:00 pm	
8:30 pm	
9:00 pm	
9:30 pm	
10:00 pm	

DAILY PLANNER

DECEMBER 4, 2024

Wednesday

TODAY'S AFFIRMATION

WEATHER

MOOD

TOP 3 PRIORITIES

1

2

3

TO-DO LIST

- ☐
- ☐
- ☐
- ☐
- ☐
- ☐
- ☐
- ☐

DON'T FORGET

TIME	PLANS & SCHEDULE
6:00 am	
6:30 am	
7:00 am	
7:30 am	
8:00 am	
8:30 am	
9:00 am	
9:30 am	
10:00 am	
10:30 am	
11:00 am	
11:30 am	
12:00 pm	
12:30 pm	
1:00 pm	
1:30 pm	
2:00 pm	
2:30 pm	
3:00 pm	
3:30 pm	
4:00 pm	
4:30 pm	
5:00 pm	
5:30 pm	
6:00 pm	
6:30 pm	
7:00 pm	
7:30 pm	
8:00 pm	
8:30 pm	
9:00 pm	
9:30 pm	
10:00 pm	

DAILY PLANNER

DECEMBER 5, 2024

Thursday

TODAY'S AFFIRMATION

WEATHER

MOOD

TOP 3 PRIORITIES

1
2
3

TO-DO LIST

-
-
-
-
-
-
-
-

DON'T FORGET

TIME	PLANS & SCHEDULE
6:00 am	
6:30 am	
7:00 am	
7:30 am	
8:00 am	
8:30 am	
9:00 am	
9:30 am	
10:00 am	
10:30 am	
11:00 am	
11:30 am	
12:00 pm	
12:30 pm	
1:00 pm	
1:30 pm	
2:00 pm	
2:30 pm	
3:00 pm	
3:30 pm	
4:00 pm	
4:30 pm	
5:00 pm	
5:30 pm	
6:00 pm	
6:30 pm	
7:00 pm	
7:30 pm	
8:00 pm	
8:30 pm	
9:00 pm	
9:30 pm	
10:00 pm	

DAILY PLANNER

DECEMBER 6, 2024

Friday

TODAY'S AFFIRMATION

WEATHER

MOOD

TOP 3 PRIORITIES

1
2
3

TO-DO LIST

-
-
-
-
-
-
-
-

DON'T FORGET

TIME	PLANS & SCHEDULE
6:00 am	
6:30 am	
7:00 am	
7:30 am	
8:00 am	
8:30 am	
9:00 am	
9:30 am	
10:00 am	
10:30 am	
11:00 am	
11:30 am	
12:00 pm	
12:30 pm	
1:00 pm	
1:30 pm	
2:00 pm	
2:30 pm	
3:00 pm	
3:30 pm	
4:00 pm	
4:30 pm	
5:00 pm	
5:30 pm	
6:00 pm	
6:30 pm	
7:00 pm	
7:30 pm	
8:00 pm	
8:30 pm	
9:00 pm	
9:30 pm	
10:00 pm	

DAILY PLANNER

DECEMBER 7, 2024

Saturday

TODAY'S AFFIRMATION

WEATHER	
MOOD	

TOP 3 PRIORITIES

1.
2.
3.

TO-DO LIST

- ▪
- ▪
- ▪
- ▪
- ▪
- ▪
- ▪
- ▪

DON'T FORGET

TIME	PLANS & SCHEDULE
6:00 am	
6:30 am	
7:00 am	
7:30 am	
8:00 am	
8:30 am	
9:00 am	
9:30 am	
10:00 am	
10:30 am	
11:00 am	
11:30 am	
12:00 pm	
12:30 pm	
1:00 pm	
1:30 pm	
2:00 pm	
2:30 pm	
3:00 pm	
3:30 pm	
4:00 pm	
4:30 pm	
5:00 pm	
5:30 pm	
6:00 pm	
6:30 pm	
7:00 pm	
7:30 pm	
8:00 pm	
8:30 pm	
9:00 pm	
9:30 pm	
10:00 pm	

DAILY PLANNER

DECEMBER 8, 2024

Sunday

TODAY'S AFFIRMATION

TOP 3 PRIORITIES

1

2

3

TO-DO LIST

-
-
-
-
-
-
-
-

DON'T FORGET

WEATHER

MOOD

TIME	PLANS & SCHEDULE
6:00 am	
6:30 am	
7:00 am	
7:30 am	
8:00 am	
8:30 am	
9:00 am	
9:30 am	
10:00 am	
10:30 am	
11:00 am	
11:30 am	
12:00 pm	
12:30 pm	
1:00 pm	
1:30 pm	
2:00 pm	
2:30 pm	
3:00 pm	
3:30 pm	
4:00 pm	
4:30 pm	
5:00 pm	
5:30 pm	
6:00 pm	
6:30 pm	
7:00 pm	
7:30 pm	
8:00 pm	
8:30 pm	
9:00 pm	
9:30 pm	
10:00 pm	

DAILY PLANNER

DECEMBER 9, 2024

Monday

TODAY'S AFFIRMATION

WEATHER

MOOD

TOP 3 PRIORITIES

1.
2.
3.

TO-DO LIST

- ■
- ■
- ■
- ■
- ■
- ■
- ■
- ■

DON'T FORGET

TIME	PLANS & SCHEDULE
6:00 am	
6:30 am	
7:00 am	
7:30 am	
8:00 am	
8:30 am	
9:00 am	
9:30 am	
10:00 am	
10:30 am	
11:00 am	
11:30 am	
12:00 pm	
12:30 pm	
1:00 pm	
1:30 pm	
2:00 pm	
2:30 pm	
3:00 pm	
3:30 pm	
4:00 pm	
4:30 pm	
5:00 pm	
5:30 pm	
6:00 pm	
6:30 pm	
7:00 pm	
7:30 pm	
8:00 pm	
8:30 pm	
9:00 pm	
9:30 pm	
10:00 pm	

DAILY PLANNER

DECEMBER 10, 2024

Tuesday

TODAY'S AFFIRMATION

WEATHER

MOOD

TOP 3 PRIORITIES

1

2

3

TO-DO LIST

-
-
-
-
-
-
-
-

DON'T FORGET

TIME	PLANS & SCHEDULE
6:00 am	
6:30 am	
7:00 am	
7:30 am	
8:00 am	
8:30 am	
9:00 am	
9:30 am	
10:00 am	
10:30 am	
11:00 am	
11:30 am	
12:00 pm	
12:30 pm	
1:00 pm	
1:30 pm	
2:00 pm	
2:30 pm	
3:00 pm	
3:30 pm	
4:00 pm	
4:30 pm	
5:00 pm	
5:30 pm	
6:00 pm	
6:30 pm	
7:00 pm	
7:30 pm	
8:00 pm	
8:30 pm	
9:00 pm	
9:30 pm	
10:00 pm	

DAILY PLANNER

DECEMBER 11, 2024

Wednesday

TODAY'S AFFIRMATION

TOP 3 PRIORITIES

1 ....
....

2 ....
....

3 ....
....

TO-DO LIST

- ■
- ■
- ■
- ■
- ■
- ■
- ■
- ■

DON'T FORGET

WEATHER

MOOD

TIME	PLANS & SCHEDULE
6:00 am	
6:30 am	
7:00 am	
7:30 am	
8:00 am	
8:30 am	
9:00 am	
9:30 am	
10:00 am	
10:30 am	
11:00 am	
11:30 am	
12:00 pm	
12:30 pm	
1:00 pm	
1:30 pm	
2:00 pm	
2:30 pm	
3:00 pm	
3:30 pm	
4:00 pm	
4:30 pm	
5:00 pm	
5:30 pm	
6:00 pm	
6:30 pm	
7:00 pm	
7:30 pm	
8:00 pm	
8:30 pm	
9:00 pm	
9:30 pm	
10:00 pm	

DAILY PLANNER

DECEMBER 12, 2024

Thursday

WEATHER

MOOD

TOP 3 PRIORITIES

1

2

3

TO-DO LIST

-
-
-
-
-
-
-
-

DON'T FORGET

TIME	PLANS & SCHEDULE
6:00 am	
6:30 am	
7:00 am	
7:30 am	
8:00 am	
8:30 am	
9:00 am	
9:30 am	
10:00 am	
10:30 am	
11:00 am	
11:30 am	
12:00 pm	
12:30 pm	
1:00 pm	
1:30 pm	
2:00 pm	
2:30 pm	
3:00 pm	
3:30 pm	
4:00 pm	
4:30 pm	
5:00 pm	
5:30 pm	
6:00 pm	
6:30 pm	
7:00 pm	
7:30 pm	
8:00 pm	
8:30 pm	
9:00 pm	
9:30 pm	
10:00 pm	

DAILY PLANNER

DECEMBER 13, 2024

Friday

TODAY'S AFFIRMATION

WEATHER

MOOD

TOP 3 PRIORITIES

1
2
3

TO-DO LIST

-
-
-
-
-
-
-
-

DON'T FORGET

TIME	PLANS & SCHEDULE
6:00 am	
6:30 am	
7:00 am	
7:30 am	
8:00 am	
8:30 am	
9:00 am	
9:30 am	
10:00 am	
10:30 am	
11:00 am	
11:30 am	
12:00 pm	
12:30 pm	
1:00 pm	
1:30 pm	
2:00 pm	
2:30 pm	
3:00 pm	
3:30 pm	
4:00 pm	
4:30 pm	
5:00 pm	
5:30 pm	
6:00 pm	
6:30 pm	
7:00 pm	
7:30 pm	
8:00 pm	
8:30 pm	
9:00 pm	
9:30 pm	
10:00 pm	

DAILY PLANNER

DECEMBER 14, 2024

Saturday

TODAY'S AFFIRMATION

WEATHER

MOOD

TOP 3 PRIORITIES

1

2

3

TO-DO LIST

-
-
-
-
-
-
-
-

DON'T FORGET

TIME	PLANS & SCHEDULE
6:00 am	
6:30 am	
7:00 am	
7:30 am	
8:00 am	
8:30 am	
9:00 am	
9:30 am	
10:00 am	
10:30 am	
11:00 am	
11:30 am	
12:00 pm	
12:30 pm	
1:00 pm	
1:30 pm	
2:00 pm	
2:30 pm	
3:00 pm	
3:30 pm	
4:00 pm	
4:30 pm	
5:00 pm	
5:30 pm	
6:00 pm	
6:30 pm	
7:00 pm	
7:30 pm	
8:00 pm	
8:30 pm	
9:00 pm	
9:30 pm	
10:00 pm	

DAILY PLANNER

DECEMBER 15, 2024

Sunday

TODAY'S AFFIRMATION

TOP 3 PRIORITIES

1
2
3

TO-DO LIST

- ■
- ■
- ■
- ■
- ■
- ■
- ■
- ■

DON'T FORGET

WEATHER

MOOD

TIME	PLANS & SCHEDULE
6:00 am	
6:30 am	
7:00 am	
7:30 am	
8:00 am	
8:30 am	
9:00 am	
9:30 am	
10:00 am	
10:30 am	
11:00 am	
11:30 am	
12:00 pm	
12:30 pm	
1:00 pm	
1:30 pm	
2:00 pm	
2:30 pm	
3:00 pm	
3:30 pm	
4:00 pm	
4:30 pm	
5:00 pm	
5:30 pm	
6:00 pm	
6:30 pm	
7:00 pm	
7:30 pm	
8:00 pm	
8:30 pm	
9:00 pm	
9:30 pm	
10:00 pm	

DECEMBER 16, 2024

Monday

TODAY'S AFFIRMATION

WEATHER

MOOD

TOP 3 PRIORITIES

1

2

3

TO-DO LIST

-
-
-
-
-
-
-
-

DON'T FORGET

TIME	PLANS & SCHEDULE
6:00 am	
6:30 am	
7:00 am	
7:30 am	
8:00 am	
8:30 am	
9:00 am	
9:30 am	
10:00 am	
10:30 am	
11:00 am	
11:30 am	
12:00 pm	
12:30 pm	
1:00 pm	
1:30 pm	
2:00 pm	
2:30 pm	
3:00 pm	
3:30 pm	
4:00 pm	
4:30 pm	
5:00 pm	
5:30 pm	
6:00 pm	
6:30 pm	
7:00 pm	
7:30 pm	
8:00 pm	
8:30 pm	
9:00 pm	
9:30 pm	
10:00 pm	

DECEMBER 17, 2024

Tuesday

TODAY'S AFFIRMATION

WEATHER

MOOD

TOP 3 PRIORITIES

1 _____

2 _____

3 _____

TO-DO LIST

- ▪ _____
- ▪ _____
- ▪ _____
- ▪ _____
- ▪ _____
- ▪ _____
- ▪ _____
- ▪ _____

DON'T FORGET

TIME	PLANS & SCHEDULE
6:00 am	
6:30 am	
7:00 am	
7:30 am	
8:00 am	
8:30 am	
9:00 am	
9:30 am	
10:00 am	
10:30 am	
11:00 am	
11:30 am	
12:00 pm	
12:30 pm	
1:00 pm	
1:30 pm	
2:00 pm	
2:30 pm	
3:00 pm	
3:30 pm	
4:00 pm	
4:30 pm	
5:00 pm	
5:30 pm	
6:00 pm	
6:30 pm	
7:00 pm	
7:30 pm	
8:00 pm	
8:30 pm	
9:00 pm	
9:30 pm	
10:00 pm	

DAILY PLANNER

DECEMBER 18, 2024

Wednesday

TODAY'S AFFIRMATION

TOP 3 PRIORITIES

1

2

3

TO-DO LIST

-
-
-
-
-
-
-

DON'T FORGET

WEATHER

MOOD

TIME	PLANS & SCHEDULE
6:00 am	
6:30 am	
7:00 am	
7:30 am	
8:00 am	
8:30 am	
9:00 am	
9:30 am	
10:00 am	
10:30 am	
11:00 am	
11:30 am	
12:00 pm	
12:30 pm	
1:00 pm	
1:30 pm	
2:00 pm	
2:30 pm	
3:00 pm	
3:30 pm	
4:00 pm	
4:30 pm	
5:00 pm	
5:30 pm	
6:00 pm	
6:30 pm	
7:00 pm	
7:30 pm	
8:00 pm	
8:30 pm	
9:00 pm	
9:30 pm	
10:00 pm	

DAILY PLANNER

DECEMBER 19, 2024

Thursday

TODAY'S AFFIRMATION

WEATHER	

MOOD	

TOP 3 PRIORITIES

1.
2.
3.

TO-DO LIST

- ■
- ■
- ■
- ■
- ■
- ■
- ■
- ■

DON'T FORGET

TIME	PLANS & SCHEDULE
6:00 am	
6:30 am	
7:00 am	
7:30 am	
8:00 am	
8:30 am	
9:00 am	
9:30 am	
10:00 am	
10:30 am	
11:00 am	
11:30 am	
12:00 pm	
12:30 pm	
1:00 pm	
1:30 pm	
2:00 pm	
2:30 pm	
3:00 pm	
3:30 pm	
4:00 pm	
4:30 pm	
5:00 pm	
5:30 pm	
6:00 pm	
6:30 pm	
7:00 pm	
7:30 pm	
8:00 pm	
8:30 pm	
9:00 pm	
9:30 pm	
10:00 pm	

DECEMBER 20, 2024

Friday

TODAY'S AFFIRMATION

WEATHER

MOOD

TOP 3 PRIORITIES

1

2

3

TO-DO LIST

-
-
-
-
-
-
-
-

DON'T FORGET

TIME	PLANS & SCHEDULE
6:00 am	
6:30 am	
7:00 am	
7:30 am	
8:00 am	
8:30 am	
9:00 am	
9:30 am	
10:00 am	
10:30 am	
11:00 am	
11:30 am	
12:00 pm	
12:30 pm	
1:00 pm	
1:30 pm	
2:00 pm	
2:30 pm	
3:00 pm	
3:30 pm	
4:00 pm	
4:30 pm	
5:00 pm	
5:30 pm	
6:00 pm	
6:30 pm	
7:00 pm	
7:30 pm	
8:00 pm	
8:30 pm	
9:00 pm	
9:30 pm	
10:00 pm	

DAILY PLANNER

DECEMBER 21, 2024

Saturday

TODAY'S AFFIRMATION

WEATHER

MOOD

TOP 3 PRIORITIES

1
2
3

TO-DO LIST

-
-
-
-
-
-
-
-

DON'T FORGET

TIME	PLANS & SCHEDULE
6:00 am	
6:30 am	
7:00 am	
7:30 am	
8:00 am	
8:30 am	
9:00 am	
9:30 am	
10:00 am	
10:30 am	
11:00 am	
11:30 am	
12:00 pm	
12:30 pm	
1:00 pm	
1:30 pm	
2:00 pm	
2:30 pm	
3:00 pm	
3:30 pm	
4:00 pm	
4:30 pm	
5:00 pm	
5:30 pm	
6:00 pm	
6:30 pm	
7:00 pm	
7:30 pm	
8:00 pm	
8:30 pm	
9:00 pm	
9:30 pm	
10:00 pm	

DAILY PLANNER

DECEMBER 22, 2024

Sunday

TODAY'S AFFIRMATION

TOP 3 PRIORITIES

1

2

3

TO-DO LIST

- ☐
- ☐
- ☐
- ☐
- ☐
- ☐
- ☐
- ☐

DON'T FORGET

WEATHER

MOOD

TIME	PLANS & SCHEDULE
6:00 am	
6:30 am	
7:00 am	
7:30 am	
8:00 am	
8:30 am	
9:00 am	
9:30 am	
10:00 am	
10:30 am	
11:00 am	
11:30 am	
12:00 pm	
12:30 pm	
1:00 pm	
1:30 pm	
2:00 pm	
2:30 pm	
3:00 pm	
3:30 pm	
4:00 pm	
4:30 pm	
5:00 pm	
5:30 pm	
6:00 pm	
6:30 pm	
7:00 pm	
7:30 pm	
8:00 pm	
8:30 pm	
9:00 pm	
9:30 pm	
10:00 pm	

DAILY PLANNER

DECEMBER 23, 2024

Monday

TODAY'S AFFIRMATION

WEATHER	

MOOD	

TOP 3 PRIORITIES

1
2
3

TO-DO LIST

- ▪
- ▪
- ▪
- ▪
- ▪
- ▪
- ▪
- ▪

DON'T FORGET

TIME	PLANS & SCHEDULE
6:00 am	
6:30 am	
7:00 am	
7:30 am	
8:00 am	
8:30 am	
9:00 am	
9:30 am	
10:00 am	
10:30 am	
11:00 am	
11:30 am	
12:00 pm	
12:30 pm	
1:00 pm	
1:30 pm	
2:00 pm	
2:30 pm	
3:00 pm	
3:30 pm	
4:00 pm	
4:30 pm	
5:00 pm	
5:30 pm	
6:00 pm	
6:30 pm	
7:00 pm	
7:30 pm	
8:00 pm	
8:30 pm	
9:00 pm	
9:30 pm	
10:00 pm	

DAILY PLANNER

DECEMBER 24, 2024

Tuesday

TODAY'S AFFIRMATION

WEATHER

MOOD

TOP 3 PRIORITIES

1
2
3

TO-DO LIST

-
-
-
-
-
-
-
-

DON'T FORGET

TIME	PLANS & SCHEDULE
6:00 am	
6:30 am	
7:00 am	
7:30 am	
8:00 am	
8:30 am	
9:00 am	
9:30 am	
10:00 am	
10:30 am	
11:00 am	
11:30 am	
12:00 pm	
12:30 pm	
1:00 pm	
1:30 pm	
2:00 pm	
2:30 pm	
3:00 pm	
3:30 pm	
4:00 pm	
4:30 pm	
5:00 pm	
5:30 pm	
6:00 pm	
6:30 pm	
7:00 pm	
7:30 pm	
8:00 pm	
8:30 pm	
9:00 pm	
9:30 pm	
10:00 pm	

DAILY PLANNER

DECEMBER 25, 2024

Wednesday

TODAY'S AFFIRMATION

WEATHER

MOOD

TOP 3 PRIORITIES

1
2
3

TO-DO LIST

-
-
-
-
-
-
-
-

DON'T FORGET

TIME	PLANS & SCHEDULE
6:00 am	
6:30 am	
7:00 am	
7:30 am	
8:00 am	
8:30 am	
9:00 am	
9:30 am	
10:00 am	
10:30 am	
11:00 am	
11:30 am	
12:00 pm	
12:30 pm	
1:00 pm	
1:30 pm	
2:00 pm	
2:30 pm	
3:00 pm	
3:30 pm	
4:00 pm	
4:30 pm	
5:00 pm	
5:30 pm	
6:00 pm	
6:30 pm	
7:00 pm	
7:30 pm	
8:00 pm	
8:30 pm	
9:00 pm	
9:30 pm	
10:00 pm	

DAILY PLANNER

DECEMBER 26, 2024

Thursday

TODAY'S AFFIRMATION

WEATHER

MOOD

TOP 3 PRIORITIES

1

2

3

TO-DO LIST

-
-
-
-
-
-
-
-

DON'T FORGET

TIME	PLANS & SCHEDULE
6:00 am	
6:30 am	
7:00 am	
7:30 am	
8:00 am	
8:30 am	
9:00 am	
9:30 am	
10:00 am	
10:30 am	
11:00 am	
11:30 am	
12:00 pm	
12:30 pm	
1:00 pm	
1:30 pm	
2:00 pm	
2:30 pm	
3:00 pm	
3:30 pm	
4:00 pm	
4:30 pm	
5:00 pm	
5:30 pm	
6:00 pm	
6:30 pm	
7:00 pm	
7:30 pm	
8:00 pm	
8:30 pm	
9:00 pm	
9:30 pm	
10:00 pm	

DAILY PLANNER

DECEMBER 27, 2024

Friday

TODAY'S AFFIRMATION

WEATHER	

MOOD	

TOP 3 PRIORITIES

1
2
3

TO-DO LIST

- ◼
- ◼
- ◼
- ◼
- ◼
- ◼
- ◼
- ◼

DON'T FORGET

TIME	PLANS & SCHEDULE
6:00 am	
6:30 am	
7:00 am	
7:30 am	
8:00 am	
8:30 am	
9:00 am	
9:30 am	
10:00 am	
10:30 am	
11:00 am	
11:30 am	
12:00 pm	
12:30 pm	
1:00 pm	
1:30 pm	
2:00 pm	
2:30 pm	
3:00 pm	
3:30 pm	
4:00 pm	
4:30 pm	
5:00 pm	
5:30 pm	
6:00 pm	
6:30 pm	
7:00 pm	
7:30 pm	
8:00 pm	
8:30 pm	
9:00 pm	
9:30 pm	
10:00 pm	

DAILY PLANNER

DECEMBER 28, 2024

Saturday

TODAY'S AFFIRMATION

TOP 3 PRIORITIES

1

2

3

TO-DO LIST

-
-
-
-
-
-
-
-

DON'T FORGET

WEATHER

MOOD

TIME	PLANS & SCHEDULE
6:00 am	
6:30 am	
7:00 am	
7:30 am	
8:00 am	
8:30 am	
9:00 am	
9:30 am	
10:00 am	
10:30 am	
11:00 am	
11:30 am	
12:00 pm	
12:30 pm	
1:00 pm	
1:30 pm	
2:00 pm	
2:30 pm	
3:00 pm	
3:30 pm	
4:00 pm	
4:30 pm	
5:00 pm	
5:30 pm	
6:00 pm	
6:30 pm	
7:00 pm	
7:30 pm	
8:00 pm	
8:30 pm	
9:00 pm	
9:30 pm	
10:00 pm	

DAILY PLANNER

DECEMBER 29, 2024

Sunday

TODAY'S AFFIRMATION

TOP 3 PRIORITIES

1
2
3

TO-DO LIST

-
-
-
-
-
-
-
-

DON'T FORGET

WEATHER

MOOD

TIME	PLANS & SCHEDULE
6:00 am	
6:30 am	
7:00 am	
7:30 am	
8:00 am	
8:30 am	
9:00 am	
9:30 am	
10:00 am	
10:30 am	
11:00 am	
11:30 am	
12:00 pm	
12:30 pm	
1:00 pm	
1:30 pm	
2:00 pm	
2:30 pm	
3:00 pm	
3:30 pm	
4:00 pm	
4:30 pm	
5:00 pm	
5:30 pm	
6:00 pm	
6:30 pm	
7:00 pm	
7:30 pm	
8:00 pm	
8:30 pm	
9:00 pm	
9:30 pm	
10:00 pm	

DAILY PLANNER

DECEMBER 30, 2024

Monday

TODAY'S AFFIRMATION

TOP 3 PRIORITIES

1
2
3

TO-DO LIST

-
-
-
-
-
-
-
-

DON'T FORGET

WEATHER

MOOD

TIME	PLANS & SCHEDULE
6:00 am	
6:30 am	
7:00 am	
7:30 am	
8:00 am	
8:30 am	
9:00 am	
9:30 am	
10:00 am	
10:30 am	
11:00 am	
11:30 am	
12:00 pm	
12:30 pm	
1:00 pm	
1:30 pm	
2:00 pm	
2:30 pm	
3:00 pm	
3:30 pm	
4:00 pm	
4:30 pm	
5:00 pm	
5:30 pm	
6:00 pm	
6:30 pm	
7:00 pm	
7:30 pm	
8:00 pm	
8:30 pm	
9:00 pm	
9:30 pm	
10:00 pm	

DAILY PLANNER

DECEMBER 31, 2024

Tuesday

TODAY'S AFFIRMATION

TOP 3 PRIORITIES

1
2
3

TO-DO LIST

-
-
-
-
-
-
-
-

DON'T FORGET

WEATHER

MOOD

TIME	PLANS & SCHEDULE
6:00 am	
6:30 am	
7:00 am	
7:30 am	
8:00 am	
8:30 am	
9:00 am	
9:30 am	
10:00 am	
10:30 am	
11:00 am	
11:30 am	
12:00 pm	
12:30 pm	
1:00 pm	
1:30 pm	
2:00 pm	
2:30 pm	
3:00 pm	
3:30 pm	
4:00 pm	
4:30 pm	
5:00 pm	
5:30 pm	
6:00 pm	
6:30 pm	
7:00 pm	
7:30 pm	
8:00 pm	
8:30 pm	
9:00 pm	
9:30 pm	
10:00 pm	

MONTHLY BUDGET PLANNER

Budget Goal: Month:

Income

Date	Description	Amount
Total		

Fixed Expenses

Date	Description	Amount
Total		

Other Expenses

Date	Description	Amount
Total		

Bills

Date	Description	Amount
Total		

Recap

	Goal	Actual	Difference
Earnt			
Spent			
Debt			
Saved			

Notes

Date:

GRATITUDE JOURNAL

DATE: _____   S M T W T F S

TODAY I'M GRATEFUL FOR

- _____
- _____
- _____

WATER INTAKE

◊◊◊◊   ◊◊◊◊   ◊◊
      1L   2L   3L

WEATHER

NOTES / REMINDERS

TODAY'S AFFIRMATION

- _____
- _____
- _____
- _____

SOMETHING I'M PROUD OF

- _____
- _____
- _____
- _____

TOMORROW I LOOK FORWARD TO

- _____
- _____
- _____
- _____

30 DAY
Self-Care Challenge

DAY 1	DAY 2	DAY 3	DAY 4	DAY 5
Start a gratitude journal	Learn to meditate	Spend the day social media free	Call someone you love	Take a 15 minute walk outdoors
DAY 6	**DAY 7**	**DAY 8**	**DAY 9**	**DAY 10**
Listen to a podcast	Learn to cook a new recipe	Stretch for 10-15 minutes	Listen to your favorite song	Practice deep breathing
DAY 11	**DAY 12**	**DAY 13**	**DAY 14**	**DAY 15**
Try a free online workout	Read a book for 15 minutes	Write a list of short-term goals	De-clutter a room or desk	Go to bed 30 minutes earlier
DAY 16	**DAY 17**	**DAY 18**	**DAY 19**	**DAY 20**
Have a game night	Wake up 15 minutes earlier	Make your favorite meal	Buy yourself something nice	Create a bucket list
DAY 21	**DAY 22**	**DAY 23**	**DAY 24**	**DAY 25**
Watch a movie or series	Write down your thoughts	Take a long shower or bath	Have a home spa day	Read inspirational quotes
DAY 26	**DAY 27**	**DAY 28**	**DAY 29**	**DAY 30**
Create a vision board	Spend some time outside	Do a hair mask	Write it all down in a journal	Take a power nap

Notes

Date:

Notes

Date:

Notes

Date:

- [ ]
- [ ]
- [ ]
- [ ]
- [ ]

Notes

Date:

Notes

Date:

Notes

Date:

Notes

Date:

Notes

Date:

Notes

Date:

Notes

Date:

Notes

Date:

Notes

Date:

(Daily)
SELF–CARE

DATE ___ /___ /___

S M T W T F S

CHECKLIST

- ◯ MAKE YOUR BED
- ◯ TAKE YOUR MEDICATIONS & VITAMINS
- ◯ SKINCARE ROUTINE
- ◯ HEALTHY MEALS
- ◯ GO FOR A WALK
- ◯ CLEANING HOUSE
- ◯ WASHING CLOTHES
- ◯ LISTEN TO MUSIC
- ◯ HAVE A POWER NAP
- ◯ SOCIAL MEDIA BREAK

- ◯ TAKE A LONG BATH
- ◯ DO A FACE MASK
- ◯ CALL A FRIEND OR FAMILY
- ◯ MEDITATION
- ◯ WATCH A MOVIE
- ◯ CUDDLE A PET OR HUMAN
- ◯ TRY A NEW RESTAURANT
- ◯ MAKE TIME TO READ
- ◯ TRY A NEW RECIPE
- ◯ NO PHONE 30 MINS BEFORE BED

WORKOUT

- ◯ CARDIO
- ◯ WEIGHT
- ◯ YOGA
- ◯ STRETCH
- ◯ REST DAY
- ◯ OTHER

HOURS OF SLEEP   (Hours)

1 2 3 4 5 6 7 8

WATER BALANCE   (Glass)

1 2 3 4 5 6 7 8

THINGS THAT MAKE ME HAPPY TODAY

MOOD

ANGRY   TIRED   SAD   GREAT   FUN

(Daily)
SELF—CARE

DATE ___ / ___ / ___

S M T W T F S

CHECKLIST

- ○ MAKE YOUR BED
- ○ TAKE YOUR MEDICATIONS & VITAMINS
- ○ SKINCARE ROUTINE
- ○ HEALTHY MEALS
- ○ GO FOR A WALK
- ○ CLEANING HOUSE
- ○ WASHING CLOTHES
- ○ LISTEN TO MUSIC
- ○ HAVE A POWER NAP
- ○ SOCIAL MEDIA BREAK

- ○ TAKE A LONG BATH
- ○ DO A FACE MASK
- ○ CALL A FRIEND OR FAMILY
- ○ MEDITATION
- ○ WATCH A MOVIE
- ○ CUDDLE A PET OR HUMAN
- ○ TRY A NEW RESTAURANT
- ○ MAKE TIME TO READ
- ○ TRY A NEW RECIPE
- ○ NO PHONE 30 MINS BEFORE BED

WORKOUT

- ○ CARDIO
- ○ WEIGHT
- ○ YOGA
- ○ STRETCH
- ○ REST DAY
- ○ OTHER

THINGS THAT
MAKE ME
HAPPY TODAY

HOURS OF SLEEP (Hours)

1 2 3 4 5 6 7 8

WATER BALANCE (Glass)

1 2 3 4 5 6 7 8

MOOD

ANGRY   TIRED   SAD   GREAT   FUN

(Daily)
SELF-CARE

DATE ____ /____ /____

S   M   T   W   T   F   S

C H E C K L I S T

- ◯ MAKE YOUR BED
- ◯ TAKE YOUR MEDICATIONS & VITAMINS
- ◯ SKINCARE ROUTINE
- ◯ HEALTHY MEALS
- ◯ GO FOR A WALK
- ◯ CLEANING HOUSE
- ◯ WASHING CLOTHES
- ◯ LISTEN TO MUSIC
- ◯ HAVE A POWER NAP
- ◯ SOCIAL MEDIA BREAK

- ◯ TAKE A LONG BATH
- ◯ DO A FACE MASK
- ◯ CALL A FRIEND OR FAMILY
- ◯ MEDITATION
- ◯ WATCH A MOVIE
- ◯ CUDDLE A PET OR HUMAN
- ◯ TRY A NEW RESTAURANT
- ◯ MAKE TIME TO READ
- ◯ TRY A NEW RECIPE
- ◯ NO PHONE 30 MINS BEFORE BED

WORKOUT

- ◯ CARDIO
- ◯ WEIGHT
- ◯ YOGA
- ◯ STRETCH
- ◯ REST DAY
- ◯ OTHER

HOURS OF SLEEP   (Hours)

1   2   3   4   5   6   7   8

WATER BALANCE   (Glass)

1   2   3   4   5   6   7   8

THINGS THAT MAKE ME HAPPY TODAY

MOOD

ANGRY   TIRED   SAD   GREAT   FUN

(Daily)
SELF-CARE

CHECKLIST

○ MAKE YOUR BED
○ TAKE YOUR MEDICATIONS & VITAMINS
○ SKINCARE ROUTINE
○ HEALTHY MEALS
○ GO FOR A WALK
○ CLEANING HOUSE
○ WASHING CLOTHES
○ LISTEN TO MUSIC
○ HAVE A POWER NAP
○ SOCIAL MEDIA BREAK

○ TAKE A LONG BATH
○ DO A FACE MASK
○ CALL A FRIEND OR FAMILY
○ MEDITATION
○ WATCH A MOVIE
○ CUDDLE A PET OR HUMAN
○ TRY A NEW RESTAURANT
○ MAKE TIME TO READ
○ TRY A NEW RECIPE
○ NO PHONE 30 MINS BEFORE BED

WORKOUT

○ CARDIO   ○ WEIGHT   ○ YOGA

○ STRETCH   ○ REST DAY   ○ OTHER

HOURS OF SLEEP   (Hours)

1 2 3 4 5 6 7 8

WATER BALANCE   (Glass)

1 2 3 4 5 6 7 8

MOOD

ANGRY   TIRED   SAD   GREAT   FUN

THINGS THAT MAKE ME HAPPY TODAY

(Daily)
SELF-CARE

DATE ___ / ___ / ___

S M T W T F S

C H E C K L I S T

- ◯ MAKE YOUR BED
- ◯ TAKE YOUR MEDICATIONS & VITAMINS
- ◯ SKINCARE ROUTINE
- ◯ HEALTHY MEALS
- ◯ GO FOR A WALK
- ◯ CLEANING HOUSE
- ◯ WASHING CLOTHES
- ◯ LISTEN TO MUSIC
- ◯ HAVE A POWER NAP
- ◯ SOCIAL MEDIA BREAK

- ◯ TAKE A LONG BATH
- ◯ DO A FACE MASK
- ◯ CALL A FRIEND OR FAMILY
- ◯ MEDITATION
- ◯ WATCH A MOVIE
- ◯ CUDDLE A PET OR HUMAN
- ◯ TRY A NEW RESTAURANT
- ◯ MAKE TIME TO READ
- ◯ TRY A NEW RECIPE
- ◯ NO PHONE 30 MINS BEFORE BED

WORKOUT

- ◯ CARDIO
- ◯ WEIGHT
- ◯ YOGA
- ◯ STRETCH
- ◯ REST DAY
- ◯ OTHER

THINGS THAT
MAKE ME
HAPPY TODAY

HOURS OF SLEEP (Hours)

1 2 3 4 5 6 7 8

WATER BALANCE (Glass)

1 2 3 4 5 6 7 8

MOOD

ANGRY   TIRED   SAD   GREAT   FUN

(Daily) SELF-CARE

CHECKLIST

○ MAKE YOUR BED
○ TAKE YOUR MEDICATIONS & VITAMINS
○ SKINCARE ROUTINE
○ HEALTHY MEALS
○ GO FOR A WALK
○ CLEANING HOUSE
○ WASHING CLOTHES
○ LISTEN TO MUSIC
○ HAVE A POWER NAP
○ SOCIAL MEDIA BREAK

○ TAKE A LONG BATH
○ DO A FACE MASK
○ CALL A FRIEND OR FAMILY
○ MEDITATION
○ WATCH A MOVIE
○ CUDDLE A PET OR HUMAN
○ TRY A NEW RESTAURANT
○ MAKE TIME TO READ
○ TRY A NEW RECIPE
○ NO PHONE 30 MINS BEFORE BED

WORKOUT

○ CARDIO   ○ WEIGHT   ○ YOGA
○ STRETCH   ○ REST DAY ○ OTHER

THINGS THAT MAKE ME HAPPY TODAY

HOURS OF SLEEP   (Hours)

1 2 3 4 5 6 7 8

WATER BALANCE   (Glass)

1 2 3 4 5 6 7 8

MOOD

ANGRY   TIRED   SAD   GREAT   FUN

(Daily)
SELF-CARE

DATE ___ / ___ / ___

S M T W T F S

CHECKLIST

- ◯ MAKE YOUR BED
- ◯ TAKE YOUR MEDICATIONS & VITAMINS
- ◯ SKINCARE ROUTINE
- ◯ HEALTHY MEALS
- ◯ GO FOR A WALK
- ◯ CLEANING HOUSE
- ◯ WASHING CLOTHES
- ◯ LISTEN TO MUSIC
- ◯ HAVE A POWER NAP
- ◯ SOCIAL MEDIA BREAK

- ◯ TAKE A LONG BATH
- ◯ DO A FACE MASK
- ◯ CALL A FRIEND OR FAMILY
- ◯ MEDITATION
- ◯ WATCH A MOVIE
- ◯ CUDDLE A PET OR HUMAN
- ◯ TRY A NEW RESTAURANT
- ◯ MAKE TIME TO READ
- ◯ TRY A NEW RECIPE
- ◯ NO PHONE 30 MINS BEFORE BED

WORKOUT

- ◯ CARDIO
- ◯ WEIGHT
- ◯ YOGA
- ◯ STRETCH
- ◯ REST DAY
- ◯ OTHER

THINGS THAT
MAKE ME
HAPPY TODAY

HOURS OF SLEEP (Hours)

1 2 3 4 5 6 7 8

WATER BALANCE (Glass)

1 2 3 4 5 6 7 8

MOOD

ANGRY   TIRED   SAD   GREAT   FUN

(Daily)
SELF-CARE

C H E C K L I S T

- ◯ MAKE YOUR BED
- ◯ TAKE YOUR MEDICATIONS & VITAMINS
- ◯ SKINCARE ROUTINE
- ◯ HEALTHY MEALS
- ◯ GO FOR A WALK
- ◯ CLEANING HOUSE
- ◯ WASHING CLOTHES
- ◯ LISTEN TO MUSIC
- ◯ HAVE A POWER NAP
- ◯ SOCIAL MEDIA BREAK

- ◯ TAKE A LONG BATH
- ◯ DO A FACE MASK
- ◯ CALL A FRIEND OR FAMILY
- ◯ MEDITATION
- ◯ WATCH A MOVIE
- ◯ CUDDLE A PET OR HUMAN
- ◯ TRY A NEW RESTAURANT
- ◯ MAKE TIME TO READ
- ◯ TRY A NEW RECIPE
- ◯ NO PHONE 30 MINS BEFORE BED

WORKOUT

- ◯ CARDIO
- ◯ WEIGHT
- ◯ YOGA
- ◯ STRETCH
- ◯ REST DAY
- ◯ OTHER

HOURS OF SLEEP   (Hours)

1   2   3   4   5   6   7   8

WATER BALANCE   (Glass)

1   2   3   4   5   6   7   8

THINGS THAT
MAKE ME
HAPPY TODAY

MOOD

ANGRY   TIRED   SAD   GREAT   FUN

(Daily)
SELF-CARE

DATE ___ / ___ / ___

S M T W T F S

CHECKLIST

- ◯ MAKE YOUR BED
- ◯ TAKE YOUR MEDICATIONS & VITAMINS
- ◯ SKINCARE ROUTINE
- ◯ HEALTHY MEALS
- ◯ GO FOR A WALK
- ◯ CLEANING HOUSE
- ◯ WASHING CLOTHES
- ◯ LISTEN TO MUSIC
- ◯ HAVE A POWER NAP
- ◯ SOCIAL MEDIA BREAK

- ◯ TAKE A LONG BATH
- ◯ DO A FACE MASK
- ◯ CALL A FRIEND OR FAMILY
- ◯ MEDITATION
- ◯ WATCH A MOVIE
- ◯ CUDDLE A PET OR HUMAN
- ◯ TRY A NEW RESTAURANT
- ◯ MAKE TIME TO READ
- ◯ TRY A NEW RECIPE
- ◯ NO PHONE 30 MINS BEFORE BED

WORKOUT

- ◯ CARDIO
- ◯ WEIGHT
- ◯ YOGA
- ◯ STRETCH
- ◯ REST DAY
- ◯ OTHER

THINGS THAT MAKE ME HAPPY TODAY

HOURS OF SLEEP (Hours)

🌙 🌙 🌙 🌙 🌙 🌙 🌙 🌙
1 2 3 4 5 6 7 8

WATER BALANCE (Glass)

🥛 🥛 🥛 🥛 🥛 🥛 🥛 🥛
1 2 3 4 5 6 7 8

MOOD

ANGRY   TIRED   SAD   GREAT   FUN

(*Daily*)
SELF–CARE

DATE ___ / ___ / ___

S M T W T F S

CHECKLIST

- ○ MAKE YOUR BED
- ○ TAKE YOUR MEDICATIONS & VITAMINS
- ○ SKINCARE ROUTINE
- ○ HEALTHY MEALS
- ○ GO FOR A WALK
- ○ CLEANING HOUSE
- ○ WASHING CLOTHES
- ○ LISTEN TO MUSIC
- ○ HAVE A POWER NAP
- ○ SOCIAL MEDIA BREAK

- ○ TAKE A LONG BATH
- ○ DO A FACE MASK
- ○ CALL A FRIEND OR FAMILY
- ○ MEDITATION
- ○ WATCH A MOVIE
- ○ CUDDLE A PET OR HUMAN
- ○ TRY A NEW RESTAURANT
- ○ MAKE TIME TO READ
- ○ TRY A NEW RECIPE
- ○ NO PHONE 30 MINS BEFORE BED

WORKOUT

- ○ CARDIO
- ○ WEIGHT
- ○ YOGA
- ○ STRETCH
- ○ REST DAY
- ○ OTHER

THINGS THAT MAKE ME HAPPY TODAY

HOURS OF SLEEP (Hours)

1 2 3 4 5 6 7 8

WATER BALANCE (Glass)

1 2 3 4 5 6 7 8

MOOD

ANGRY TIRED SAD GREAT FUN

(Daily)
SELF-CARE

DATE ___ / ___ / ___

S M T W T F S

CHECKLIST

- ○ MAKE YOUR BED
- ○ TAKE YOUR MEDICATIONS & VITAMINS
- ○ SKINCARE ROUTINE
- ○ HEALTHY MEALS
- ○ GO FOR A WALK
- ○ CLEANING HOUSE
- ○ WASHING CLOTHES
- ○ LISTEN TO MUSIC
- ○ HAVE A POWER NAP
- ○ SOCIAL MEDIA BREAK

- ○ TAKE A LONG BATH
- ○ DO A FACE MASK
- ○ CALL A FRIEND OR FAMILY
- ○ MEDITATION
- ○ WATCH A MOVIE
- ○ CUDDLE A PET OR HUMAN
- ○ TRY A NEW RESTAURANT
- ○ MAKE TIME TO READ
- ○ TRY A NEW RECIPE
- ○ NO PHONE 30 MINS BEFORE BED

WORKOUT

- ○ CARDIO
- ○ WEIGHT
- ○ YOGA
- ○ STRETCH
- ○ REST DAY
- ○ OTHER

THINGS THAT MAKE ME HAPPY TODAY

HOURS OF SLEEP (Hours)

1 2 3 4 5 6 7 8

WATER BALANCE (Glass)

1 2 3 4 5 6 7 8

MOOD

ANGRY TIRED SAD GREAT FUN

(Daily)
SELF-CARE

DATE ____ / ____ / ____

S M T W T F S

C H E C K L I S T

- ○ MAKE YOUR BED
- ○ TAKE YOUR MEDICATIONS & VITAMINS
- ○ SKINCARE ROUTINE
- ○ HEALTHY MEALS
- ○ GO FOR A WALK
- ○ CLEANING HOUSE
- ○ WASHING CLOTHES
- ○ LISTEN TO MUSIC
- ○ HAVE A POWER NAP
- ○ SOCIAL MEDIA BREAK

- ○ TAKE A LONG BATH
- ○ DO A FACE MASK
- ○ CALL A FRIEND OR FAMILY
- ○ MEDITATION
- ○ WATCH A MOVIE
- ○ CUDDLE A PET OR HUMAN
- ○ TRY A NEW RESTAURANT
- ○ MAKE TIME TO READ
- ○ TRY A NEW RECIPE
- ○ NO PHONE 30 MINS BEFORE BED

WORKOUT

- ○ CARDIO
- ○ WEIGHT
- ○ YOGA
- ○ STRETCH
- ○ REST DAY
- ○ OTHER

HOURS OF SLEEP (Hours)

1 2 3 4 5 6 7 8

WATER BALANCE (Glass)

1 2 3 4 5 6 7 8

THINGS THAT MAKE ME HAPPY TODAY

MOOD

ANGRY TIRED SAD GREAT FUN

SELF-REFLECTION

DATE _____

MON	TUE	WED	THU	FRI	SAT	SUN

INTENTIONS

NOURISHMENT

SELF-CARE

MOVEMENT

GOALS

OUTCOME I WANT TO ACHIEVE

WHY IT IS IMPORTANT

ACTION PLAN

DAILY AFFIRMATION

WHAT MADE TODAY GREAT

NOTES

SELF-REFLECTION

DATE _____
:

MON	TUE	WED	THU	FRI	SAT	SUN

INTENTIONS

NOURISHMENT

SELF-CARE

MOVEMENT

GOALS

OUTCOME I WANT TO ACHIEVE

WHY IT IS IMPORTANT

ACTION PLAN

DAILY AFFIRMATION

WHAT MADE TODAY GREAT

NOTES

SELF-REFLECTION

DATE —————

MON	TUE	WED	THU	FRI	SAT	SUN

INTENTIONS

NOURISHMENT

SELF-CARE

MOVEMENT

GOALS

OUTCOME I WANT TO ACHIEVE

WHY IT IS IMPORTANT

ACTION PLAN

DAILY AFFIRMATION

WHAT MADE TODAY GREAT

NOTES

SELF-REFLECTION

DATE _____

MON	TUE	WED	THU	FRI	SAT	SUN

INTENTIONS

NOURISHMENT

SELF-CARE

MOVEMENT

GOALS

OUTCOME I WANT TO ACHIEVE

WHY IT IS IMPORTANT

ACTION PLAN

DAILY AFFIRMATION

WHAT MADE TODAY GREAT

NOTES

SELF-REFLECTION

DATE ———————

MON	TUE	WED	THU	FRI	SAT	SUN

INTENTIONS

NOURISHMENT

SELF-CARE

MOVEMENT

GOALS

OUTCOME I WANT TO ACHIEVE

WHY IT IS IMPORTANT

ACTION PLAN

DAILY AFFIRMATION

WHAT MADE TODAY GREAT

NOTES

SELF-REFLECTION

DATE ————————

MON	TUE	WED	THU	FRI	SAT	SUN

INTENTIONS

NOURISHMENT

SELF-CARE

MOVEMENT

GOALS

OUTCOME I WANT TO ACHIEVE

WHY IT IS IMPORTANT

ACTION PLAN

DAILY AFFIRMATION

WHAT MADE TODAY GREAT

NOTES

SELF-REFLECTION

DATE _____

MON	TUE	WED	THU	FRI	SAT	SUN

INTENTIONS

NOURISHMENT

SELF-CARE

MOVEMENT

GOALS

OUTCOME I WANT TO ACHIEVE

WHY IT IS IMPORTANT

ACTION PLAN

DAILY AFFIRMATION

WHAT MADE TODAY GREAT

NOTES

SELF-REFLECTION

DATE ————————

MON	TUE	WED	THU	FRI	SAT	SUN

INTENTIONS

NOURISHMENT

SELF-CARE

MOVEMENT

GOALS

OUTCOME I WANT TO ACHIEVE

WHY IT IS IMPORTANT

ACTION PLAN

DAILY AFFIRMATION

WHAT MADE TODAY GREAT

NOTES

SELF-REFLECTION

DATE———

MON	TUE	WED	THU	FRI	SAT	SUN

INTENTIONS

NOURISHMENT

SELF-CARE

MOVEMENT

GOALS

OUTCOME I WANT TO ACHIEVE

WHY IT IS IMPORTANT

ACTION PLAN

DAILY AFFIRMATION

WHAT MADE TODAY GREAT

NOTES

SELF-REFLECTION

DATE _____

:

MON	TUE	WED	THU	FRI	SAT	SUN

INTENTIONS

NOURISHMENT

SELF-CARE

MOVEMENT

GOALS

OUTCOME I WANT TO ACHIEVE

WHY IT IS IMPORTANT

ACTION PLAN

DAILY AFFIRMATION

WHAT MADE TODAY GREAT

NOTES

SELF-REFLECTION

DATE_____

MON	TUE	WED	THU	FRI	SAT	SUN

INTENTIONS

NOURISHMENT

SELF-CARE

MOVEMENT

GOALS

OUTCOME I WANT TO ACHIEVE

WHY IT IS IMPORTANT

ACTION PLAN

DAILY AFFIRMATION

WHAT MADE TODAY GREAT

NOTES

SELF-REFLECTION

DATE _____

MON	TUE	WED	THU	FRI	SAT	SUN

INTENTIONS

NOURISHMENT

SELF-CARE

MOVEMENT

GOALS

OUTCOME I WANT TO ACHIEVE

WHY IT IS IMPORTANT

ACTION PLAN

DAILY AFFIRMATION

WHAT MADE TODAY GREAT

NOTES

I hope that this year was all that you dreamed and hoped. I hope that this year was a year of focus and enlightenment, perspective and resourcefulness. This is just the start of the best you have to offer. Take the lessons and successes into 2025. Leave everything else behind.

2024

PLANNER

PURPLE INK, INC

www.ingramcontent.com/pod-product-compliance
Lightning Source LLC
Chambersburg PA
CBHW080414030426
42335CB00020B/2451